A TEXT BOOK OF

THERMODYNAMICS-I

For

Semester - I

SECOND YEAR DEGREE COURSE IN MECHANICAL ENGINEERING AND AUTOMOBILE ENGINEERING

As Per the New Revised Syllabus of
Dr. Babasaheb Ambedkar Marathwada University, Aurangabad
(2013-2014)

Dr. S. N. SAPALI
B.E. (Mech), M.E. (Mech) Ph.D. (IIT) Kharagpur
Professor & Head of Mechanical Engg. Dept.,
College of Engineering (COEP), Pune.
(An Autonomous Institute of Government of Maharashtra)

Dr. S. S. KORE
B.E. (Mech.), M.E. (Mech.), Ph.D.
Associate Professor,
Sinhgad Academy of Engineering,
Kondhwa (Bk.), Pune.

Prof. S. S. GHORPADE
B.E. (Mech.), M.E. (Mech.)
Assistant Professor,
Sinhgad Academy of Engineering
Kondhwa (Bk.), Pune.

NIRALI PRAKASHAN

N2649

THERMODYNAMICS-I (SE Mechanical - BAMU)　　　　　ISBN 978-93-83525-42-3
First Edition : September 2013
© : **Authors**

The text of this publication, or any part thereof, should not be reproduced or transmitted in any form or stored in any computer storage system or device for distribution including photocopy, recording, taping or information retrieval system or reproduced on any disc, tape, perforated media or other information storage device etc., without the written permission of Authors with whom the rights are reserved. Breach of this condition is liable for legal action.

Every effort has been made to avoid errors or omissions in this publication. In spite of this, errors may have crept in. Any mistake, error or discrepancy so noted and shall be brought to our notice shall be taken care of in the next edition. It is notified that neither the publisher nor the authors or seller shall be responsible for any damage or loss of action to any one, of any kind, in any manner, therefrom.

Published By :　　　　　　　　　　　　　　　　　　　　　　　　　　　　　**Printed at**
NIRALI PRAKASHAN　　　　　　　　　　　　　　　　　　　**Repro Knowledgecast Limited**
Abhyudaya Pragati, 1312, Shivaji Nagar,　　　　　　　　　　　　　　　　　　　　　**India**
Off J.M. Road, PUNE – 411005
Tel - (020) 25512336/37/39, Fax - (020) 25511379
Email : niralipune@pragationline.com

DISTRIBUTION CENTRES
PUNE

Nirali Prakashan　　　　　　　　　　　　　　　*Nirali Prakashan*
119, Budhwar Peth, Jogeshwari Mandir Lane　　　S. No. 28/25, Dhyari,
Pune 411002, Maharashtra　　　　　　　　　　　Near Pari Company, Pune 411041
Tel : (020) 2445 2044, 66022708, Fax : (020) 2445 1538　　Tel : (022) 24690204 Fax : (020) 24690316
Email : bookorder@pragationline.com　　　　　　Email : dhyari@pragationline.com
　　　　　　　　　　　　　　　　　　　　　　　　bookorder@pragationline.com

MUMBAI
Nirali Prakashan
385, S.V.P. Road, Rasdhara Co-op. Hsg. Society Ltd.,
Girgaum, Mumbai 400004, Maharashtra
Tel : (022) 2385 6339 / 2386 9976, Fax : (022) 2386 9976
Email : niralimumbai@pragationline.com

DISTRIBUTION BRANCHES

NAGPUR　　　　　　　　　　　　　　　　　　　　**JALGAON**
Pratibha Book Distributors　　　　　　　　　　　　*Nirali Prakashan*
Above Maratha Mandir, Shop No. 3, First Floor,　　　34, V. V. Golani Market, Navi Peth, Jalgaon 425001,
Rani Jhanshi Square, Sitabuldi, Nagpur 440012,　　　Maharashtra, Tel : (0257) 222 0395
Maharashtra, Tel : (0712) 254 7129　　　　　　　　Mob : 94234 91860

BENGALURU　　　　　　　　　　　　　　　　　　**KOLHAPUR**
Pragati Book House　　　　　　　　　　　　　　　*Nirali Prakashan*
House No. 1, Sanjeevappa Lane, Avenue Road Cross,　New Mahadvar Road,
Opp. Rice Church, Bengaluru – 560002.　　　　　　Kedar Plaza, 1st Floor Opp. IDBI Bank
Tel : (080) 64513344, 64513355,　　　　　　　　　Kolhapur 416 012, Maharashtra. Mob : 9855046155
Mob : 9880582331, 9845021552
Email:bharatsavla@yahoo.com

CHENNAI
Pragati Books
9/1, Montieth Road, Behind Taas Mahal, Egmore,
Chennai 600008 Tamil Nadu, Tel : (044) 6518 3535,
Mob : 94440 01782 / 98450 21552 / 98805 82331, Email : bharatsavla@yahoo.com

RETAIL OUTLETS
PUNE

Pragati Book Centre　　　　　　　　　　　　　　　*Pragati Book Centre*
157, Budhwar Peth, Opp. Ratan Talkies,　　　　　　676/B, Budhwar Peth, Opp. Jogeshwari Mandir,
Pune 411002, Maharashtra　　　　　　　　　　　Pune 411002, Maharashtra
Tel : (020) 2445 8887 / 6602 2707, Fax : (020) 2445 8887　Tel : (020) 6601 7784 / 6602 0855

Pragati Book Centre　　　　　　　　　　　　　　　*PBC Book Sellers & Stationers*
Amber Chamber, 28/A, Budhwar Peth,　　　　　　152, Budhwar Peth, Pune 411002, Maharashtra
Appa Balwant Chowk, Pune : 411002, Maharashtra,　Tel : (020) 2445 2254 / 6609 2463
Tel : (020) 20240335 / 66281669
Email : pbcpune@pragationline.com

MUMBAI
Pragati Book Corner
Indira Niwas, 111 - A, Bhavani Shankar Road, Dadar (W), Mumbai 400028, Maharashtra
Tel : (022) 2422 3526 / 6662 5254, Email : pbcmumbai@pragationline.com

Preface ...

It gives us an immense pleasure to present this Text Book of **"Thermodynamics-I"** for the students of Second Year Degree Course in Mechanical and Production Engineering. This book is strictly written as per the new revised syllabus of Dr. Babasaheb Ambedkar Marathwada University, Aurangabad.

Thermodynamics has been a part of the curricula of many disciplines like Mechanical, Automobile, and Chemical Engineering students. The object of this book is to present the subject matter in the most precise, compact and in a lucid manner.

Authors have tried to introduce the subject to the average students, with a large number of solved examples. The subject matter has been developed in a logical and coherent manner with neat illustrations along with a fairly large number of solved examples and exercises. Answers to many unsolved numerical problems are also given.

The main objectives of this text are :

- **To cover the basic principles of thermodynamics.**
- **To develop a very good understanding of the subject matter.**
- **To give practice to solve the numerical examples in thermodynamics.**

We are very much thankful to Shri. Dineshbhai Furia and Shri. Jignesh Furia of M/s Nirali Prakashan, Pune for giving a platform to provide good inputs the students community. We are grateful to Mr. Mallikarjun Munde, a Senior Manager for his endless efforts to make this book as best as it can be. We are also thankful to Mr. Malik Shaikh and Miss. Chaitali Takale for their co-operation throughout the work.

We also thankful to Mr. Kumbeshwar Vibhute for his help and efforts for promotion of the book.

Although every care has been taken to check mistakes, and errors, yet it is difficult to claim perfection. Any errors, mistakes and suggestions for the improvement of this book, brought to our notice will be thankfully acknowledged and incorporated in the next edition.

30th August 2013   **Authors**
Pune.

Syllabus ...

Unit I : First Laws or Thermodynamics Applied to Flow Process (7 Hrs.)
Concept of Flow Work, Control Volume and Steady Flow Process, Assumptions, Steady Flow Energy Equation on Time and Mass Basis, Difference between Steady Flow and Non-flow process, Study and Applications of SFEE to some steady flow devices viz. Nozzles, Diffusers, Throttling Valve, Turbine, Compressors, I.C. Engine, Heat Exchangers etc. Limitations of First Law of Thermodynamics, Concept of PMM-I (Descriptive and Numerical Treatment).

Unit II : Second Law of Thermodynamics (7 Hrs.)
Various Statements, Heat Engine, Refrigerator and Heat Pump, COP of Heat Pump and Refrigerator, Reversed Heat Engine, Equivalence of Kelvin-Planck and Clausius Statements, PMM-II, Carnot Theorem, Thermodynamic Temperature Scale (Descriptive and Numerical Treatment).

Unit III : Entropy (7 Hrs.)
Concept of Entropy, Clausius Theorem, Clausius Inequality, Temperature-Entropy Diagrams, Entropy changes for an Ideal Gas during Reversible Process, Entropy of Isolated System in Real Processes, Principle of increase of Entropy, Total Entropy Changes, Applications of Entropy Principle, Available and Unavailable Energy. (Descriptive Treatment).

Unit IV : Power Cycle (7 Hrs.)
Concept of Air Standard Cycle, Assumptions, Carnot, Otto, Diesel and Dual Air Standard Cycles with Representation on P-V and T-S Planes, Mathematical Analysis or Efficiency, Mean Effective Pressure and Power Output, Comparison, Brayton Cycles, Atkinson Cycle, Ericsson Cycle (Descriptive and Numerical Treatment).

Unit V : Properties of Steam or Pure Substance (7 Hrs.)
Pure Substances, Phase, Phase Transformation of Water at Constant Pressure, P-V Phase Diagram, Critical Point, Triple Point, Different Stages, Entropy of Steam, Steam Tables, Processes of Steam, Enthalpy-Entropy Diagram, Steady Flow Process and Determination of Dryness Fraction of Steam. (Descriptive and Numerical Treatment).

Unit VI : Fuels and Combustion (6 Hrs.)
Definition of Fuel, Calorific Values, Definition of Combustion, Mass Fraction, Mol Fraction, Combustion and Volumetric Air, Excess Air and Deficient Air, Analysis of Product of Combustion, Gravimetric and Volumetric Analysis and their Conversion, Determination of Actual and Excess Air Quantity from Combustion Analysis and Stoichiometric and Actual Air to Fuel Ratios, Orsat Apparatus, Method to determine Flue Gas Analysis – CO/CO_2, CO_2. (Descriptive and Numerical Treatment).

***

Contents ...

Unit I : First Laws or Thermodynamics Applied to Flow Process
1.1. - 1.28

1.1	Introduction	1.1
1.2	First Law of Thermodynamics	1.1
	1.2.1 First Law of Thermodynamics and Joule's Experiment	1.1
1.3	First Law Applied to a Closed System Undergoing a Change of State	1.3
1.4	Internal Energy	1.4
1.5	Steady Flow Process	1.5
	1.5.1 Flow Work	1.5
	1.5.2 Mass Balance	1.6
1.6	First Law Applied to a Steady Flow Process	1.6
1.7	Application to Different Devices	1.8
1.8	Work Done in a Reversible Steady Flow Process	1.11
1.9	Significance of $\int_1^2 PdV$ in Case of Steady Flow Process	1.12
1.10	Perpetual Motion Machine of First Kind, PMM - I	1.13
1.11	Limitations of First Law of Thermodynamics	1.14
•	Solved Problems	1.15
•	Exercise	1.23

Unit II : Second Law of Thermodynamics
2.1 - 2.28

2.1	Limitations of First Law of Thermodynamics	2.1
2.2	Terminology	2.2
	2.2.1 Thermal Energy Reservoirs	2.2
	2.2.2 Heat Engine or Carnot Engine	2.2
	2.2.3 Refrigerator	2.3
	2.2.4 Heat Pump (HP)	2.4
2.3	The Second Law of Thermodynamics	2.5
2.4	Equivalence of Kelvin-Planck and Clausius Statements	2.6
2.5	PPM II (Perpetual Motion Machine of Type II)	2.7
	2.5.1 Different Forms of PMM II	2.7
	2.5.2 Converse of PMM II	2.7
2.6	Concept of Reversibility and Irreversiblity	2.8
	2.6.1 Causes of Irreversibility	2.8
	2.6.2 Conditions for Reversibility	2.13
	2.6.3 Types of Irreversibility	2.14
2.7	Carnot's Theorem	2.14
2.8	Definition of Thermodynamic Temperature	2.17
•	Exercise	2.26

Unit III : Entropy   3.1 - 3.22

- 3.1 Introduction   3.1
- 3.2 Clausius Inequality   3.3
- 3.3 Principle of Increase of Entropy   3.5
- 3.4 Entropy Changes for a Closed System   3.6
  - 3.4.1 The Tds Relations   3.6
  - 3.4.2 Change of Entropy of a Gas   3.7
  - 3.4.3 Entropy Changes for an Open System   3.14
  - 3.4.4 The Entropy Change of Solids and Liquids   3.15
- 3.5 Introduction   3.16
- 3.6 Available and Unavailable Energy   3.16
- 3.7 Available Energy Referred to a Cycle   3.17
- 3.8 Decrease in Available Energy in a Heat Transfer Process Through a Finite Temperature Difference   3.19
- • Exercise   3.21

Unit IV : Power Cycle   4.1 - 4.34

- 4.1 Introduction   4.1
- 4.2 Ideal or Air Standard Cycle   4.2
- 4.3 Carnot Cycle (Reversible Cycle)   4.2
- 4.4 Otto Cycle   4.4
- 4.5 The Diesel Cycle   4.8
  - 4.5.1 MEP of Diesel Cycle   4.10
  - 4.5.2 Effect of Compression Ratio on Diesel Cycle Efficiency   4.10
- 4.6 The Dual Cycle of Limited Pressure Cycle   4.11
  - 4.6.1 Mean Effective Pressure of Limited Pressure Cycle   4.13
- 4.7 Brayton Cycle   4.13
  - 4.7.1 Assumptions for Ideal Cycle Analysis   4.14
  - 4.7.2 Thermal Efficiency and Work Ratio   4.15
- 4.8 Atkinson Cycle   4.18
- 4.9 Ericsson Cycle   4.19
- • Solved Problems   4.20
- • Exercise   4.33

Unit V : Properties of Steam or Pure Substance   5.1 - 5.46

- 5.1 Phase Transformation of Water AT Constant Pressure   5.1
- 5.2 Effect of Pressure on Boiling Point   5.4
- 5.3 Property Diagrams   5.4
  - 5.3.1 p–v Diagram of Water   5.4
  - 5.3.2 Temperature Specific Volume Diagram of Water   5.5
  - 5.3.3 Enthalpy – Entropy (h–s) Diagram of Water   5.6
  - 5.3.4 T-s Diagram for Water   5.6
- 5.4 Properties of Steam   5.7
- • Solved Problems   5.10
- 5.5 Thermodynamic Processes   5.12
  - 5.5.1 Constant Volume Heating or Cooling   5.12
- • Solved Problems   5.14
  - 5.5.2 Constant Pressure Process   5.17
- • Solved Problems   5.17

	5.5.3	Constant Temperature (Isothermal) Process	5.19
•		Solved Problems	5.20
	5.5.4	Polytropic Process	5.21
	5.5.5	Adiabatic Process	5.23
•		Solved Problems	5.24
	5.5.6	Throttling Process	5.25
•		Solved Problems	5.26
5.6		Measurement of Dryness Fraction of Steam	5.27
	5.6.1	Barrel or Tank Calorimeter	5.28
	5.6.2	Separating Calorimeter	5.29
	5.6.3	Throttling Calorimeter	5.31
	5.6.4	Separating and Throttling Calorimeter	5.32
•		Additional Solved Problems	5.34
•		Exercise	5.45
•		Examples for Practice	5.45

Unit VI : Fuels and Combustion   6.1 - 6.68

9.1		Calorific Value of a Fuel	6.1
9.2		Types of Fuels	6.3
9.3		Solid Fuels	6.3
	9.3.1	Coal Analysis	6.4
	9.3.2	Proximate Analysis	6.4
	9.3.3	Ultimate Analysis	6.5
	9.3.4	Types of Coal	6.5
	9.3.5	Liquid Fuels	6.7
	9.3.6	Gaseous Fuels	6.9
9.4		Mass and Mol Fraction	6.13
9.5		Stoichiometric Combustion Equation	6.17
9.6		Minimum Air Requirement on Mass Basis	6.19
9.7		Actual Air	6.21
9.8		Air : Fuel Ratio	6.21
9.9		Products of Combustion	6.22
	9.9.1	Products of Combustion with Stoichiometric Air	6.22
	9.9.2	Products of Combustion with Excess Air	6.23
	9.9.3	Volumetric Analysis of Products	6.23
9.10		Incomplete Combustion	6.26
9.11		Effect of Air : Fuel Ratio on Products of Combustion	6.26
9.12		Orsat Apparatus	6.27
9.13		Determination of Carbon from Fuel Burning to CO or CO_2 from Orsat Analysis	6.31
9.14		Determination of Calorific Value of Fuels	6.33
	9.14.1	Bomb Calorimeter	6.33
	9.14.2	Boy's Gas Calorimeter	6.37
•		Solved Problems	6.39
•		Exercise	6.68

***

Unit I

Chapter 1: FIRST LAW OF THERMODYNAMICS APPLIED TO FLOW PROCESSES

1.1 Introduction

Thermodynamics is a science that deals with matter, energy and interactions between matter and energy.
The subject of thermodynamics is based essentially on three main concepts, these are
  (i) **Energy**, is an idea central to the development of all branches of science and engineering. A fundamental postulate of thermodynamics is that matter has energy (which can be in several forms) and energy is conserved.
  (ii) **Thermodynamic Equilibrium**; a state which every isolated system with no internal constraints eventually attains.
  (iii) **Entropy**; which determines whether a specified type of the change can occur or not.

1.2 First Law of Thermodynamics

Heat and work, the forms of energy which are discussed in the earlier articles, are related by the first law of thermodynamics. This is a law of conservation of energy which states that 'energy can neither be created nor be destroyed'. This law cannot be proved mathematically, but no exception has been observed.

1.2.1 First Law of Thermodynamics and Joule's Experiment

Before defining the first law of thermodynamics, it is better to discuss some experimental results on which it is based. Such an experiment was carried out by a scientist J. P. Joule, during the period 1840-1849. In one of the experiment, he used the apparatus similar to that shown in Fig. 1.1.

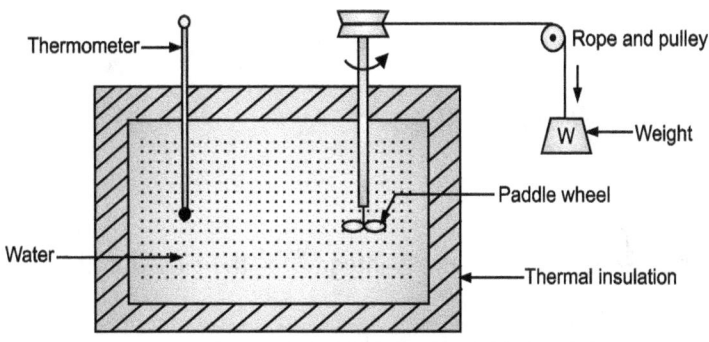

Fig. 1.1: Joule's Experiment

It consists of a closed container insulated from outside, filled with certain amount of water, having thermometer and a paddle wheel.

The temperature of water is measured before and after the work is done on it through a paddle wheel, which rotates due to the weight moving down. The rise in the temperature of water is always proportional to the work done on it due to the potential energy lost by the weight.

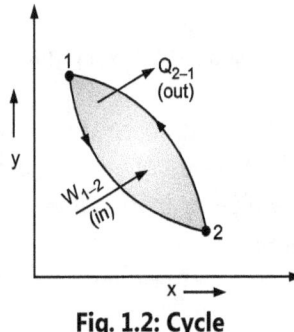

Fig. 1.2: Cycle

Let W_{1-2} is the work done on the water (system), t_1 = initial temperature of water, t_2 = temperature of water after the work is done ($t_2 > t_1$). This process is as shown in Fig. 1.2.

Now, assume the insulation is removed, therefore heat transfer takes place from the system to the surroundings. Therefore, its temperature reaches to the original temperature t_1. The amount of heat Q_{2-1} is transferred to the surroundings. Thus, a system completes a cycle, with definite amount of work W_{1-2} input to the system and followed by Q_{2-1}, amount of heat dissipated from the system.

Joule had conducted this experiment number of times for different weights moving through different distances. Each time he measured the temperature rise of the system.

He found that Q_{1-2} is proportional to W_{1-2}. ($Q_{1-2} \propto W_{1-2}$). This constant of proportionality is known as **'Joule's equivalent or the mechanical equivalent of heat'**.

In SI units, work is measured in N-m and heat in joules (J) and the relation is
1 N-m = 1 joule and hence Joule's constant is unity.

If the cycle shown in Fig. 1.2 involves many more heat and work transfers, the same conclusion will be found. Expressed mathematically,

$$(\Sigma W)_{cycle} = J \, (\Sigma Q)_{cycle} \qquad \ldots (1.1)$$

It can be written as $\oint \delta W = J \oint \delta Q$

As $J = 1$, $\qquad \oint \delta W = \oint \delta Q \qquad \ldots (1.2)$

where the symbol $\oint$ denotes the cyclic integral for the closed path. This is the first law applied to a closed system undergoing a cyclic process.

Other Statements of First Law of Thermodynamics:

(i) Principle of Energy Conservation:

According to this concept, energy can neither be created nor be destroyed. This implies that the sum of the energies of a system at the microscopic and macroscopic levels is fixed, unless there is an interaction with the surroundings, involving an energy exchange.

This can be simply stated as

"The total energy of an isolated system, measured with respect to any given frame of reference remains constant." Mathematically, for an isolated system,

$$E \text{ (total)} = U + K.E. + P.E. + \text{Chemical energy} + \ldots\ldots$$
$$= \text{Constant}$$

1.3 First Law Applied to a Closed System Undergoing a Change of State

The expression $(\Sigma W)_{cycle} = (\Sigma Q)_{cycle}$ applies only to a system undergoing a cyclic process. But in practice, a system may undergo a *non-cyclic* process which produces a change of state in the system.

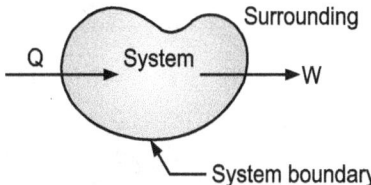

Fig. 1.3: A system interacting with the surroundings which involves work and heat transfer

Let us consider a system interacting with surroundings which involves work and heat transfer (Fig. 1.3).

If Q is the amount of heat transferred to the system and W is the work obtained from it, then Q – W is the energy stored in the system. This stored energy in the system is not a heat or work but referred as internal energy or simply energy of the system.

ΔE = Q – W, where ΔE is the increase in internal energy of the system.

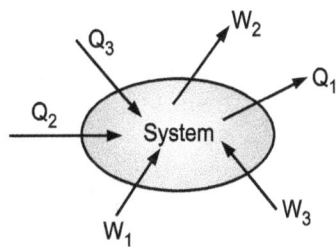

Fig. 1.4: System interacting with the surroundings involving more energy transfers

If more energy transfers are involved in the process, as shown in Fig. 1.4, the first law gives
$(Q_2 + Q_3 - Q_1) = \Delta E + (W_2 + W_1 - W_3)$

Energy is conserved in this operation also.

1.4 Internal Energy

Let a system undergoes a cyclic process as shown in Fig. 1.5. Consider this system changes its state from state 1 to state 2 following the path A. Apply first law to this process.

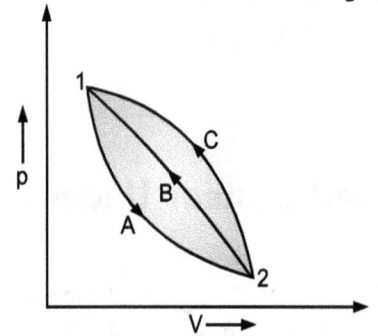

Fig. 1.5: Energy - a property of a system

$$Q_A = \Delta E_A + W_A \quad \ldots (1.1)$$

The system returns from state 2 to state 1 along the path B.

$$\therefore \quad Q_B = \Delta E_B + W_B \quad \ldots (1.2)$$

These two processes form a cycle, for which,

$$(\Sigma W)_{cycle} = (\Sigma Q)_{cycle}$$

$$\therefore \quad W_A + W_B = Q_A + Q_B$$

$$\therefore \quad Q_A - W_A = W_B - Q_B \quad \ldots (1.3)$$

From equations (1.10), (1.2) and (1.3), it results,

$$\Delta E_A = -\Delta E_B \quad \ldots (1.4)$$

Similarly, if we consider the cycle as 1 – A – 2 – C – 1, then,

$$\Delta E_A = -\Delta E_C \quad \ldots (1.5)$$

Comparison of the equations (1.4) and (1.5) will lead to,

$$\Delta E_B = \Delta E_C \quad \ldots (1.6)$$

Hence, the change in energy between the states 1 and 2 is same for the paths B and C. It means the internal energy is independent of the path of the process. It is fixed for a particular state of the system. Therefore, one can conclude that internal energy is a point function and property of the system.

We have, $\delta Q - \delta W = dE$

The total energy change, $\delta E = \delta U + \delta KE + \delta PE$

where, $\delta KE \rightarrow$ change in K.E.

$\delta PE \rightarrow$ change in P.E.

$\delta U \rightarrow$ change in internal energy

If there is no change in K.E. and P.E., then

$\delta PE = \delta KE = 0$,

hence, $\delta Q - \delta W = \delta U \quad \ldots (1.7)$

As $(\delta Q - \delta W)$ is independent of path and depends only on end states, the internal energy $U = \int (\delta Q - \delta W)$ is also independent of path and therefore, a property of the system.

1.5 Steady Flow Process

A steady flow process is said to exist when the working substance flows in and out of the control volume and the properties of the working substance at any section of flow do not vary with time. A steady flow process must satisfy the following conditions:

(i) The rates of work and heat transferred across the control surface do not change with time.

(ii) The mass flow rates at entrance and exit sections of the control volume are equal and do not change with time. Naturally, the mass within the control volume does not change with time and there is no change in energy within the system.

(iii) The state of the working substance at any section within the control volume or at entrance or exit sections does not change with respect to time.

1.5.1 Flow Work

Unlike closed systems, control volumes involve mass flow across their boundaries, and some work is required to push the mass into or out of the control volume. This work is known as the flow work or flow energy and is necessary for maintaining a continuous flow through a control volume (open system).

To obtain a relation for flow work, consider a volume 'V' of the fluid element shown in Fig. 1.6. The fluid immediately upstream will force this fluid element to enter the control volume, thus it can be regarded as an imaginary piston. The fluid element can be chosen to be sufficiently small.

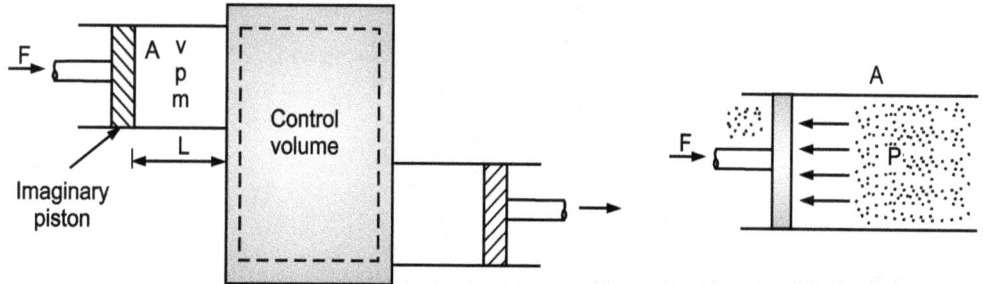

Fig. 1.6: Schematic for flow work

Fig. 1.7: The force applied on a fluid by a piston is equal to the force applied on the piston by a fluid

If the fluid pressure is P and cross-sectional area of the fluid element is A, (Fig. 1.7), the force applied on the fluid element by the imaginary piston is $F = P \cdot A$.

To push the entire fluid element into the control volume, this force must act through a distance L. Thus the work done in pushing the fluid element across the boundary (i.e. the flow work) is

$$W_{flow} = F \cdot L = P \cdot A \cdot L = PV, \text{ kJ} \qquad \ldots (1.8)$$

The flow work per unit mass is obtained by dividing both sides of this equation by the mass of the fluid element.

$$W_{flow} = PV_s \text{ (kJ/kg)} \qquad \ldots (1.9)$$

where V_s = Specific volume of fluid, m³/kg

The total energy of the flowing fluid is

$$= PV_s + (U + KE + PE)$$

But, $\quad U + PV_s = $ enthalpy h

∴ Total energy of flowing fluid per unit mass

$$= h + KE + PE \qquad \ldots (1.10)$$

$$= h + \frac{V^2}{2} + gZ \qquad \ldots (1.11)$$

1.5.2 Mass Balance

By the conservation of mass, for steady flow, the mass flow rate entering the control volume must be equal to the mass flow rate leaving the control volume. (Volume flow rate at entry and exit of control volume may be different). See Fig. 1.8.

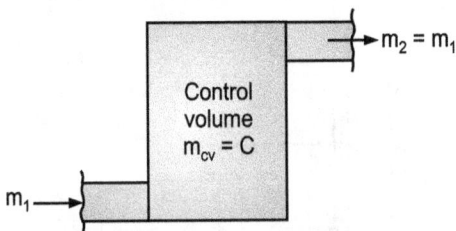

Fig. 1.8: During a steady flow process, the amount of mass entering the control volume equals the amount of mass leaving

1.6 First Law Applied to a Steady Flow Process

A steady flow system is shown in Fig. 1.9, where one stream of fluid enters the control volume at section 1 – 1 and other stream of the fluid leaves the control volume at section 2 – 2. The properties at any location within the control volume are steady with time.

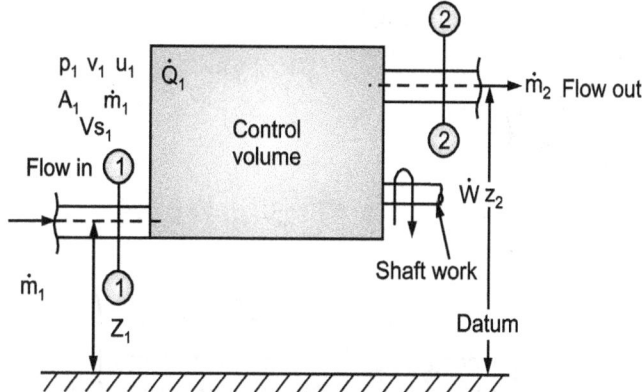

Fig. 1.9: Steady flow process

The following quantities are expressed with reference to Fig. 1.9.

A_1, A_2 — cross section of stream, m²
m_1, m_2 — mass flow rate, kg/s
P_1, P_2 — absolute pressure, N/m²
V_{s1}, V_{s2} — specific volume, m³/kg
u_1, u_2 — specific internal energy, J/kg
V_1, V_2 — velocity of fluid, m/s
Z_1, Z_2 — elevation above an arbitrary datum, m
Q — net rate of heat flow into control volume, J/s
W — net rate of work transfer through control volume, J/s

Subscripts 1 and 2 refer to the inlet and outlet sections.

The sum of energy quantities entering into the system

$$= Q + m_1 \left(u_1 + \frac{V_1^2}{2} + gz_1 + PV_{s1} \right) \qquad \ldots (1.12)$$

$$= Q + m_1 \left(h_1 + \frac{V_1^2}{2} + gz_1 \right) \qquad \ldots (1.13)$$

The sum of energy quantities leaving the control volume

$$= W + m_2 \left(h_2 + \frac{V_2^2}{2} + gz_2 \right) \qquad \ldots (1.14)$$

The change in energy ΔE of the control volume (system) is zero for **steady state conditions**.

Apply first law, i.e. the total energy entering the control volume is equal to the total energy leaving the control volume plus ΔE.

For steady flow, $m_1 = m_2 = m$ and $\Delta E = 0$.

$$\therefore Q + m\left(h_1 + \frac{V_1^2}{2} + gz_1\right) = W + m\left(h_2 + \frac{V_2^2}{2} + gz_2\right) \text{ J/s}$$

$$\therefore Q - W = m\left(h_2 + \frac{V_2^2}{2} + gz_2\right) - m\left(h_1 + \frac{V_1^2}{2} + gz_1\right) \text{ J/s} \qquad \ldots(1.15)$$

In words,

$$\begin{pmatrix} \text{Total energy} \\ \text{crossing boundary} \\ \text{as heat-work} \\ \text{per unit time} \end{pmatrix} = \begin{pmatrix} \text{Total energy} \\ \text{transported out} \\ \text{of CV with mass} \\ \text{per unit time} \end{pmatrix} - \begin{pmatrix} \text{Total energy} \\ \text{transported into} \\ \text{CV with mass} \\ \text{per unit time} \end{pmatrix} \qquad \ldots(1.16)$$

It can be expressed as

$$Q - W = m\left[(h_2 - h_1) + \frac{V_2^2 - V_1^2}{2000} + \frac{g(z_2 - z_1)}{1000}\right] \text{ kW} \qquad \ldots(1.17)$$

$$Q - W = m\,(\Delta h + \Delta KE + \Delta PE) \text{ kW} \qquad \ldots(1.18)$$

Dividing these equations by m, we obtain the "steady flow energy equation (SFEE)" on a unit mass basis as

$$q = Q/m, \qquad w = W/m \text{ kJ/kg}$$

$$q - w = h_2 - h_1 + \frac{V_2^2 - V_1^2}{2000} + g\frac{(z_2 - z_1)}{1000} \text{ kJ/kg}$$

1.7 Application to Different Devices

(a) Nozzle and Diffuser:

A nozzle is a device used to accelerate the fluid flow while the diffuser is a device used to convert the kinetic energy of a flowing fluid into pressure head.

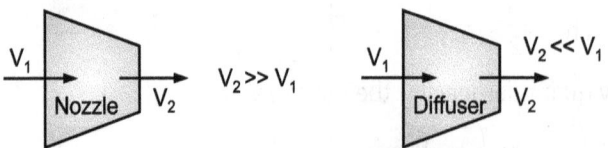

Fig. 1.10: Nozzle and Diffuser

$Q = 0$, The rate of heat transfer between the fluid and surroundings is very small and neglected.

W = 0, As there is no shaft work available from these or even work is not supplied.

ΔPE ≈ 0, The fluid usually experiences no change of elevation.

The SFEE equation (1.34) reduces to

$$0 = h_2 - h_1 + \frac{v_2^2 - v_1^2}{2000}$$

Usually v_1 is very small ($v_1 << v_2$) for nozzle,

$$\therefore v_2 = \sqrt{2000(h_1 - h_2)} \text{ m/s} \qquad \ldots (1.19)$$

Here $(h_1 - h_2)$ is in J/kg.

(b) Turbine and Compressor:

Turbines are prime-movers which generate power, whereas compressors and pumps require power input.

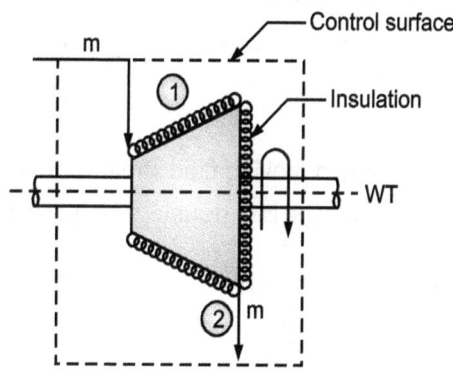

Fig. 1.11: Flow through a turbine

As the turbine is insulated, no heat exchange takes place, therefore, Q = 0. The flow velocities are often small in steam turbines, and K.E. term can be neglected. Also for steam turbines, ΔPE = 0.

∴ SFEE then becomes $h_1 = h_2 + W$

or $W = h_1 - h_2$ kJ/kg

$= m(h_1 - h_2)$ kW ... (1.20)

where m = mass flow rate in kg/s.

Similarly, for an adiabatic pump or compressor, the SFEE is,

$W = (h_2 - h_1) \cdot m$ kW ... (1.21)

where 'h_1' and 'h_2' are in kJ/kg.

(c) Throttling Valves:

Throttling valves are a kind of flow restricting devices that cause a significant pressure drop in the fluid. Some familiar examples are ordinary adjustable valves, capillary tubes and porous plugs. Unlike turbines, they produce a pressure drop without involving any work. The pressure drop in the fluid is often accompanied by a large drop in temperature and for that reason throttling devices are commonly used in refrigeration and air conditioning applications.

Throttling devices are very small in size, therefore flow through them is adiabatic (Q = 0). No work is involved, hence W = 0. Change in potential energy, $\Delta PE \approx 0$, Increase in KE of the fluid is insignificant, $\Delta KE = 0$.

$$\therefore \quad Q - W = \Delta h + \Delta KE + \Delta PE$$
$$0 = \Delta h + 0 + 0$$
$$\therefore \quad 0 = \Delta h$$
i.e. $\quad h_1 = h_2 \text{ kJ/kg} \quad \ldots (1.22)$

i.e. enthalpy values at the inlet and exit of a throttling valve are same.

(d) Heat Exchanger:

Heat exchanger is a device, where two moving fluid streams exchange heat without mixing. The simplest form of a heat exchanger is a double tube (also called tube and shell) heat exchanger shown in Fig. 1.12.

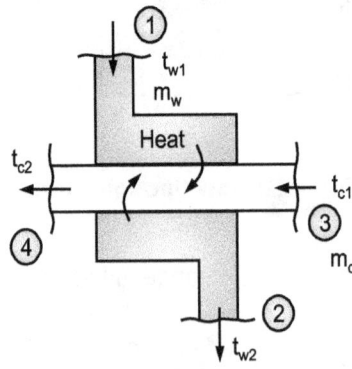

Fig. 1.12

$W = 0, \Delta PE = 0, \Delta KE = 0$

$$m_w h_1 + m_c h_3 = m_w h_2 + m_c h_4$$
$$\therefore \quad m_w (h_1 - h_2) = m_c (h_4 - h_3) \quad \ldots (1.23)$$

c = cold fluid, w = water (hot fluid)

1.8 Work Done in a Reversible Steady Flow Process
Refer Fig. 1.13.

We know that SFEE is

$$Q + \left(h_1 + \frac{v_1^2}{2000} + \frac{gz_1}{1000}\right) = W + \left(h_2 + \frac{v_2^2}{2000} + \frac{gz_2}{1000}\right)$$

$$\therefore \quad Q - W = \Delta h + \Delta PE + \Delta KE \text{ kJ/kg}$$

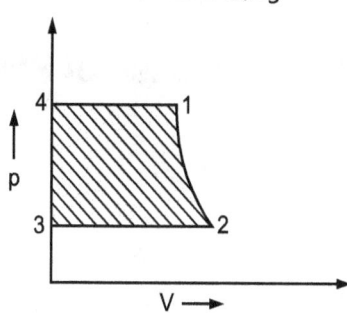

Fig. 1.13: Meaning of $-\int V dP$

In the differential form,

$$\delta q = \delta W + dh + dPE + dKE \quad \ldots (I)$$

From first law, $\quad \delta q = \delta W + dU$

and $\delta W = P\, dV$ for a reversible work

$$\delta q = PdV + dU \quad \ldots (II)$$

Enthalpy, $\quad h = U + PV$

$$dh = dU + PdV + VdP \quad \ldots (III)$$

Substituting values of δq and dh from equations (II) and (III) in equation (I),

$PdV + dU = \delta W + dU + PdV + VdP + dPE + dKE$

$$\therefore \quad -\int VdP = \int \delta W + \Delta PE + \Delta KE \quad \ldots (1.24)$$

which is to say that, in a reversible steady flow process, $-\int VdP$ equals the shaft work 'W' plus changes in KE and PE.

(a) If ΔPE is negligible,

$$-\int V\, dP = W + \Delta KE$$

(b) If ΔKE is negligible,

$$-\int V\, dP = W + \Delta PE$$

(c) If ΔKE and ΔPE both are negligible, then

$$-\int V\, dP = W_{shaft} \qquad \ldots (1.25)$$

i.e. in a reversible steady flow process, $-\int V\, dP$ equals shaft work 'W' when changes in kinetic energy and potential energy are neglected.

1.9 Significance of $\int_1^2 PdV$ in Case of Steady Flow Process

Refer Fig. 1.14.

The SFEE is

$$Q + \left(h_1 + \frac{v_1^2}{2} + gz_1\right) = W + \left(h_2 + \frac{v_2^2}{2} + gz_2\right)$$

$$\therefore \quad Q + \left(U_1 + P_1V_1 + \frac{v_1^2}{2000} + \frac{gz_1}{1000}\right) = W + \left(U_2 + P_2V_2 + \frac{v_2^2}{2000} + \frac{gz_2}{1000}\right) \text{ kJ/kg}$$

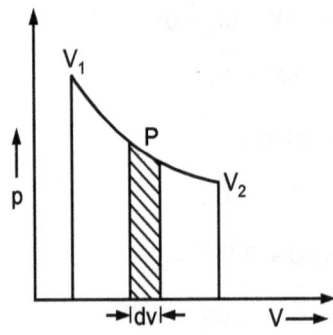

Fig. 1.14

$$Q = \Delta U + \Delta(PV) + \Delta KE + \Delta PE + W$$

In differential form, $\quad \delta Q = dU + d(PV) + d(KE) + d(PE) + \delta W$

For any reversible process,

$$\delta Q = dU + PdV$$

$\therefore \qquad dU + PdV = dU + d(PV) + d(KE) + d(PE) + \delta W$

$\therefore \qquad PdV = d(PV) + d(KE) + d(PE) + \delta W$

Integrating

$$\therefore \int_1^2 PdV = \Delta PV + \Delta KE + \Delta PE + W \qquad \ldots (1.26)$$

$\int_1^2 PdV$ for a steady flow process is sum of change in flow work plus change in kinetic energy, plus change in potential energy and shaft work.

Note: For **non-flow** reversible process, $\int_1^2 P\, dV$ is the area under the curve and it represents shaft work when the pressure changes from P_1 to P_2 and volume from V_1 to V_2.

$$\int_1^2 P\, dv = W_{1-2} \qquad \ldots (1.27)$$

1.10 Perpetual Motion Machine of First Kind, PMM - I

First law states that energy can neither be created nor be destroyed but only gets transformed from one form to another.

A device which violates the first law of thermodynamics is called as perpetual motion machine of first kind.

A device which continuously produces work without consuming any energy, is known as perpetual motion machine of first kind. This is illustrated in Fig. 1.15. PMM - I is against first law, hence PMM - I is impossible.

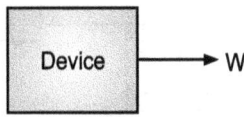

Fig. 1.15: PMM - I

The converse of PMM - I is, there can be no machine which would continuously consume work without some other form of energy appearing simultaneously (Fig. 1.16).

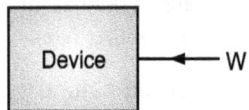

Fig. 1.16: Converse of PMM - I

This is also not possible.

1.11 Limitations of First Law of Thermodynamics

(i) First law of thermodynamics tells that energy can be transformed from one form to another, but it does not tell how much energy can be transformed from one form to another. It means it is not quantitative law.

(ii) Energy of an isolated system remains constant, as stated by first law. But it does not give information regarding whether a system which undergoes a process or not.

(iii) Let us consider the following examples. Let a room is heated by an electric resistor (Fig. 1.17).

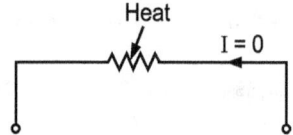

Fig. 1.17: Transferring heat to the wire will not generate electricity

Again the first law dictates that the amount of electrical energy supplied to the resistance wire be equal to the amount of energy transformed to the room air as heat. Now, attempt to reverse this process. If the same amount of heat supplied to the resistance wire will not generate electric energy, still it will not violate first law.

Again consider a paddle - wheel mechanism that is operated by the fall of mass. (Fig. 1.18).

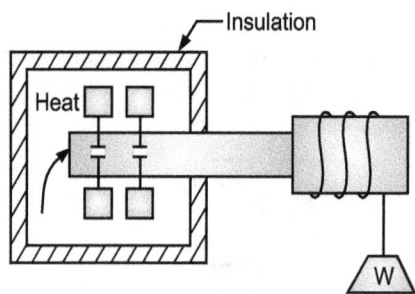

Fig. 1.18: Transferring heat to paddle wheel does not cause it to rotate

As the weight falls, paddle wheel rotates, stirring the fluid. Therefore, fluid gets heated. Now, attempt to reverse the process. That is transferring heat from the fluid to the paddle wheel, does not make the paddle wheel to rotate in reverse direction raising the weight from lower level to higher level. Still it will not violate the first law.

It is clear from above, that processes proceed naturally in a **certain** direction and not in the reverse direction. The first law places no restriction on the direction of a process; but satisfying the first law does not ensure that process will actually occur.

These limitations of first law make necessary to study second law of thermodynamics.

SOLVED PROBLEMS

Problem 1.1: Air at 100 kPa and 280 K is compressed steadily to 600 kPa and 400 K. The mass flow rate of the air is 0.02 kg/s and a heat loss of 16 kJ/kg occurs during the process. Assuming the changes in kinetic and potential energies are negligible, determine the necessary power input to the compressor.

Assume enthalpy of air at inlet and exit as 280.13 kJ/kg and 400.98 kJ/kg respectively.

Solution: Steady flow energy equation is

$$q + \left(h_1 + \frac{v_1^2}{2} + gz_1\right) = w + \left(h_2 + \frac{v_2^2}{2} + gz_2\right)$$

$$q - w = \Delta h + \Delta PE + \Delta KE$$
∴ $$q - w = \Delta h + 0 + 0$$
∴ $$q - w = h_2 - h_1$$
∴ $$-16 - w = (400.98 - 280.13)$$
$$w = -136.85 \text{ kJ/kg}$$

This is the work done on the air per unit mass. The power input to the compressor is determined by multiplying this value by the mass flow rate.

$$W = m \cdot w = (-136.85) \times (0.02) = -2.74 \text{ kW} \quad \textbf{Ans.}$$

Problem 1.2: A water turbine receives water through a nozzle at the rate of 36000 kg/min. The head of water from the centre of the turbine is 300 m and discharge 5 m below the centre line of turbine. The velocity of water at outlet is 8 m/s. Neglecting the initial velocity of water, find the power output of the turbine.

Solution: Given: $m_w = \dfrac{3600}{60}$ kg/s = 600 kg/s, $v_1 = 0$, $v_2 = 8$ m/s

SFEE is,

$$Q + \left(h_1 + \frac{v_1^2}{2} + gz_1\right) = W + \left(h_2 + \frac{v_2^2}{2} + gz_2\right)$$

$h_1 = h_2 = 0$, $Q = 0$, $v_1 = 0$, $z_2 = 0$

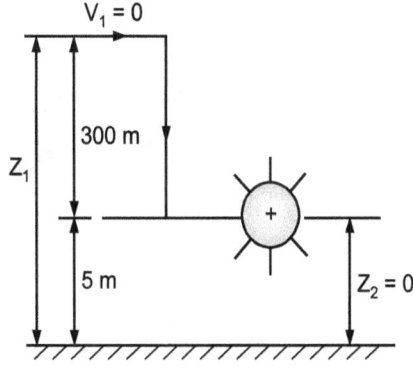

Fig. 1.19

$$\therefore \quad W = gz_1 - \frac{V_2^2}{2} \text{ J/kg}$$

$$= 9.81 \times (305) - \frac{8^2}{2} = 2960 \text{ J/kg}$$

$$\text{Power output} = 2960 \times m_w = \frac{2960 \times 600}{1000} = 1776 \text{ kW} \quad \text{... Ans.}$$

Problem 1.3: In a steady flow machine, 405 kW of work is done by the machine. The flow of fluid is 3 kg/s. The specific volume of the fluid, pressure and velocity at inlet are 0.37 m³/kg, 6 bar and 16 m/s respectively. The inlet is 32 m above the floor and discharge pipe is at the level of floor. The discharge conditions are 0.62 m²/kg, 1 bar and 270 m/s respectively. The total heat loss between the inlet and discharge is 9 kJ/kg of the fluid. Find the change in specific internal energy.

Solution: Refer Fig. 1.20.

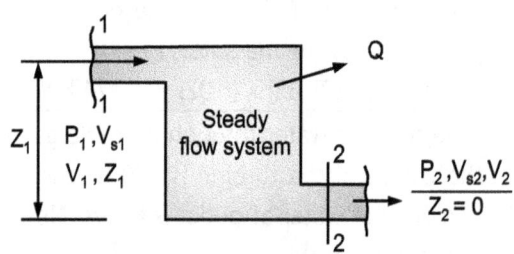

Fig. 1.20

Given: W = 405/3 = 135 kJ/kg

m = 3 kg/s $\quad z_1 = 32$ m

$V_{s1} = 0.37$ m³/kg $\quad V_{s2} = 0.62$ m³/kg

$P_1 = 6$ bar $\quad P_2 = 1$ bar

$V_1 = 16$ m/s $\quad V_2 = 270$ m/s, $z_2 = 0$

$Q = 9$ kJ/kg $\quad u_2 - u_1 = ?$

Using SFEE

$$Q + \left(u_1 + P_1 V_{s1} + \frac{V_1^2}{2} + gz_1\right) = W + \left(u_2 + P_2 V_{s2} + \frac{V_2^2}{2} + gz_2\right)$$

$$-9 + (u_1 + 6 \times 10^5 \times 0.37 + \frac{16^2}{2} + 9.81 \times 32)$$

$$= 135 + (u_2 + 1 \times 10^5 \times 0.62 + \frac{270^2}{2} + 9.81 \times 0)$$

$\therefore \quad u_2 - u_1 = -20$ kJ/kg

$\therefore \quad$ Total $\Delta U = -20 \times m = -20 \times 3 = -60$ kJ/s = -60 kW ... **Ans.**

Problem 1.4: Air flows steadily at the rate of 0.5 kg/s, through an air compressor entering at 7 m/s velocity, 100 kPa and 0.95 m³/kg and leaving at 5 m/s, 700 kPa and 0.19 m³/kg respectively. The internal energy of the air leaving is 90 kJ/kg greater than that of air entering. Cooling water in the compressor jacket absorbs heat from the air at the rate of 58 kW.
  (a) Compute the rate of shaft work input to the compressor in kW.
  (b) Find the ratio of inlet and outlet pipe diameter.

Solution:

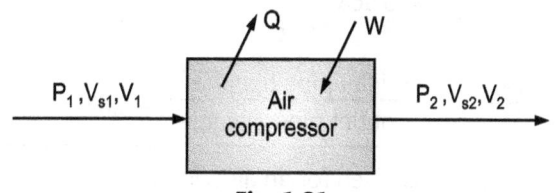

Fig. 1.21

Given: m = 0.5 kg/s

v_1 = 7 m/s $\qquad$ v_2 = 5 m/s

V_{s1} = 0.95 m³/kg $\qquad$ V_{s2} = 0.19 m³/kg

P_1 = 100 × 10³ N/m² $\qquad$ P_2 = 700 × 10³ N/m²

$u_2 - u_1$ = 90 kJ/kg $\qquad$ Q = − 5.8 kW

$$Q = \frac{-58}{m} = \frac{-58}{0.5} = -116 \text{ kJ/kg}$$

$$Q + \left(u_1 + P_1 V_{s1} + \frac{v_1^2}{2} + gz_1\right) = W + \left(u_2 + P_2 V_{s2} + \frac{v_2^2}{2} + gz_2\right)$$

(a) $W = \left[(u_1 - u_2) + P_1 V_{s1} - P_2 V_{s2} + \frac{v_1^2}{2} - \frac{v_2^2}{2}\right] + Q$

$\quad = \left[-90 \times 10^3 + 100 \times 10^3 \times 0.95 - 700 \times 10^3 \times 0.19 + \frac{7^2}{2} - \frac{5^2}{2}\right] - 116 \text{ J/kg}$

$\quad = [-90 + 95 - 133 + 0.012 - 116] \text{ kJ/kg}$

$\quad = -223.98 \text{ kJ/kg}$

Mass flow rate is m = 0.5 kg/s

Net work done/s = W × m = − 223.98 × 0.5 = − 112 kW **... Ans.**

(b) m × V_{s1} = A_1 v_1 ∴ $\quad A_1 = \dfrac{m \cdot V_{s1}}{v_1} = \dfrac{0.5 \times 0.95}{7} = 0.0678 \text{ m}^2$

$$A_2 = \frac{m \cdot V_{s2}}{V_2} = \frac{0.5 \times 0.19}{5} = 0.019 \text{ m}^2$$

$$\frac{A_1}{A_2} = \frac{\frac{\pi}{4} \cdot d_1^2}{\frac{\pi}{4} \cdot d_2^2} = \frac{0.0678}{0.019} = 3.568$$

$$\therefore \quad \frac{d_1^2}{d_2^2} = 3.568$$

$$\therefore \quad \frac{d_1}{d_2} = \frac{\text{inlet pipe diameter}}{\text{outlet pipe diameter}} = 1.889 \quad \text{... Ans.}$$

Problem 1.5: The following data is given for an air compressor:

(i) Rate of air flow 5 kg/s

	Inlet	Outlet
Pressure	80 kPa	600 kPa
Sp. volume	0.65 m³/kg	0.12
Sp. internal energy	40 kJ/kg	140 kJ/kg
Velocity	6 m/s	4 m/s

Heat rejected to cooling water is 50 kW.

Find (i) Power required to drive the compressor in kW.

(ii) Ratio of inlet pipe diameter to outlet pipe diameter.

Solution: $\Delta PE = 0$, $Q = \frac{50}{5} = 10$ kJ/kg

The SFEE is

$$Q + \left(u_1 + P_1 V_{s1} + \frac{V_1^2}{2} + gz_1\right) = W + \left(u_2 + P_2 V_{s2} + \frac{V_2^2}{2} + gz_2\right) \text{ J/kg}$$

$$Q + \left(u_1 + P_1 V_{s1} + \frac{V_1^2}{2}\right) = W + \left(u_2 + P_2 V_{s2} + \frac{V_2^2}{2}\right)$$

$$10 + \left(40 + 80 \times 0.65 + \frac{6^2}{2} \times 10^{-3}\right)$$

$$= W + \left(140 + 600 \times 0.12 + \frac{4^2}{2} \times 10^{-3}\right) \text{ kJ/kg}$$

$$\therefore \quad W = -129.99 \text{ kJ/kg} \quad \text{... Ans.}$$

For determining the ratio of diameters, use continuity equation.

$$\dot{m} = \frac{A_1 V_1}{V_{s1}} = \frac{A_2 V_2}{V_{s2}}$$

$$\therefore \frac{A_1}{A_2} = \frac{V_{s1}}{V_{s2}} \times \frac{V_2}{V_1}$$

$$= \frac{0.65}{0.12} \times \frac{4}{6} = 3.611$$

$$\therefore \frac{d_1}{d_2} = \sqrt{\frac{A_1}{A_2}} = \sqrt{3.611} = 1.9 \quad \text{... Ans.}$$

Problem 1.6: Air flows in a compressor at a rate of 0.7 kg/sec. The air enters at 5 m/sec velocity, 100 kPa pressure, 0.85 m³/kg, volume leaving at 3 m/sec, 700 kPa and 0.17 m³/kg. The internal energy of the air leaving is 80 kJ/kg greater than that of air entering. Cooling water in the compressor jacket absorb heat from air at the rate of 60 kW.

(a) Determine the rate of shaft work input to the air in kW.

(b) Find the ratio of inlet pipe diameter to outlet pipe diameter.

Solution:

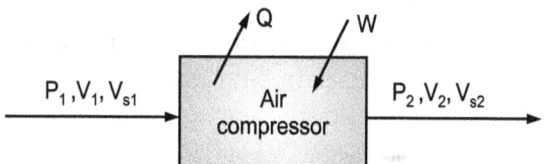

Fig. 1.22: Block diagram of a compressor

Given:
$\dot{m} = 0.7$ kg/sec.
$V_1 = 5$ m/sec, $V_2 = 3$ m/sec
$V_{s1} = 0.85$ m³/kg, $V_{s2} = 0.17$ m³/kg
$P_1 = 100 \times 10^3$ N/m², $P_2 = 700 \times 10^3$ N/m²
$u_2 - u_1 = 80$ kJ/kg, $Q = \frac{-60}{0.7} = -85.7$ kJ/kg

(a) **Shaft work:** Steady flow energy equation:

$$Q + \left(u_1 + P_1 V_{s1} + \frac{V_1^2}{2} + gz_1 \right) = W + \left(u_2 + P_2 V_{s2} + \frac{V_2^2}{2} + gz_2 \right)$$

$$\therefore W = \left[(u_1 - u_2) + P_1 V_{s1} - P_2 V_{s2} + \frac{V_1^2}{2} - \frac{V_2^2}{2} \right] + Q$$

$$= \left[-80 \times 10^3 + 100 \times 10^3 \times 0.85 - 700 \times 10^3 \times 0.17 + \frac{5^2}{2} - \frac{3^2}{2} \right] - 85.7$$

$$= -80 + 85 - 119 - 0.008 - 85.7$$
$$= -199.7 \text{ kJ/kg}$$

Mass flow rate of air = 0.7 kg/sec.

Net work = $m \times W = 0.7 \times (-199.7) = -139.8$ kW ... **Ans.**

(b) Ratio of inlet to outlet pipe diameter

$$= m v_{s_1} = A_1 v_1$$

$$\therefore \quad A_1 = \frac{m \cdot v_{s_1}}{v_1} = \frac{0.7 \times 0.85}{5} = 0.119 \text{ m}^2$$

Similarly, $\quad A_2 = \dfrac{m \cdot v_{s_2}}{v_2} = \dfrac{0.7 \times 0.17}{3} = 0.0396$

$$\therefore \quad \frac{A_1}{A_2} = \frac{\frac{\pi}{4} \cdot d_1^2}{\frac{\pi}{4} \cdot d_2^2} = \frac{0.119}{0.0396} = 3$$

$$\therefore \quad \frac{d_1}{d_2} = \frac{\text{Inlet pipe diameter}}{\text{Outlet pipe diameter}} = 1.732 \quad \text{... \textbf{Ans.}}$$

Problem 1.7: Air at 100 kPa and 280 K is compressed steadily to 600 kPa and 400 K. The mass flow rate of air is 0.02 kg/s and heat loss 16 kJ/kg occurs during the process. Assuming changes in kinetic and potential energies to be negligible, determine the necessary power input to the compressor. Assume enthalpy of air at inlet and exit at 280.13 kJ/kg and 400.98 kJ/kg respectively.

Solution: Given:
$P_1 = 100$ kPa $\quad\quad \dot{m}_{air} = 0.02$ kg/s
$T_1 = 280$ K $\quad\quad Q = -16$ kJ/kg
$P_2 = 600$ kPa $\quad\quad h_1 = 280.13$ kJ/kg
$T_2 = 400$ K $\quad\quad h_2 = 400.98$ kJ/kg

The steady flow energy equation is

$$q + \left(h_1 + \frac{v_1^2}{2} + gz_1 \right) = w + \left(h_2 + \frac{v_2^2}{2} + gz_2 \right)$$

Change in K.E. and P.E. are negligible.

$$\therefore \quad q - w = \Delta h$$
$$w = q - \Delta h$$
$$= -16 - (400.98 - 280.13)$$
$$= -136.85 \text{ kJ/kg}$$

Power input, $W = m \cdot w$

$$= 0.02 \frac{kg}{s} \times (-136.85) \frac{kJ}{kg} = -2.737 \text{ kW} \quad \text{... Ans.}$$

Problem 1.8: A gas turbine receives gases at 7.2 bar and 850°C and velocity of 160 m/s. The gases come out of turbine at 1.15 bar and 450°C and a velocity of 250 m/s. Find out the work output from the gas turbine in kW/kg. The process may be assumed as adiabatic. Take C_p = 1.04 kJ/kg-°C for gas.

Solution: The general energy equation on the basis of 1 kg flow can be written as

$$\left(\frac{V_1^2}{2} + gZ_1 + h_1\right) \pm Q \pm W = \left[\frac{V_2^2}{2} + gZ_2 + h_2\right]$$

For the gas turbine, $Z_1 = Z_2$, $Q = 0$

(as the flow is adiabatic (given))

Gas turbine is work developing system.

∴ $\left(\frac{V_1^2}{2} + h_1\right) - W = \left(\frac{V_2^2}{2} + h_2\right)$

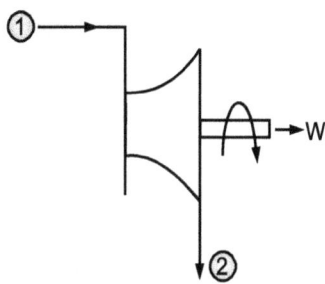

Fig. 1.23

∴ $W = \frac{V_1^2 - V_2^2}{2} + (h_1 - h_2) = \frac{V_1^2 - V_2^2}{2} + C_p (T_1 - T_2)$

$$= \left[\frac{(160)^2 - (250)^2}{2}\right] + 1.04 \times 10^3 \times (850 - 450) \text{ joules}$$

$$= (-18450 + 416 \times 10^3) \text{ joules} = -18.45 + 416 = 397.55 \text{ kJ/kg}$$

... Ans.

FIRST LAW OF THERMODYNAMICS APPLIED TO FLOW PROCESSES

Problem 1.9: A turbine operates under steady flow conditions with the following inlet and outlet conditions of the working fluid.

Property	Inlet	Outlet
Pressure (kPa)	1177	19.6
Specific volume (m³/kg)	0.218	7.79
Velocity (m/s)	35	100
Internal energy (kJ/kg)	2792.7	2456.5
Elevation (m)	3	0.0

Heat lost to the surrounding is 25 kJ/min. If the rate of steam flow through the turbine is 240 kg/min, what is the power output of the turbine?

Solution: The general flow energy equation considering mass flow rate m kg/sec can be written as

$$m\left[\frac{V_1^2}{2} + Z_1 g + u_1 + p_1 v_{s1}\right] - Q - W = m\left[\frac{V_2^2}{2} + Z_2 g + u_2 + p_2 v_{s2}\right]$$

where m is mass flow in kg/sec and Q and W are also on second basis.

where Q is heat rejected in J/sec = $\dfrac{25 \times 1000}{60}$ = 416.6 J/s

and W is the work developed in J/sec = watts

and m is mass of working fluid passing through the turbine = $\dfrac{240}{60}$ = 4 kg/sec

$$\therefore \quad W = m\left[\frac{V_1^2 - V_2^2}{2} + g(Z_1 - Z_2) + (u_1 - u_2) + (p_1 v_{s1} - p_2 v_{s2})\right] - Q$$

Substituting the given values in proper units,

$$W = 4\left[\frac{(35)^2 - (100)^2}{2} + 9.81(3-0) + 10^3(2792.7 - 2456.5) + (0.1177 \times 0.218 - 19.6 \times 7.79) \times 10^3\right] - 416.6$$

$$\therefore \quad W = 4 \times [-4387.5 + 29.43 + 10^3 \times 336.2 + 10^3 \times 103.9] - 416.6$$

$$= 4 \times 10^3 [-4.38 + 0.029 + 336.2 + 103.9] - 416.6$$

$$= 4 \times 10^3 [435.8] - 416.6$$

$$= 1742.6 \text{ kWz} \qquad \text{... Ans.}$$

Problem 1.11: A gas at pressure of 1500 kPa is expanded in a cylinder - piston arrangement. The piston has a diameter of 10 cm. The expansion curve is a straight line. At the end of expansion, the pressure of the gas is 120 kPa. Find the work done by the gas on the piston if stroke length is 0.25 m.

Solution:

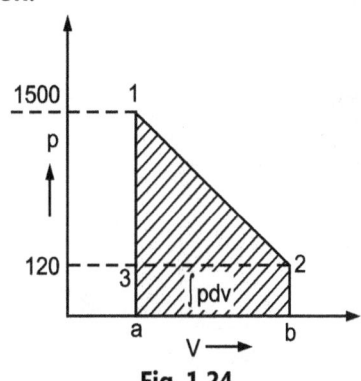

Fig. 1.24

$$W = \int_1^2 P\, dV$$

= Area under the curve

$\therefore \quad V_b - V_a = \dfrac{\pi}{4} d^2 \cdot L = \dfrac{\pi}{4}(0.1)^2 \times 0.25 = 1.96 \times 10^{-3} \text{ m}^3$

$\therefore \quad W = \text{Area } 1-2-3 + \text{Area } a-b-2-3$

$= \dfrac{1}{2} \times (1500 - 120) \times V_s + 120 \times V_s$

$= \left[\dfrac{1}{2}(1500 - 120) + 120\right] \times 1.96 \times 10^{-3}$

$= 1.355$ kN-m ... **Ans.**

EXERCISE

1. What is energy? What are the forms of energy?
2. What do you understand by internal energy?
3. What is the outcome of Joule's experiment?
4. Give different statements of first law of thermodynamics.
5. Prove that energy is a property of the system.
6. What is meant by steady flow process?
7. Explain the meaning of flow work.
8. Apply first law of thermodynamics to steady flow process.
9. Explain few examples of steady flow process with the assumptions.
10. What are the limitations of first law of thermodynamics?

11. What is the meaning of $-\int V\, dP$ in a steady flow process?
12. What is meant by perpetual motion machine of first kind?
13. The power output of an adiabatic steam turbine is 5 MW and the inlet and exit conditions of steam are as under.

	Pressure	Temp.	Velocity	Elevation
Inlet	2 MPa	400°C	50 m/s	10 m
Exit	15 kPa	0.9 dry	180 m/s	6 m

Determine the work done / kg of steam and the mass flow rate in kg/s.

(**Ans.** W_s = 871.91 kJ/kg, $\dot{m}$ = 5.734 kg/s)

14. A centrifugal pump operates under steady flow conditions. It delivers 0.3 m³ of water per minute at 20°C. The suction pressure is 80 kPa, and the delivery pressure is 3 bar. Diameters of suction and delivery pipes are 15 cm and 10 cm respectively. The pump axis is 5 m above the sump level and is 15 m below the level in the overhead tank. Neglecting change of internal energy, calculate the power required to operate the pump. Given: g = 9.81 m/s², e_w = 1000 kg/m³. (**Ans.** w_s = – 2.1623 kW)

15. In a steady flow machine 405 kW of work is done by the machine. The flow of the fluid is 3 kg/sec. The specific volume of fluid, pressure and velocity at inlet are 0.37 m³/kg, 6 bar and 16 m/sec. The inlet is 32 m above the floor and the discharge pipe is at the floor level. The discharge conditions are 0.62 m³/kg, 1 bar and 270 m/sec respectively. The total heat loss between the inlet and discharge is 9 kJ/kg of the fluid. Find the change in specific internal energy. **Ans.** – 20.01 kg

16. The following data refers to a steady flow process.

	At entrance	At exit
Enthalpy (kJ/kg)	4000	4100
Velocity (m/sec)	50	20
Height (m) above datum	50	10

Mass flow rate – 1 kg/sec.

Heat transfer rate is 200 kJ/sec to the system. Determine the power capacity of the system and state whether it is a power producing system or otherwise.

Ans. Power capacity = $\dfrac{\delta W}{dt}$ = + 101.442 kW

(It is power generating system)

17. A room is fitted with two fans each consuming 0.2 kW power. There are three lamps in the room each consuming 200 W. Ventilation air enters the room with enthalpy of 85 kJ/kg and leaves the room with enthalpy of 60 kJ/kg. The rate of air flow is 100 kg/hour. There are five persons in the room and heat generated by each person is 600 kJ/hour. Determine the rate at which the heat is to be removed by a room cooler, so that steady state is maintained in the room. **Ans.** 2.52 kW

Hint: Equation for steady state flow is $\dot{m}(h_1 - h_2) + q = w$

$$\therefore \dot{m}(h_1 - h_2) + \begin{pmatrix} \text{Heat added} \\ \text{due to lamps} \end{pmatrix} + \begin{pmatrix} \text{Heat generated} \\ \text{by five persons} \end{pmatrix} - \begin{pmatrix} \text{Heat removed} \\ \text{by cooler} \end{pmatrix}$$

= Work supplied by fan (which should be negative)

18. In a steam turbine, steam flows at a rate of 2 kg/s and the heat transfer from the turbine is 10 kW. The steam enters the turbine with enthalpy of 3138.6 kJ/kg and leaves the turbine with enthalpy of 2675.4 kJ/kg. The inlet and outlet velocities of steam are 50 m/s and 200 m/s respectively. The inlet pipe is 3 m above the outlet pipe. Take $g = 9.8066$ m/sec².

Calculate the output of the turbine in kW. **Ans.** 878.84 kW

19. The following data refers to a centrifugal air compressor of a gas turbine.

   (1) Inlet air condition   -   Pressure 1 bar, Temperature 350 K.

   (2) Outlet air condition   -   Pressure 5 bar, Temperature 530 K.

   (3) Outlet air velocity.   -   100 m/sec.

   The mass rate of flow into the compressor is 10 kg/s. Determine power required to drive the compressor. Assume that the compression is adiabatic and compressor is horizontal. Take C_p for air as 1.0035 kJ/kg K. **Ans.** – 1856.3 kW

20. A steam power plant consists of a boiler, a turbine, a condenser and a feed pump. The steam is generated in the boiler. The steam leaving the boiler enters the turbine and expands in the turbine. The exhaust steam from turbine is condensed in the condenser. The condensed steam is pumped by feed pump into the boiler.

   The block diagram of the steam plant is as shown in the *Fig. 1.25*. The following observations were taken during a trial on the steam plant.

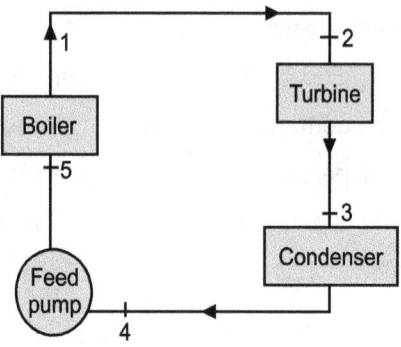

Fig. 1.25

		Pressure	Temperature
1.	Condition of steam leaving the boiler (Location 1)	24 bar	300°C
2.	Condition of steam entering the turbine (Location 2)	22 bar	290°C
3.	Condition of steam leaving the turbine, entering condenser (Location 3)	14 kPa,	0.95 dry
4.	Condition of steam leaving the condenser entering feed pump (Location 4)	13 kPa	40°C

5. C_p of superheated steam — 2.1 kJ/kg K
6. Specific heat of water 4.18 kJ/kg K
7. Power required to drive the 5 kJ/kg pump.

Assume that turbine walls are insulated.

Find following quantities per kilogram of fluid flowing through the plant.

(a) Heat transferred to the atmosphere from the pipe line between boiler and turbine in kJ/kg.

(b) Power output of the turbine in kJ/kg.

(c) Heat transfer in condenser in kJ/kg.

(d) Heat transfer in boiler in kJ/kg.

Ans. (a) – 61.42 kJ/kg, (b) + 474.12 kJ/kg, (c) – 2310.66 kJ/kg, (d) 2841.2 kJ/kg.

21. A fluid system undergoes a non-flow frictionless process from $V_1 = 0.15$ m³ to $V_2 = 0.5$ m³. The relation between pressure and volume is given by the expression, $P = \dfrac{1.5}{V} + 2$ bar, where V is in m³. During this process the system rejects 22.4 kJ of heat. Find the change in enthalpy.   **Ans.** $\Delta H = 142.39$ kJ

22. During a non-flow process, work per degree temperature increase, is $\dfrac{\delta W}{dt} = 190$ kJ/°C and the internal energy is expressed as $U = 50 + 14\,T$ kJ/°C.
Determine the heat if the temperature changes from 25°C to 50°C.   **Ans.** 5150 kJ.

23. In a reversible process for a closed system, the pressure and volume vary according to the law $PV^n = C$. If $Q = 15$ kJ, $U = 45$ kJ, $P_1 = 1.4$ bar, $P_2 = 8.4$ bar, $V_1 = 0.15$ m³ and $V_2 = 0.0357$ m³, determine index 'n'.   **Ans. :** 1.2996

24. In a vertical cylinder, air below a frictionless piston occupies a volume of 0.09 m³ at a pressure of 10 bar. The diameter of the cylinder is 0.6 m. The mass of the piston is 90 kg. A stopper which keeps the piston in this position is suddenly removed. The piston moves upwards through a distance of 1.5 m.

The pressure of air above the piston is 1 bar.

The air expands according to law $Pv^{1.3}$ = constant.

Neglect velocity of air and calculate velocity of the piston when it has risen 1.5 m.

Ans. Velocity of piston = 41.74 m/sec.

25. An internally reversible process occurs in a system during which $Q = -12$ kJ, $\Delta U = -79$ kJ and $\Delta H = -111$ kJ.

Determine

(a) Work done if the system is non-flow.

(b) Shaft work and change of flow energy if the system is steady state-steady flow with $\Delta K = 4$ kJ for system.

(c) With $\Delta K = 4$ kJ, evaluate $\int P\,dV$ and $-\int V\,dP$ in kJ

Ans. (a) $W_{(non-flow)} = 67$ kJ,

(b) $W_{(shaft)} = 95$ kJ, $\Delta PV = -32$ kJ

(c) $\int P\,dV = 67$ kJ, $-\int v\,dP = 99$ kJ

26. A fluid system undergoes a non-flow frictionless process from $V_1 = 6$ m³ to $V_2 = 2$ m³. The pressure and volume relation during the process is given by

$P = \left(\dfrac{1500}{V} + 200\right) \dfrac{kN}{m^2}$, when V is in m³. The heat rejected during the process is 210 kJ. Determine the change in internal energy.

Ans. + 2237.94 kJ.

Unit II

SECOND LAW OF THERMODYNAMICS

2.1 Limitations of First Law of Thermodynamics

- First law of thermodynamics tells that energy can be transformed from one form to another, but it does not tell how much energy can be transformed from one form to another. It means it is not quantitative law.

- Energy of an isolated system remains constant, as stated by first law. But it does not give information regarding whether a system which undergoes a process or not.

- Let us consider the following examples. Let a room is heated by an electric resistor (Fig. 2.1).

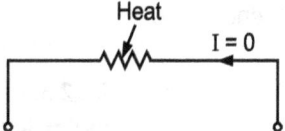

Fig. 2.1: Transferring heat to the wire will not generate electricity

Again the first law dictates that the amount of electrical energy supplied to the resistance wire be equal to the amount of energy transformed to the room air as heat. Now, attempt to reverse this process. If the same amount of heat supplied to the resistance wire will not generate electric energy, still it will not violate first law.

Again consider a paddle - wheel mechanism that is operated by the fall of mass. (Fig. 2.2).

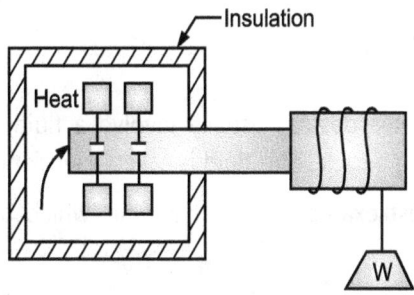

Fig. 2.2: Transferring heat to paddle wheel does not cause it to rotate

2.2 Terminology

2.2.1 Thermal Energy Reservoirs

A hypothetical body with a large thermal capacity (mass × specific heat) that can supply or absorb finite amount of heat energy without undergoing a change in temperature is termed as **thermal energy reservoir**. In practice, large bodies of water such as oceans, lakes and rivers as well as the atmospheric air are considered as thermal reservoirs.

A reservoir that supplies energy in the form of heat is called a **source** and one that absorbs energy in the form of heat is called a **sink**.

2.2.2 Heat Engine or Carnot Engine

Work can easily be converted into other forms of energy, but converting other forms of energy into work is not that easy. A device used to convert heat energy to work is known as **heat engine**.

Heat engines differ considerably from one another, but all are characterised by the following (Fig. 2.3).

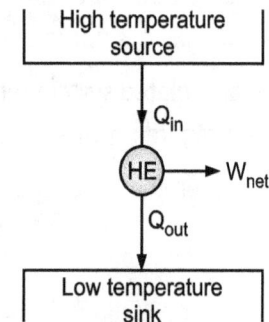

Fig. 2.3: Part of the heat received by a heat engine is converted to work while the rest is rejected)

(1) They receive heat from a high temperature source (solar energy, oil furnace, nuclear reactor, etc.)
(2) They convert part of this heat to work (usually in the form of a rotating shaft).
(3) They reject the remaining waste heat to a low temperature sink (the atmosphere, rivers, oceans etc.)
(4) They operate on a cycle.

Heat engines and other cyclic devices usually involve a fluid to and from which heat is transferred while undergoing a cycle. This fluid is called a working substance.

A steam power plant is best example of heat engine, which operates on thermodynamic cycle.

The work developing devices such as Internal combustion type (gas turbines and car engines) are also heat engines but they operate on mechanical cycle.

Let, Q_{in} = amount of heat supplied to heat engine, kJ

Q_{out} = amount of heat rejected to heat engine, kJ

The net work output, $W_{net} = Q_{in} - Q_{out}$ kJ

Thermal Efficiency:

Q_{out} is never zero. Therefore, W_{net} of heat engine is always less than Q_{in}.

∴ Thermal efficiency = $\dfrac{\text{net work output}}{\text{total heat input}}$

$$\eta_{th} = \dfrac{W_{net}}{Q_{in}} = \dfrac{Q_{in} - Q_{out}}{Q_{in}}$$

$$= 1 - \dfrac{Q_{out}}{Q_{in}} \qquad \ldots (2.1)$$

2.2.3 Refrigerator

A device which transfers heat from a low temperature body (medium) to a high temperature one is called as a **refrigerator**.

A refrigerator is a cyclic device which uses refrigerant as a working fluid. The most frequently used refrigeration is a vapour - compression refrigeration cycle.

A refrigerator is shown schematically in Fig. 2.4. Here Q_L is the amount of heat removed from the refrigerated space at temperature T_L, Q_H is the amount of heat rejected to the warm environment at temperature T_H and W_{net} is the net work input to the refrigerator.

The efficiency of a refrigerator is expressed in terms of the *coefficient of performance* (COP), denoted by COP_R.

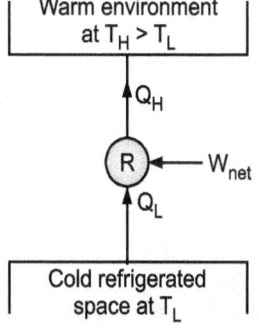

Fig. 2.4: Schematic of refrigerator

Coefficient of Performance:

The objective of a refrigerator is to remove heat (Q_L) from the refrigerated space. To accomplish this, it requires W_{net} work as input. Therefore, COP of a refrigerator is

$$COP_R = \frac{\text{desired effect}}{\text{required input}} = \frac{Q_L}{W_{net}} \quad \ldots (2.2)$$

but,
$$W_{net} = Q_H - Q_L$$

∴
$$COP_R = \frac{Q_L}{Q_H - Q_L} = \frac{1}{(Q_H/Q_L) - 1} \quad \ldots (2.3)$$

COP may be greater than unity also.

2.2.4 Heat Pump (HP)

Another device that transfers heat from a low temperature space to a high temperature one is the heat pump. (Fig. 2.5). The objective of a heat pump is to maintain a heated space at high temperature.

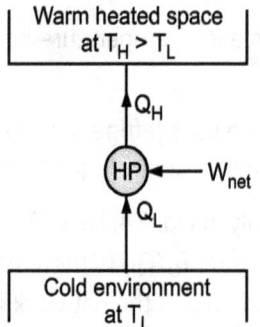

Fig. 2.5: Schematic of heat pump

The measure of performance of a heat pump is also expressed in terms of the coefficient of performance (COP_{HP}), defined as

$$COP_{HP} = \frac{\text{desired output}}{\text{required input}} = \frac{Q_H}{W_{net}} \quad \ldots (2.4)$$

$$= \frac{Q_H}{Q_H - Q_L} = \frac{1}{1 - \frac{Q_L}{Q_H}} \quad \ldots (2.5)$$

A comparison of equations (2.3) and (2.5) reveals that

$$COP_{HP} = COP_R + 1$$

2.3 The Second Law of Thermodynamics

In the last section, it is discussed that heat engine must reject some heat to a low temperature reservoir to complete the cycle, i.e. no heat engine can convert all the heat it receives to useful work. This limitation on the thermal efficiency of heat engine forms the basis for the *Kelvin-Planck statement*.

(a) Kelvin - Planck - Statement:

"It is impossible to construct a device that operates on a cycle and produces no effect other than withdrawal energy as heat from a single reservoir and converting all of it into work".

Simply, it can also be stated as "It is impossible for any device that operates on a cycle to receive heat from a single reservoir and produce an equivalent amount of work."

It can also be stated as "No engine can have thermal efficiency of 100 percent" [Fig. 2.6 (a)].

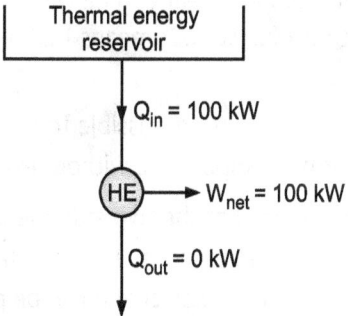

Fig. 2.6 (a): A heat engine that violates Kelvin-Planck statement of second law (PMM - II)

A device that violates the second law of thermodynamics is called a perpetual motion machine of the second kind (PMM - II).

PMM - II is practically impossible.

(b) Clausius - Statement (Second Law of Thermodynamics)

"It is impossible to construct a device that operates in a cycle and produces no effect other than the transfer of heat from a low temperature body to a higher temperature body without external aid".

It simply states that a refrigerator will not operate unless its compressor is driven by an external power (electric motor). It means a device requires external energy to transfer heat from a low temperature body to a higher temperature body.

A device that violates Clausius statement is shown in Fig. 2.6 (b).

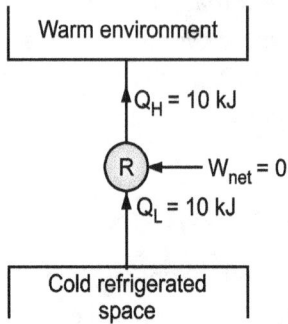

Fig. 2.6 (b): A refrigerator that violates the Clausius statement of the second law (PMM - II)

2.4 Equivalence of Kelvin-Planck and Clausius Statements

- Kelvin-Planck statement tells that any heat engine will not convert the thermal energy of heat source completely into useful work. It means that a heat engine does not have 100 percent efficiency.

- Clausius statement tells that it will not be possible to transfer heat from a body at lower temperature to a body at higher temperature without external aid (energy input).

- From above paragraphs, one feels that the two statements are totally different and have no way interlinked. But conceptually the two statements of second law of thermodynamics are equivalent in all respect and can be proved here.

- The proof is not in the form of mathematical steps but violation of one statement implies the violation of the second and vice-versa.

(a) Consider a cyclic heat pump 'P' shown in Fig. 2.7 which transfers heat from a low temperature reservoir (T_2) to a high temperature reservoir (T_1) with no other effect i.e. with no expenditure of work, violating Clausius statement.

Let us assume a heat engine 'E' working between the same thermal reservoirs producing net work (W_{net}) in a thermodynamic cycle. Assume that the rate of working of the heat engine is such that it draws an amount of heat Q_1 from the reservoir equal to that discharged by the heat pump (P). It means there is no need of high temperature reservoir and the heat Q_1 discharged by the heat pump (P) is directly fed to the heat engine. So one concludes that heat pump 'P' and the heat engine 'E' working together constitute a heat engine operating in cycles and producing net work while exchanging heat only with one body at a single fixed temperature. This violates the Kelvin-Planck statement.

(b) Let us consider a perpetual motion machine of second kind (PMM-II) 'E' which produces net work in a cycle by exchanging heat with only one thermal energy reservoir (at T_1) and thus violates the Kelvin-Planck statement (See Fig. 2.8).

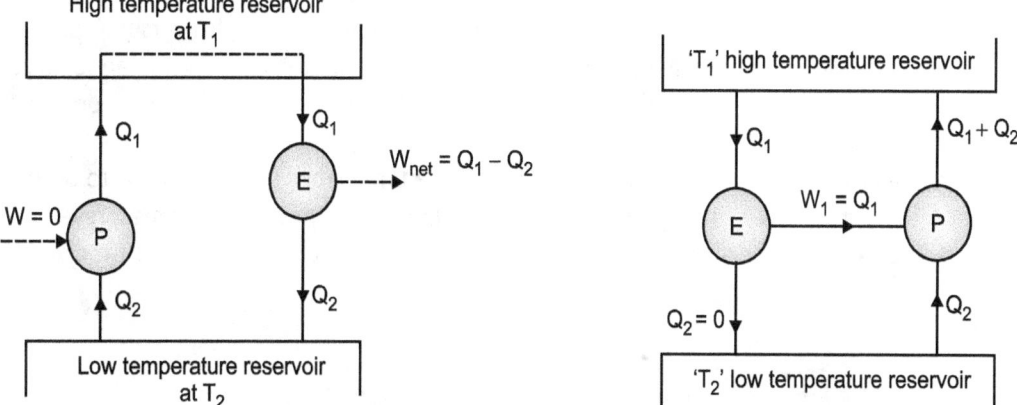

Fig. 2.7: Violation of Clausius statement   Fig. 2.8: Violation of Kelvin-Planck statement

Now, consider a cyclic heat pump (P) extracting heat Q_2 from a low temperature reservoir at T_2 and discharging heat to the high temperature reservoir at T_1 with the expenditure of work 'W' equal to that of the PMM-II delivers to a complete cycle. So E and P together constitute a heat pump working in cycles and producing the sole effect of transferring heat from a body at low temperature to a body at high temperature, thus violating the Clausius statement.

2.5 PPM II (Perpetual Motion Machine of Type II)
- It is a device which violates the second law of thermodynamics.
- Such a device is hypothetical and not practically possible.

2.5.1 Different Forms of PMM II
(a) A device which is operating in a cycle producing work by exchanging heat with a single reservoir. (Therefore, violates Kelvin-Plank Statement).
(b) A heat engine which is converting heat completely into work i.e. a heat engine with q = 100%.
(c) A heat pump which is transferring heat from a sink (L) to source (HTR) without any work input (violation of class).
(d) A refrigerator working without compressor.

2.5.2 Converse of PMM II
(a) For a heat engine efficiency is always less than unity.
(b) Heat pump or refrigerator must have work input for working.
(c) For a heat engine to work, some heat must be to a sink.

2.6 Concept of Reversibility and Irreversiblity

1. A reversible process is carried out infinitely slowly with an infinitesimal gradient, so that every state passed through by the system is an equilibrium state.
2. Any natural process carried out with a finite gradient is an irreversible process. A reversible process consists of a succession of equilibrium states. So it is an idealized hypothetical process. It is said to be an asymptote to reality. All spontaneous processes are irreversible.
3. Time has an important effect on reversibility. If the time allowed for a process to occur is infinitely large, even though the gradient is finite, the process becomes reversible. However, if this time allowed is reduced to a finite value, the finite gradient makes the process irreversible.

2.6.1 Causes of Irreversibility

The irreversibility of a process may be due to either lack of equilibrium during the process or involvement of dissipative effects.

(a) Irreversibility Due to Lack of Equilibrium

When there is no thermodynamic equilibrium (mechanical, thermal or chemical) between the system and its surroundings, or between two systems, or two parts of the same system, causes a continuous change which is irreversible. The following are few specific examples in this regard:

(i) Heat Transfer through a Finite Temperature Difference: To transfer a finite amount of heat through an infinitesimal temperature difference would require an infinite amount of time, or infinite area. All actual heat transfer processes are through a finite temperature difference and are, therefore, irreversible, and greater the temperature difference, the greater is the irreversibility.

We can demonstrate by the second law that heat transfer through a finite temperature difference is irreversible.

- Let us assume that a source at T_A and a sink at T_B ($T_A > T_B$) are available, and let Q_{A-B} be the amount of heat flowing from A and B (See Fig. 2.9).
- Let us assume engine operating between A and B, taking heat Q_1 from A and discharging heat Q_2 to B.
- Let the heat transfer process be reversed, and Q_{B-A} be the heat flowing from B to A (See Fig. 2.10) and let the rate of working of the engine be such that

$$Q_2 = Q_{B-A}$$

Then the sink B may be eliminated. The net result is that E produces net work W in a cycle by exchanging heat only with A, thus violating the Kelvin-Plank statement. So the heat transfer process Q_{A-B} is irreversible, and Q_{B-A} is not possible.

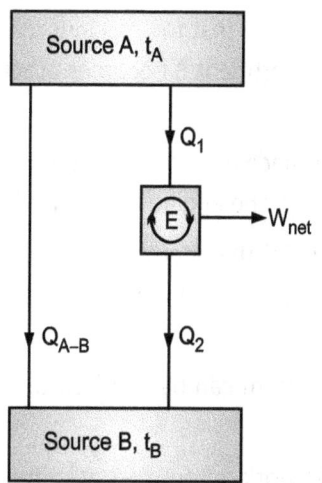

Fig. 2.9: Heat transfer through a finite temperature difference

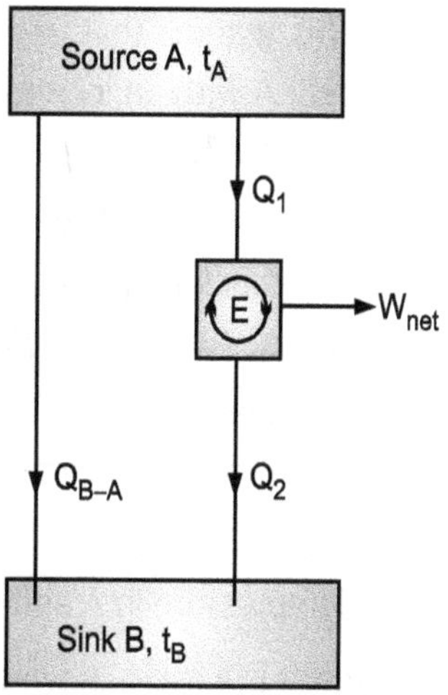

Fig. 2.10: Heat transfer through a finite temperature difference is irreversible

(ii) Lack of pressure: Equilibrium within the Interior of the System or between the System and the Surroundings: When there exists a difference in pressures between the system and the surroundings, or within the system itself, then both the system and its surroundings, will undergo a change of state. For example, let any system is at a pressure p_1 greater than the surrounding. In this case, a process occurs wherein the system pressure reduces to surrounding pressure resulting into the mechanical equilibrium. The reverse of this process is not possible spontaneously without producing any other effect.

(iii) Free Expansion: Let us consider an insulated container (See Fig. 2.11) which is divided into two compartments A and B by a thin diaphragm. Compartment A contains a mass of gas, while compartment B is completely evacuated. If a hole is made in the diaphragm, the gas in A will expand into B until the pressures in A and B compartments become equal. This is known as free or unrestrained expansion. We can demonstrate by the second law, that the process of free expansion is irreversible.

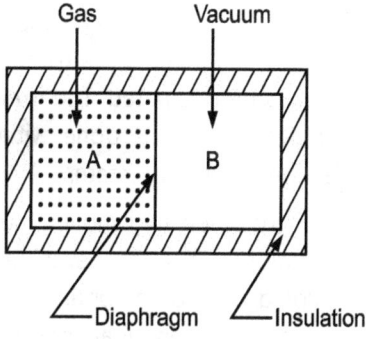

Fig. 2.11: Free expansion

- To prove this, assume that free expansion is reversible, and that the gas in B returns into compartment A with an increase in pressure, and compartment B becomes evacuated as before (See Fig. 2.12).
- There is no other effect. Let us install an engine (a machine, not a cyclic heat engine) between A and B, and permit the gas to expand through the engine from A to B.
- The engine develops a work output W at the expense of the internal energy of the gas. The internal energy of the gas (system) in B can be resorted to its initial value by heat transfer Q (=W) from a source.
- Now, by the use of the reverse free expansion, the system can be resorted to the initial state of high pressure in A and vacuum in B.
- The net result is a cycle, in which we observe that net work output W is accomplished by exchanging heat with a single reservoir.
- This violates the Kelvin-Planck statement. Hence, free expansion is irreversible. The same argument will hold if the compartment B is not in vacuum but at a pressure lower than that in compartment A (case b).

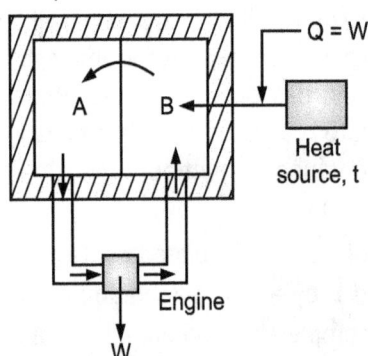

Fig. 2.12: Second law demonstrates that free expansion is irreversible

(b) Reversibility due to Dissipative Effects

The transformation of work into molecular internal energy either of the system or of the reservoir takes place through the agency of such phenomena as friction, viscosity, inelasticity, electrical resistance, and magnetic hysteresis. These effects are known as dissipative effects, and work is said to be dissipated. The irreversibility of a process may be due to the dissipative effects in which work is done without producing an equivalent increase in the kinetic or potential energy of any system.

(i) Friction: Friction is always present when two moving surfaces are in contact. Friction may be reduced by suitable lubrication, but it can never be completely eliminated. If this were possible, a movable device could be kept in continual motion without violating either of the two laws of thermodynamics. The continual motion of a movable device in the complete absence of friction is known as perpetual motion of the third kind.

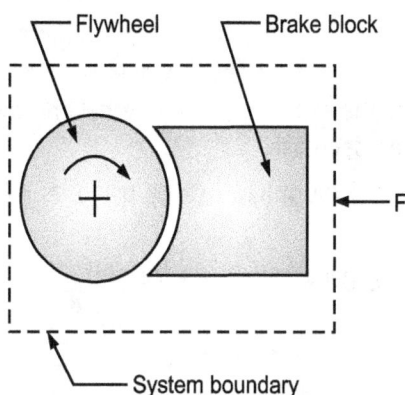

Fig. 2.13: System consists of Flywheel and Brake

- That friction makes a process irreversible can be demonstrated by the second law. Let us consider a system consisting of a flywheel and a brake block (See Fig. 2.13).
- The flywheel was rotating with a certain rpm, and it was brought to rest by applying the friction brake.
- The distance moved by the brake block is very small, so work transfer is very nearly equal to zero.
- If the braking process occurs very rapidly, there is little heat transfer. Using suffix 2 after braking and suffix 1 before braking, and applying the first law, we have

$$Q_{1-2} = E_2 - E_1 + W_{1-2}$$
$$0 = E_2 - E_1 + 0$$
$$\therefore \quad E_2 = E_1 \qquad \ldots (2.6)$$

The energy of the system (isolated) remains constant. Since the energy may exist in the forms of kinetic, potential, and molecular internal energy, we have,

$$U_2 + \frac{mV_2^2}{2} + mZ_{2g} = U_1 + \frac{mV_1^2}{2} + mZ_{1g}$$

Since the wheel is brought to rest, $V_2 = 0$, and there is no change in P.E.

$$U_1 = U_1 + \frac{mV_1^2}{2} \qquad \ldots (2.7)$$

Therefore, the molecular internal energy of the system (i.e., of the brake and the wheel) increases by absorption if the K.E. of the wheel. The reverse process, i.e., the conversion of this increase in molecular internal energy into K.E. within the system to cause the wheel to rotate is not possible to prove it by the second law, let us assume that it is possible, and imagine the following cycle with three processes.

Process A: Let initially the wheel and the brake are at high temperature as a result of the absorption of the K.E. of the wheel, and the flywheel is at rest. Let the flywheel now start rotating at a particular rpm at the expense of the internal energy of the wheel and brake, the temperature of which will then decrease.

Process B: Let the flywheel be brought to rest by using its K.E. in raising weights, with no change in temperature.

Process C: Now, let heat be supplied from a source to the flywheel and the weights, with no change in temperature.

Therefore, the processes A, B, and C together constitute a cycle producing work by exchanging heat with a single reservoir. This violates the Kelvin-Planck statement, and it will become a PMM2. So the braking process, i.e., the transformation of K.E. into molecular internal energy, is irreversible.

(ii) Paddle-Wheel Work Transfer:

- Consider an insulated tank with a fluid (system) in it. Work may be transferred into a system by means of a paddle wheel (See Fig. 2.12) which is also known as stirring work. Here work transferred is dissipated adiabatically into an increase in the molecular internal energy of the system.

- To prove the irreversibility of the process, let us assume that the same amount of work is delivered by the system at the expense of its molecular internal energy, and the temperature of the system goes down (See Fig. 2.15).

- The system is brought back to its initial state by heat transfer from a source. These two processes together constitute a cycle in which there is work output and the system exchanges heat with a single reservoir.

- It becomes a PMM2, and hence the dissipation of stirring work to internal energy is irreversible.

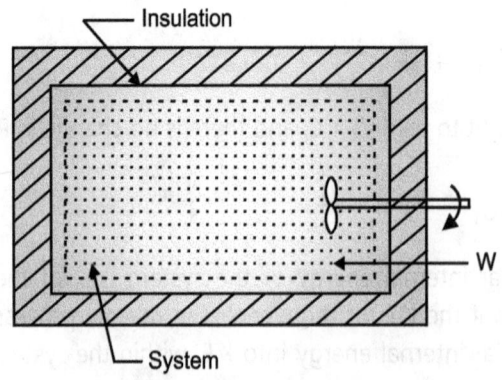

Fig. 2.14: Adiabatic work transfer

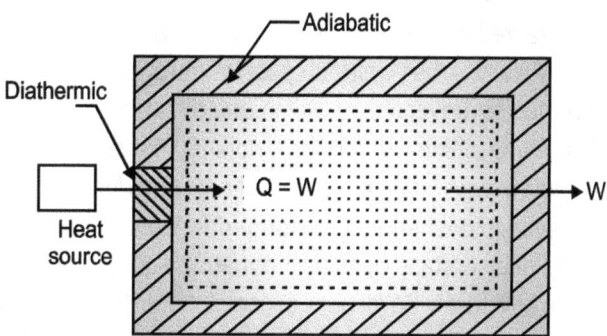

Fig. 2.15: Irreversibility due to dissipation of stirring work into internal energy

(iii) Transfer of Electricity through a Resistor: The flow of electric current through a wire represents work transfer, because the current can drive a motor which can raise a weight. Taking the wire/ the resistor as the system (See Fig. 2.14) and the first law as,

$$Q_{1-2} = U_2 - U_1 + W_{1-2}$$

Here both W_{1-2} and Q_{1-2} are negative.

$$W_{1-2} = U_2 - U_1 + Q_{1-2} \qquad \ldots (2.8)$$

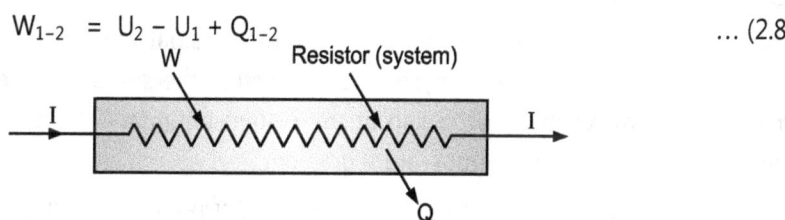

Fig. 2.16: Irreversibility due to dissipation of electrical work into internal energy

A part of the work transfer is stored as an increase in the internal energy of the wire (to give an increase in its temperature), and the remainder leaves the system as heat. At steady state, the internal energy and hence the temperature of the resistor become constant with respect to time and

$$W_{1-2} = Q_{1-2} \qquad \ldots (2.9)$$

The reverse process, i.e. the conversion of heat Q_{1-2} into electrical work W_{1-2} of the same magnitude is not possible. Let us assume that this is possible. Then heat Q_{1-2} will be absorbed and equal work W_{1-2} will be delivered. But this will become a PMM2. So the dissipation of electrical work into internal energy or heat is irreversible.

2.6.2 Conditions for Reversibility

- A natural process is irreversible because the conditions for mechanical, thermal and chemical equilibrium are not satisfied, and the dissipative effects, in which work is transformed into an increase in internal energy, are present.

- For a process to be reversible, it must not possess these features. If a process is performed quasistatically, the system passes through states of thermodynamic equilibrium, which may be traversed as well in one direction or in the opposite direction.
- *If there are no dissipative effects, all the work done by the system during the performance of a process in one direction can be returned to the system during the reverse process.*
- A process will be reversible when it is performed in such a way that the system is at all times infinitesimally near a state of thermodynamic equilibrium and in the absence of dissipative effect of any form. Reversible processes are, therefore, purely ideal, limiting cases of actual processes.

2.6.3 Types of Irreversibility

A process becomes irreversible if it occurs due to a finite potential gradient like the gradient in temperature or pressure, or if there is dissipative effect like friction, in which work is transformed into internal energy increase of the system. Two types of irreversibility can be distinguished:

(a) Internal irreversibility

(b) External irreversibility

The internal irreversibility is caused by the internal dissipative effects like friction, turbulence, electrical resistance, magnetic hysteresis, etc. within the system. The external irreversibility refers to the irreversibility occurring at the system boundary like heat interaction with the surroundings due to finite temperature gradient.

Sometimes, it is useful to make other distinctions. If the irreversibility of a process is due to the dissipation of work into the increase in internal energy of a system, or due to a finite pressure gradient, it is called mechanical irreversibility. If the process occurs in account of a finite temperature gradient, it is thermal irreversibility, and if it is due to a finite concentration gradient or a chemical reaction, it is called chemical irreversibility.

A heat engine cycle in which there is a temperature difference (i) between the source and the working fluid during heat supply, and (ii) between the working fluid and the sink during heat rejection, exhibits external thermal irreversibility. If the real source and sink are not considered and hypothetical reversible processes for heat supply and heat rejection are assumed, the cycle can be reversible. With the inclusion of the actual source and sink, however, the cycle becomes externally irreversible.

2.7 Carnot's Theorem

"It states that of all engines operating between a given constant temperature source and a given constant temperature sink, none has a higher efficiency than a reversible engine".

Proof:

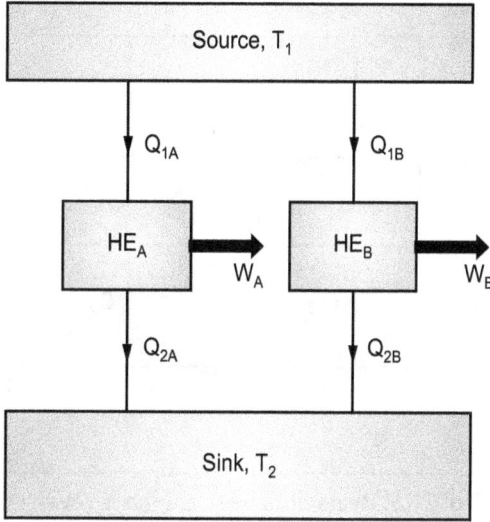

Fig. 2.17: Two cyclic heat engines

Two cyclic heat engines HE_A and HE_B operating between the same source and sink, of which HE_B is reversible.

HE_A and HE_B are the two engines operating between the given source at temperature T_1 and the given sink at temperature T_2 as shown in Fig. 2.17.

Let HE_A be any heat engine and HE_B be any reversible heat engine.

We have to prove that efficiency of HE_B is more than that of HE_A.

Let us assume that $\eta_A > \eta_B$.

Let the rates of working of the engines be such that as shown in Fig. 2.17.

$$Q_{1A} = Q_{1B} = Q_1$$

$$\eta_A > \eta_B$$

$$\frac{W_A}{Q_{1A}} = \frac{W_B}{Q_{1B}}$$

$$W_A > W_B$$

Now, let HE_B be reversed.

Since HE_B is a reversible heat engine, the magnitudes of heat and work transfer quantities will remain the same, but their directions will be reversed, as shown in Fig. 2.18.

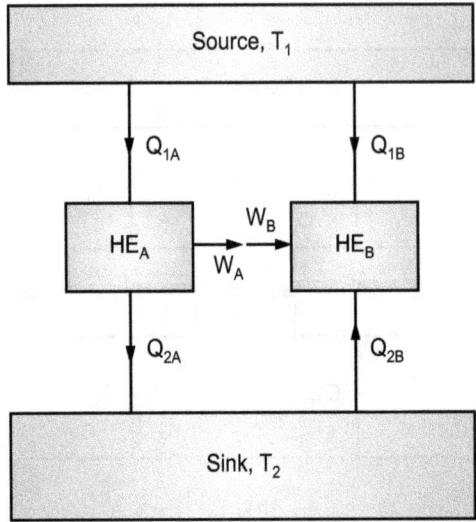

Fig. 2.18: Reversible heat engine is reversed

Now, if both the engine that is 'A' and 'reversed B' are combined together as shown in Fig. 2.19.

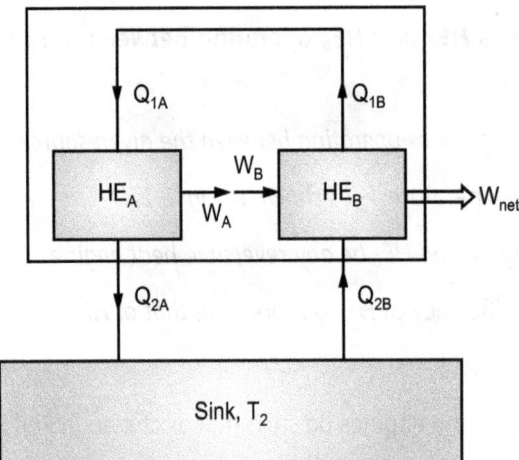

Fig. 2.19: Combined heat engine and heat pump

Thus, this combined heat engine is producing net work, $W_{net} = W_A - W_B$, by exchanging heat with a single reservoir. However it is not possible because it is thus violating Kelvine- Planck Statement of Second law of thermodynamics.

Therefore the assumption that efficiency of *irreversible heat engine is more than that of reversible heat engine is wrong.*

Therefore the efficiency of *irreversible heat engine can not be more than that of reversible heat engine.*

In other word, the efficiency of irreversible heat engine is always less than that of reversible heat engine.
Corollary1

2.8 Definition of Thermodynamic Temperature

The efficiency of the engine is the work divided by the heat introduced to the system or

$$\eta = \frac{w_{cy}}{q_H} = \frac{q_H - q_C}{q_H} = 1 - \frac{q_C}{q_H} \qquad \ldots (2.10)$$

where w_{cy} is the work done per cycle. Thus, the efficiency depends only on q_C/q_H.
Because all reversible engines operating between the same heat reservoirs are equally efficient, any reversible heat engine operating between temperatures T_1 and T_2 must have the same efficiency, meaning, the efficiency is the function of the temperatures only:

$$\frac{q_C}{q_H} = f(T_H, T_C) \qquad \ldots (2.11)$$

In addition, a reversible heat engine operating between temperatures T_1 and T_3 must have the same efficiency as one consisting of two cycles, one between T_1 and another (intermediate) temperature T_2, and the second between T_2 and T_3. This can only be the case if

$$f(T_1, T_3) = \frac{q_3}{q_1} = \frac{q_2 q_3}{q_1 q_2} = f(T_1, T_2)\, f(T_2, T_3)$$

Specializing to the case that T is a fixed reference temperature: the temperature of the triple point of water. Then for any T^2 and T_3,
Therefore, if thermodynamic temperature is defined by

$$T = 273.16 \cdot f(T_1, T)$$

then the function f, viewed as a function of thermodynamic temperature, is

$$f(T_2, T_3) = \frac{T_3}{T_2}$$

and the reference temperature T_1 has the value 273.16. (Of course any reference temperature and any positive numerical value could be used—the choice here corresponds to the Kelvin scale.)
It follows immediately that

$$\frac{q_C}{q_H} = f(T_H, T_C) = \frac{T_C}{T_H} \qquad \ldots (2.12)$$

Substituting Equation (2.13) back into Equation (2.14) gives a relationship for the efficiency in terms of temperature.

$$\eta = 1 - \frac{q_C}{q_H} = 1 - \frac{T_C}{T_H}$$

Problem 2.1: A Carnot engine which rejects heat to a cooling pond at 27°C has an efficiency of 30 percent. If the cooling pond receives 837.2 kJ/min, what is the power developed by the cycle? Find the temperature of the source.

Solution: $T_L = 27 + 273 = 300$ K

$\eta_{th} = 30\%$, $Q_L = 837.2$ kJ/min $= 139.5$ kW

$$\eta_{carnot} = \frac{T_H - T_L}{T_H}$$

$$0.3 = \frac{T_H - (300)}{T_H}$$

$\therefore \quad T_H = \mathbf{428.5 \text{ K}}$

For reversible engine,

$$\frac{Q_L}{Q_H} = \frac{T_L}{T_H}$$

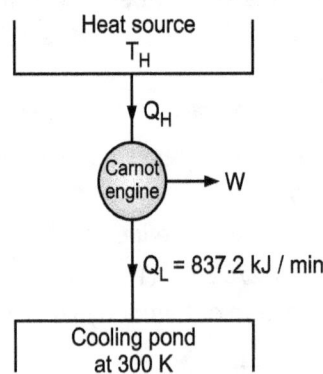

Fig. 2.20: Heat engine

$$Q_H = \frac{Q_L}{T_L} \cdot T_H$$

$$= \frac{837.2 \times 428.5}{300} = 1196 \text{ kJ/min.}$$

Power developed, $W = Q_H - Q_L$

$$= 1196 - 837.2 = 358.6 \text{ kJ/min} = \mathbf{5.97 \text{ kW}} \quad \text{... Ans.}$$

Problem 2.2: The working substance in a Carnot engine is 0.05 kg of air. The maximum cycle temperature is 900 K and maximum pressure is 8.5 MPa. The heat added per cycle is 5 kJ. Determine the maximum cylinder volume if the minimum temperature during the cycle is 300 K.

Solution: Given : $m = 0.05$ kg, $T_H = 900$ K

Maximum pressure = $p_1 = 8.5 \times 10^6$ N/m²

The maximum temperature and pressure corresponds to a point 1 on p-V diagram (See Fig. 2.20) and maximum volume at state 3.

We apply gas equation to find the volume V_1.

$$p_1 V_1 = mRT_1 \qquad \therefore V_1 = \frac{mRT_1}{p_1} = \frac{0.05 \times 0.287 \times 900}{8.5 \times 10^3} = 1.52 \times 10^{-3} \text{ m}^3$$

Heat supplied, $Q = p_1 V_1 \ln V_2/V_1$

$$5 \times 10^3 = 8.5 \times 10^6 \times 1.52 \times 10^{-3} \ln \frac{V_2}{V_1}$$

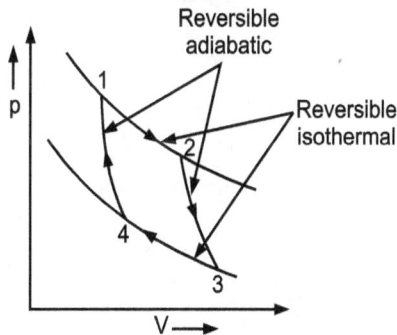

Fig. 2.21: Carnot cycle

$$\therefore \quad \log \frac{V_2}{V_1} = 0.387 \qquad \therefore \frac{V_2}{V_1} = 1.4727$$

$$\therefore \quad V_2 = 1.52 \times 10^{-3} \times 1.4727 = 2.23 \times 10^{-3} \text{ m}^3$$

But $\dfrac{V_3}{V_2} = \left(\dfrac{T_2}{T_3}\right)^{1/\gamma - 1}$

$$\therefore \quad V_3 = V_2 \left(\frac{T_2}{T_3}\right)^{1/\gamma - 1} = 2.23 \times 10^{-3} \left(\frac{900}{300}\right)^{1/1.4 - 1}$$

$$= 0.0347 \text{ m}^3$$

∴ Maximum cylinder volume = **0.0347 m³** ... **Ans.**

Problem 2.3: A reversible engine with 40% efficiency discharges 1520 kJ of heat per minute at 27°C to a water pond. Find the temperature of the source which supplies the heat to the engine and power developed by the engine.

Solution: The arrangement of the system is shown in Fig. Ex. 2.22.

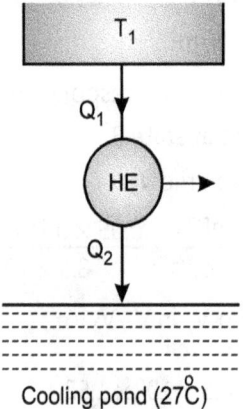

Cooling pond (27°C)

Fig. 2.22

The efficiency of the engine is given by,

$$\eta = \frac{T_1 - T_2}{T_1} = \frac{W}{Q_1} = \frac{W}{W + Q_2}$$

$T_1 = ?$, $T_2 = 27 + 273 = 300$ K

$Q_2 = $ **1520 kJ/min (given)**

Substituting the values in the above equation again

$$0.4 = \frac{T_1 - 300}{T_1} = \frac{W}{W + 1520}$$

∴ $0.4\, T_1 = T_1 - 300$

∴ $0.6\, T_1 = 300$

∴ $T_1 = $ **500 K**

     $W = 0.4\, W + 608$

∴ $0.6\, W = 608$

∴ $W = $ **1013.3 kJ/min**

∴   Power $= \dfrac{1013.3}{60}$ kW = **16.9 kW**   **... Ans.**

Problem 2.4: A reversible engine receives heat from a mixture of water vapour and liquid water under a pressure of 1.013 bar and rejects 4000 kJ/hr to a mixture of ice and liquid under the pressure of 1.013 bar. Find the power delivered by the engine.

Solution: As per the condition mentioned in the example, the given data is

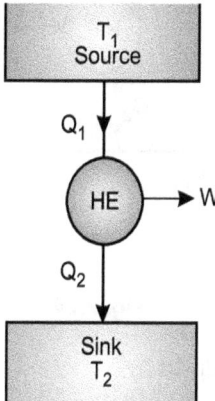

Fig. 2.23

$$T_1 = 100 + 273 = 373 \quad \text{and} \quad T_2 = 0 + 273 = 273 \text{ K}$$

The efficiency of a reversible engine is given by,

$$\eta = \frac{T_1 - T_2}{T_1} = \frac{W}{Q_1} = \frac{W}{W + 4000}$$

$$\therefore \quad \frac{373 - 273}{373} = \frac{W}{W + 4000} = \frac{100}{373} = 0.268$$

$$\therefore \quad W = 0.268\, W + 1072$$

$$\therefore \quad 0.732\, W = 1072$$

$$\therefore \quad W = \frac{1072}{0.732} = 1465 \text{ kJ/hr}$$

$$\therefore \quad \text{Power} = \frac{1465}{3600} = 0.407 \text{ kW} \quad \text{... Ans.}$$

Problem 2.5: The C.O.P. of a refrigerator operating on reversed Carnot cycle is 5.4 when it maintains −5°C in the evaporator. Determine the condenser temperature and refrigerating effect if the power required to run the refrigerator is 3.2 kW.

Solution: The arrangement of the system is shown in Fig. 2.24. In this particular system, the source is the evaporator at − 5°C and sink is the condenser at temperature T_1.

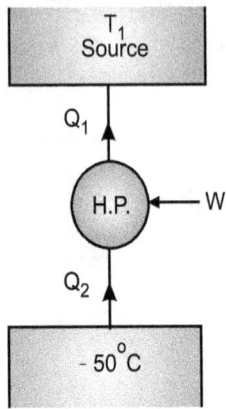

Fig. 2.24

The C.O.P. of the refrigerator is given by,

$$\text{C.O.P.} = \frac{Q_2}{W} = \frac{Q_2}{Q_1 - Q_2} = \frac{T_2}{T_1 - T_2}$$

$$T_2 = -5 + 273 = \textbf{268 K} \text{ (given)}$$

∴ $\quad 5.4 = \dfrac{268}{T_1 - 268}$

∴ $\quad T_1 = 268 + \dfrac{268}{5.4} = 268 + 49.63 = \textbf{317.63 K}$

$$Q_2 = W \times \text{C.O.P.} = 3.2 \times 5.4 = \textbf{17.3 kW}$$

Problem 2.6: A reversible heat pump is used for heating a building in the winter season. The heat is absorbed from the earth by a fluid circulating in buried pipes and delivered to the building to maintain the temperature at 23°C. Determine the amount of heat supplied to the building if one kW-hr of electrical energy is needed to operate the heat pump. The soil temperature may be taken as 0°C.

Solution: The arrangement of the system is shown in Fig. 2.25. Here source (earth) and sink (building) temperatures are 0°C and 23°C respectively.

∴ $\quad T_1 = 23 + 273 = 296 \text{ K}$

And $\quad T_2 = 0 + 273 = 273 \text{ K}$

$$\text{C.O.P.} = \frac{Q_1}{W} = \frac{Q_1}{Q_1 - Q_2} = \frac{T_1}{T_1 - T_2}$$

$$\therefore \quad \frac{Q_1}{W} = \frac{296}{296-273} = \frac{296}{23} = 12.9$$

$$W = 1 \text{ kW-hr} = \frac{1 \text{ kJ}}{\text{sec}} \times 3600 \text{ sec} = 3600 \text{ kJ}$$

$$\therefore \quad Q_1 = \qquad\qquad 12.9 \times 3600 = \textbf{46440 kJ/hr} \quad \text{... Ans.}$$

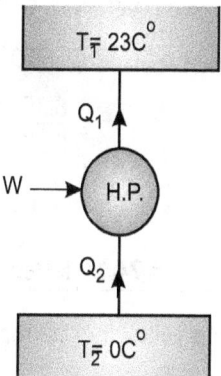

Fig. 2.25

Problem 2.7: A reversible engine is supplied with heat from two constant temperature sources at 900 K and 600 K and rejects to sink at 300 K. Assuming the engine to execute a number of complete cycles while developing 70 kW and rejecting 3200 kJ/min, calculate the heat supplied by each source and efficiency of the engine.

Solution: The arrangement of the system is shown in Fig. 2.26.

The work developed by the engine, $W = 70$ kJ/sec.

Total heat supplied to the engine = Work developed + Heat rejected

$$= 70 + \frac{3200}{60} = 123.3 \text{ kJ/sec}$$

Assume, source S_1 supplies Q kJ/sec, then the heat supplied by source S_2

$$= 123.3 - Q$$

Using the efficiency expression for a couple of each source and same sink, we can write

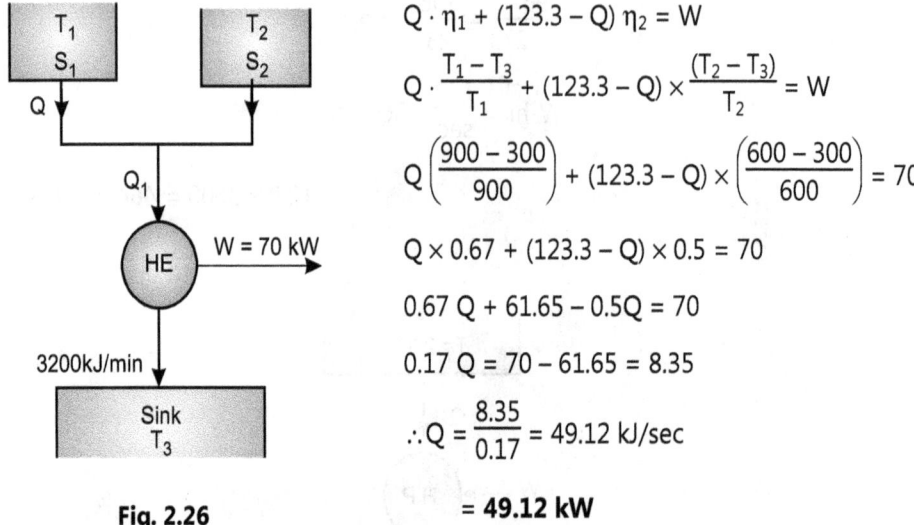

$Q \cdot \eta_1 + (123.3 - Q)\eta_2 = W$

$Q \cdot \dfrac{T_1 - T_3}{T_1} + (123.3 - Q) \times \dfrac{(T_2 - T_3)}{T_2} = W$

$Q \left(\dfrac{900 - 300}{900}\right) + (123.3 - Q) \times \left(\dfrac{600 - 300}{600}\right) = 70$

$Q \times 0.67 + (123.3 - Q) \times 0.5 = 70$

$0.67 Q + 61.65 - 0.5Q = 70$

$0.17 Q = 70 - 61.65 = 8.35$

$\therefore Q = \dfrac{8.35}{0.17} = 49.12 \text{ kJ/sec}$

Fig. 2.26 $= 49.12$ kW

∴ Heat supplied by S_2 = 123.30 − 49.12 = **74.18 kJ/sec = 74.18 kW**   ... **Ans.**

Problem 2.8: An inventor makes the following claims. Determine, whether his claims are valid or invalid? Why?

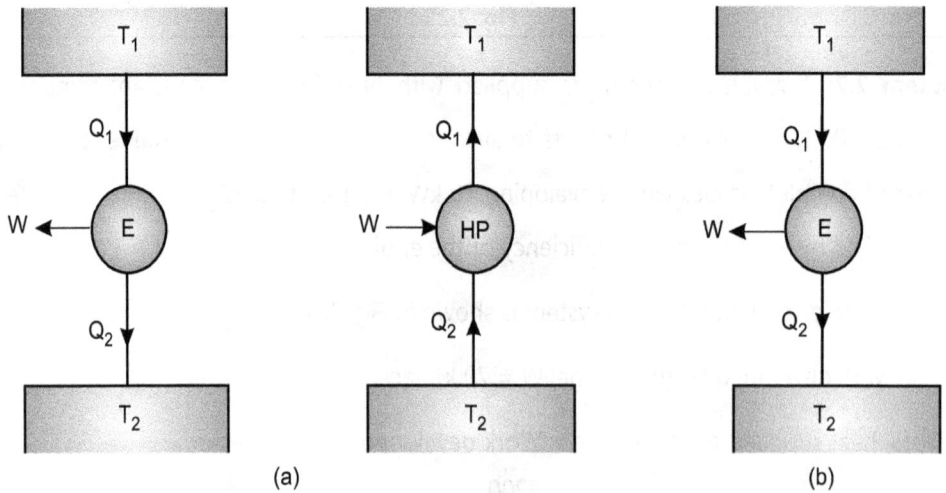

Fig. 2.27

> A flame 1500 K used as a heat source and the low temperature reservoir is at 300 K. The inventor indicates that 69% of the heat transfer to the cycle device from the flame is returned as work.

> A building receives a heat of 50000 kJ/hr from a heat pump. The inside temperature is maintained at 22°C and surroundings are at − 1°C. The inventor claims a work input of 7000 kJ/hr is sufficient.

> An engine operates between 1000 K and 400 K with a heat transfer into the engine of 500 kW capacity. The inventor states that the heat transfer to the low temperature reservoir is 250 kW and the work output is 250 kW.

Solution:

1. As per the claim of the inventor, the work output is 69% of heat transfer, that means the efficiency of engine is 69%.

    The maximum efficiency possible for the given temperature range is

    $$\eta_{max} = \frac{T_1 - T_2}{T_1} = \frac{1500 - 300}{1500} = \frac{1200}{1500} = 0.8 = 80\%$$

    The inventor claim is less than maximum possible, so it is valid.

2. The maximum C.O.P. possible for heating the building is

    $$C.O.P. = \frac{Q_1}{W} = \frac{Q_1}{Q_1 - Q_2} = \frac{T_1}{T_1 - T_2}$$

    $$\therefore \quad \frac{50000}{W} = \frac{(22 + 273)}{[22 - (-1)]} = \frac{295}{23}$$

    Therefore, the minimum work input required for the purpose is

    $$W = 50000 \times \frac{23}{295} = \mathbf{3898.3 \text{ kJ/hr}} \quad \ldots \text{ Ans.}$$

    The amount of work supplied (7000 kJ/hr) as per inventor data is greater than the minimum work required for the purpose, so his claim is valid.

3. As per inventor claim, the efficiency is given by

    $$\eta = \frac{Output}{Input} = \frac{250}{500} = 0.5 = 50\%$$

    The maximum possible efficiency for the given temperature limit is given by

    $$\eta_{max} = \frac{T_1 - T_2}{T_1} = \frac{1000 - 400}{1000} = \frac{600}{1000} = 0.6 = \mathbf{60\%} \quad \ldots \text{ Ans.}$$

    The efficiency claimed by the inventor is less than the maximum possible efficiency, so his claim is valid.

EXERCISE

1. What do you understand by thermal reservoirs?

2. What is heat engine? Explain its working with block diagram. What is its thermal efficiency?

3. Define second law of thermodynamics.

   Explain: (i) Kelvin - Planck statement, (ii) Clausius statement

   Give suitable examples.

4. What is meant by perpetual motion machine of second kind?

5. What is refrigerator and heat pump? What is meant by COP?

6. An inventor claims to have developed a refrigerating machine which operates between −20°C and +30°C and consumes 1 kW power. The machine gives a refrigerating affect of 21.6 MJ/h. Verify the validity of his claim.

7. A domestic food freezer maintains a temperature of − 15°C. The outdoor ambient is at 30°C. If the heat load on the freezer is 1.75 kW, what is the minimum power necessary to pump out this heat? If the actual C.O.P. of the freezer is half that of the ideal C.O.P., what is the actual power required?

   (**Ans.** Minimum power required = 0.305 kW, Actual power required = 0.61 kW)

8. A reversible heat pump is driven by a reversible heat engine. The heat rejected by the heat pump and by the heat engine is used to warm up a building. If the thermal efficiency of the heat engine is 27% and the C.O.P. of the heat pump is 4, find the ratio of heat supplied to building to the heat supplied to the heat engine.

   (**Ans.** Ratio = 2.08)

9. Define heat engine, refrigerator and heat pump. Explain why the performance of heat engine is measured in terms of efficiency but that of refrigerators and heat pumps in terms of C.O.P. Why does the expression for C.O.P. differ for refrigerator and heat pump?

10. Discuss whether the following processes are reversible or irreversible. Give reasons for the conclusion.

(a) Water is evaporated at constant temperature by (i) adding heat and (ii) by adding work.

(b) Air is expanded slowly against a frictionless piston in an insulated cylinder.

(c) Two gases mix in an insulated vessel (i) at same temperature (ii) at different temperatures.

(d) Water under a piston of constant weight is stirred unit and 20% of it evaporates.

(e) Gas expands through a small orifice from a high pressure chamber to low pressure chamber.

(f) A stream of water at 20°C is mixed with a stream of water at 80°C.

What is the check to decide whether a given process is reversible or irreversible?

11. Do the following occurrences violate the second law? Give reasons:

    (a) An isothermal reversible expansion of a perfect gas absorbs heat from a heat reservoir and converts it completely into work.

    (b) An electric refrigerator rejects heat to a constant temperature atmosphere while operating in a cycle.

12. Explain mechanical reversibility differs from thermodynamic reversibility? What is the difference between internal and external reversibility? Give two examples of each.

13. An inventor claims to have developed an engine working between 400 K and 200 K taking 100 kJ of energy and rejecting 40 kJ of energy and delivering 15 kWh of work. Verify whether his claim is correct or not.

14. An inventor claims to have developed an engine that takes 100 MJ of heat at 400 K and rejects 40 MJ at 150 K and delivers 15 kWh of work. Discuss the possibility of this engine on the market (1 kWh = 3600 J/s).

15. C.O.P. of a refrigerating system is 50% of the theoretical value. It removes 600 kJ/min from a reservoir at 250 K while the heat is rejected to the atmosphere at 300 K.
    (a) Determine heat rejected to high temperature reservoir. (b) If the refrigerator is reversed to operate as engine (all data remaining same what would be the power developed?

16. A household refrigerator absorbs heat at 5°C and rejects heat at 40°C. Its compressor is driven by 2 kW motor and 25 MJ heat is absorbed per hour at the low temperature. Find the amount of heat rejected per hour.

17. An inventor claims that the heat engine developed by him has the following specifications:

   Power developed = 76 kW, Fuel burned = 4 kg/hr, C.V. of fuel = 50 MJ/kg, and Working temperature limit = 700 K and 300 K.

   Check whether his claim is correct or not.

Unit III
ENTROPY

3.1 Introduction

Entropy is a useful property and serves as a valuable tool in the second law analysis of engineering devices. Entropy is not a common word as energy is. But with continued use, our understanding of entropy will deepen and we will grow in understanding entropy. In the following paragraphs, it has been tried out to introduce the entropy to the reader.

Entropy can be defined as a measure of molecular disorder or molecular randomness. Let us discuss the entropy of a fluid which could exist in three different phases. A common fluid water exists in vapour, liquid and solid phase depending upon the temperature at a fixed pressure. In vapour state, the molecular distance is more as compared with liquid and solid state. It means the molecules in vapour phase have more freedom to move in any direction, it means the molecules arranged in most disorderly manner. Hence, the entropy of a system (fluid) in vapour state is more as compared with its liquid state. Similarly, the water molecules are more systematically/orderly organised in the solid state than liquid. Therefore, the entropy of liquid water is always more compared to that it in solid state. This discussion is equally applicable to all the systems which could be in different phases. This is as shown in Fig. 3.1.

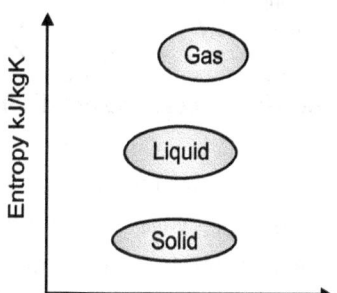

Fig. 3.1: The entropy (molecular disorder) of a substance increases as it changes its phase to liquid or gas

Molecules in the gas phase possess a considerable amount of kinetic energy. However, no matter how large their kinetic energy are, the gas molecules will not rotate a paddle wheel inserted into the container and produce work. This is so because the gas molecules and the energy they carry with them are disorganised. Probably the number of molecules which try to rotate the paddle wheel in one direction is equally opposed by the remaining gas molecules, resulting in no rotation of the paddle wheel. Hence, one cannot extract useful work directly from disorganised energy (See Fig. 3.2).

Fig. 3.2: The disorganised energy does not create useful effect
(equal and opposite forces applied to a load will not move it)

Now, consider a rotating shaft as shown in Fig. 3.3. Here all the molecules of shaft are organised and rotate in one direction. Hence, one can extract useful work from the organised molecules as exist in the form of solid shaft. The rotation of the shaft can be utilised to raise or lower the load. Being an organised form of energy, work is free of disorder or randomness and thus free of entropy. There is no transfer of entropy associated with energy transfer as work.

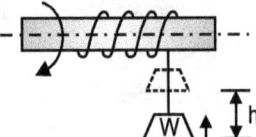

Fig. 3.3: Weight can be raised or lowered by a rotating shaft which does not create any disorder (entropy)

Let us consider one more example in which heat is transferred from a hot body to a cold body as shown in Fig. 3.4.

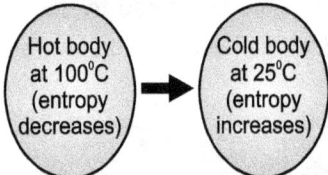

Fig. 3.4: During a heat transfer process, the net disorder (entropy) increases

Heat, a disorganized energy, and disorganization (entropy) will result with heat. As a result, the entropy of the hot body will decrease while the entropy and disorder of the cold body increase. As per second law, the increase in entropy of cold body be greater than the decrease in entropy of the hot body, and thus the net entropy of the combined system (cold body and hot body) increases. It means the combined system is at a state of greater disorder at the end state.

"Steel has got a great strength and looses all when red hot". You may be surprised at this stage to read the sentence. Let us apply entropy concept to our life style. When a person is angry it means the body organs are in the most disordered state. Therefore, when an angry person will perform badly or he does unwanted/not useful task, which may lead to any type of distruction. Therefore, every person should try to keep entropy of his body to a minimum level to do the constructive job.

3.2 Clausius Inequality

An important inequality that has major consequences in thermodynamics is the Clausius inequality, which is expressed as,

$$\oint \frac{\delta Q}{T} \leq 0 \qquad \ldots (3.1)$$

The cyclic integral of $\frac{\delta Q}{\delta T}$ is always less than or equal to zero. This inequality is valid for all cycles, reversible or irreversible. The $\oint$ is used to indicate that integration is to be carried out over the entire cycle.

The validity of the Clausius inequality can be illustrated with the help of two heat engines, one reversible and the other irreversible both operating between the same temperature limits of T_H and T_L.

Here T_H represents the temperature of high-temperature reservoir while T_L is that of low-temperature reservoir as shown in Fig. 3.5.

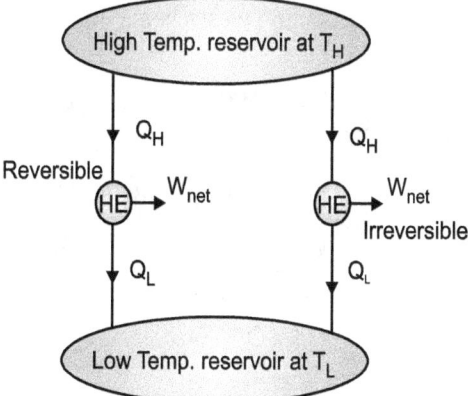

Fig. 3.5: A reversible and irreversible heat engine operating between the same temperature limits (same reservoir)

Here Q_H and Q_L are the rate of heat transfer taking place at constant temperatures T_H and T_L respectively.

(A) For reversible heat engine, the cyclic integral of $\frac{\delta Q}{T}$ becomes,

$$\oint \left(\frac{\delta Q}{T}\right)_{rev} = \int \frac{\delta Q_H}{T_H} - \int \frac{\delta Q_L}{T_L}$$

$$= \frac{1}{T_H} \oint \delta Q_H - \frac{1}{T_L} \oint \delta Q_L$$

$$= \frac{Q_H}{T_H} - \frac{Q_L}{T_L} = 0$$

Since, $\frac{Q_H}{T_H} = \frac{Q_L}{T_L}$ for reversible cycle, thus, for a reversible heat engine cycle,

$$\oint \left(\frac{\delta Q}{T}\right)_{rev} = 0 \qquad \ldots (3.2)$$

Equation (3.2) is developed for totally reversible heat engine, but is equally valid for heat engines that are only internally reversible. In such a situation, T_H and T_L can be considered as the temperature of the working fluid at locations heat is received and rejected respectively. Therefore, equation (3.2) can be written as,

$$\oint \left(\frac{\delta Q}{T}\right)_{int\ rev} = 0 \qquad \ldots (3.3)$$

(B) Now, consider the irreversible heat engine operating between the same thermal reservoirs (temperature limits) as the reversible one and receive the same amount of heat Q_H during a cyclic operation. But as per the Carnot principle, the irreversible heat engine will deliver less net work and which rejects more waste heat. Therefore,

$$Q_{L,\ irrev} > Q_L$$
$$Q_{L,\ irrev} = Q_L + Q_{diff}$$

where, Q_{diff} is a positive quantity.

Carrying out the cyclic integral of $\frac{\delta Q}{T}$ for this irreversible heat engines results,

$$\oint \left(\frac{\delta Q}{T}\right)_{irrev} = \frac{Q_H}{T_H} - \frac{Q_{L,\ irrev}}{T_L}$$

$$= \frac{Q_H}{T_H} - \frac{Q_L}{T_L} - \frac{Q_{diff}}{T_L}$$

$$= -\frac{Q_{diff}}{T_L} < 0$$

∴ For an irreversible heat engine cycle,

$$\oint \left(\frac{\delta Q}{T}\right)_{irrev} < 0 \qquad \ldots (3.4)$$

The Clausius inequality is obtained by combining the equations (3.3) and (3.4) as,

$$\oint \frac{\delta Q}{T} \leq 0 \qquad \ldots (3.5)$$

The equation (3.5) is valid for totally or just internally reversible cycles. Equality sign is for reversible engine while inequality sign is for irreversible engine.

3.3 Principle of Increase of Entropy

Consider a cycle that consists of two processes, one internally reversible and the other irreversible as shown in Fig. 3.6.

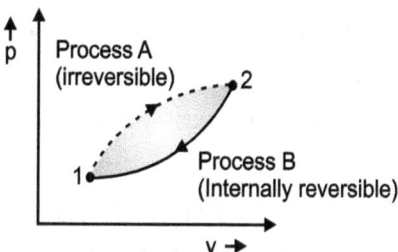

Fig. 3.6: A cycle composed of a reversible and an irreversible process

Clausius inequality tells that the cyclic integral of $\frac{\delta Q}{T}$ for the irreversible cycle is less than zero, i.e.

$$\oint \left(\frac{\delta Q}{T}\right)_{irrev} < 0$$

or

$$\int_{1,A}^{2} \left(\frac{\delta Q}{T}\right)_{irrev} + \int_{2,B}^{1} \left(\frac{\delta Q}{T}\right)_{int,\,rev} < 0$$

The second term in the above equation represents entropy change $s_1 - s_2$. Thus,

$$\int_{1,A}^{2} \left(\frac{\delta Q}{T}\right)_{irrev} + (s_1 - s_2) < 0$$

This can be rearranged as,

$$\Delta s = (s_2 - s_1) > \int_{1,A}^{2} \left(\frac{\delta Q}{T}\right)_{irrev} \qquad \ldots (3.6)$$

From equation (3.7) one can say "the entropy change of a closed system during an irreversible process is greater than the integral of $\frac{\delta Q}{T}$ evaluated for that process".

In general, the relation between the change of entropy of a closed system and the integral of $\frac{\delta Q}{T}$ can be expressed as,

$$\Delta s \geq \int_{1}^{2} \frac{\delta Q}{T} \qquad \ldots (3.7)$$

or in the differential form,

$$ds \geq \frac{\delta Q}{T} \qquad \ldots (3.8)$$

Here the equality sign holds for a totally or just internally reversible process and the inequality for an irreversible process. δQ represents a differential amount of actual heat transfer between the system and surroundings and 'T' is the absolute temperature at the boundary.

Let us now consider an isolated system. It is known that in an isolated system, matter, work and heat cannot cross the boundary of the system. Hence, according to the first law of thermodynamics, the internal energy of the system remains constant.

For isolated system, $\delta Q = 0$, from equation (3.9), we get,

$$(ds)_{isolated} \geq 0 \qquad \ldots (3.9)$$

Equation (3.10) tells that the entropy of an isolated system either increases or remains constant. This is a corollary of second law of thermodynamics. It explains the principle of increase in entropy.

3.4 Entropy Changes for a Closed System

3.4.1 The Tds Relations

Earlier in this chapter, it is shown that the quantity $\left(\frac{\delta Q}{T}\right)_{int\ rev}$ corresponds to a differential change in property, called as entropy. The entropy change for various processes like constant volume process, constant pressure process, isothermal process etc. was evaluated and shown in the preceding sections. When the temperature varies during a process, we have a relation between δQ and T to perform this integration.

Finding such relations is the task done in this section.

The differential form of the conservation of energy equation for a closed stationary system having a simple compressible fluid for internally reversible process can be written as,

$$\delta Q = \delta w + \delta u$$

But

$$\delta Q = Tds$$
$$\delta w = pdV$$

Thus

$$Tds - pdv = du$$
$$Tds = du + pdV \qquad \ldots (3.10)$$

or

$$Tds = du + pdV \qquad \text{for unit mass} \ldots (3.11)$$

This equation is known as first Tds or Gibb's equation.

The second Tds equation is obtained by eliminating du from equation (3.26) by using the definition of enthalpy (h = u + pv).

$$h = u + pV \rightarrow dh = du + pdV + Vdp$$

But
$$du + pdV = Tds$$

∴
$$Tds = dh - Vdp \qquad \ldots (3.12)$$

Equations (3.11 and 3.12) are extremely valuables as they relate entropy changes of a system to the changes in other properties.

3.4.2 Change of Entropy of a Gas

Let 1 kg of gas at a pressure p_1, volume V_1, absolute temperature T_1 and entropy s_1, be heated such that its final pressure, volume, absolute temperature and entropy are p_2, V_2, T_2 and s_2 respectively. According to first law,

$$dQ = du + dW$$

where,
- dQ = Small change of heat
- du = Small change of internal energy and
- dW = Small change of work done (pdV)

Now
$$dQ = c_v dT + pdV$$

Dividing both sides by T, we get

$$\frac{dQ}{T} = \frac{c_v dT}{T} + \frac{pdV}{T}$$

But
$$\frac{dQ}{T} = ds$$

and as
$$pV = RT$$

∴
$$\frac{p}{T} = \frac{R}{V}$$

Hence,
$$ds = \frac{c_v dT}{T} + R\frac{dV}{V}$$

Integrating both sides,

$$\int_{s_1}^{s_2} ds = c_v \int_{T_1}^{T_2} \frac{dT}{T} + R \int_{V_1}^{V_2} \frac{dV}{V}$$

or
$$(s_2 - s_1) = c_v \log_e \frac{T_2}{T_1} + R \log_e \frac{V_2}{V_1} \quad \ldots (3.13)$$

This expression can also be obtained in the following way:

According to the gas equation, we have
$$\frac{p_1 V_1}{T_1} = \frac{p_2 V_2}{T_2}$$

or
$$\frac{T_2}{T_1} = \frac{p_2}{p_1} \times \frac{V_2}{V_1}$$

Substituting the value of $\frac{T_2}{T_1}$ in equation (3.12) we get,

$$s_2 - s_1 = c_v \log_e \frac{p_2}{p_1} \times \frac{V_2}{V_1} + R \log_e \frac{V_2}{V_1}$$

$$= c_v \log_e \frac{p_2}{p_1} + c_v \log_e \frac{V_2}{V_1} + R \log_e \frac{V_2}{V_1}$$

$$= c_v \log_e \frac{p_2}{p_1} + (c_v + R) \log_e \frac{V_2}{V_1}$$

$$= c_v \log_e \frac{p_2}{p_1} + c_p \log_e \frac{V_2}{V_1}$$

$$\therefore \quad s_2 - s_1 = c_v \log_e \frac{p_2}{p_1} + c_p \log_e \frac{V_2}{V_1} \quad \ldots (3.14)$$

Again, from gas equation,
$$\frac{p_1 V_1}{T_1} = \frac{p_2 V_2}{T_2}$$

or
$$\frac{V_2}{V_1} = \frac{p_1}{p_2} \times \frac{T_2}{T_1}$$

Putting the value of $\frac{V_2}{V_1}$ in equation (3.12), we get,

$$(s_2 - s_1) = c_v \log_e \frac{T_2}{T_1} + R \log_e \frac{p_1}{p_2} \times \frac{T_2}{T_1}$$

$$= c_v \log_e \frac{T_2}{T_1} + R \log_e \frac{p_1}{p_2} + R \log_e \frac{T_2}{T_1}$$

$$= (c_v + R) \log_e \frac{T_2}{T_1} - R \log_e \frac{p_2}{p_1}$$

$$= c_p \log_e \frac{T_2}{T_1} - R \log_e \frac{p_2}{p_1}$$

$$\therefore \quad s_2 - s_1 = c_p \log_e \frac{T_2}{T_1} - R \log_e \frac{p_2}{p_1} \quad \ldots (3.15)$$

(a) Heating a Gas at Constant Volume

Refer Fig. 3.7. Let 1 kg of gas be heated at constant volume and let the change in entropy and absolute temperature be from s_1 to s_2 and T_1 to T_2 respectively.

Then
$$Q = c_v (T_2 - T_1)$$

Differentiating to find small increment of heat dQ corresponding to small rise in temperature dT,

$$dQ = c_v \, dT$$

Dividing both sides by T, we get

$$\frac{dQ}{T} = c_v \cdot \frac{dT}{T}$$

or
$$ds = c_v \cdot \frac{dT}{T}$$

Integrating both sides, we get

$$\int_{s_1}^{s_2} ds = c_v \int_{T_1}^{T_2} \frac{dT}{T}$$

or
$$s_2 - s_1 = c_v \log_e \frac{T_2}{T_1} \qquad \ldots (3.16)$$

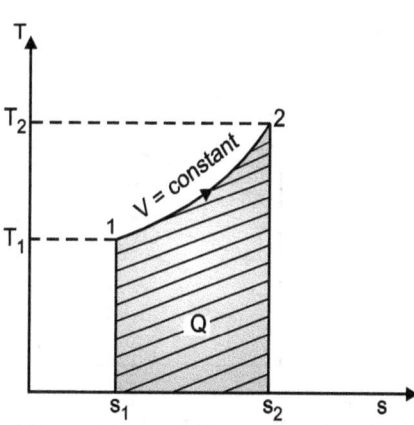

Fig. 3.7: Constant volume process on T-s diagram

(b) Heating a Gas at Constant Pressure

Refer Fig. 3.8. Let 1 kg of gas be heated at constant pressure, so that its absolute temperature changes from T_1 to T_2 and entropy s_1 to s_2.

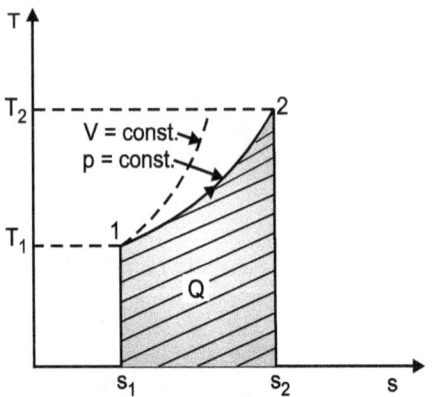

Fig. 3.8: T-s diagram: Constant pressure process

Then, $\quad Q = c_p (T_2 - T_1)$

Differentiating to find small increase in heat, dQ of this gas when the temperature rise is dT.

$$dQ = c_p \cdot dT$$

Dividing both sides by T, we get

$$\frac{dQ}{T} = \frac{dT}{T}$$

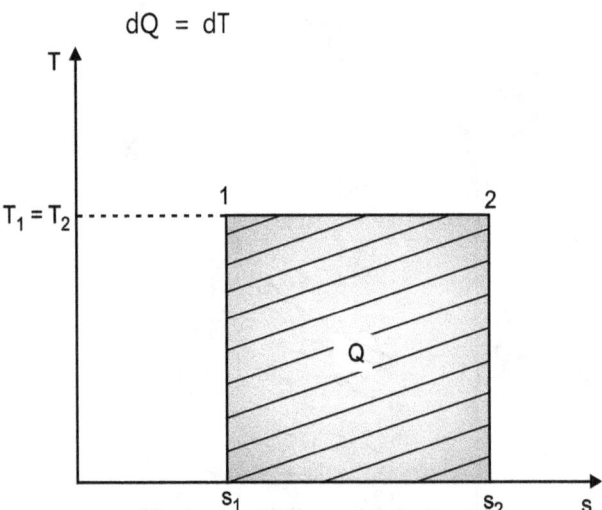

Fig. 3.9: T-s diagram: Isothermal process

$$\therefore \quad T(s_2 - s_1) = RT_1 \log_e \frac{V_2}{V_1}$$

$$s_2 - s_1 = R \log_e \frac{V_2}{V_1} \qquad [\because T_1 = T_2 = T] \ldots (3.17)$$

(c) Adiabatic Process (Reversible)

During an adiabatic process as heat is neither supplied nor rejected,

$$dQ = 0$$
$$\frac{dQ}{dT} = 0$$
$$ds = 0 \qquad \ldots (3.18)$$

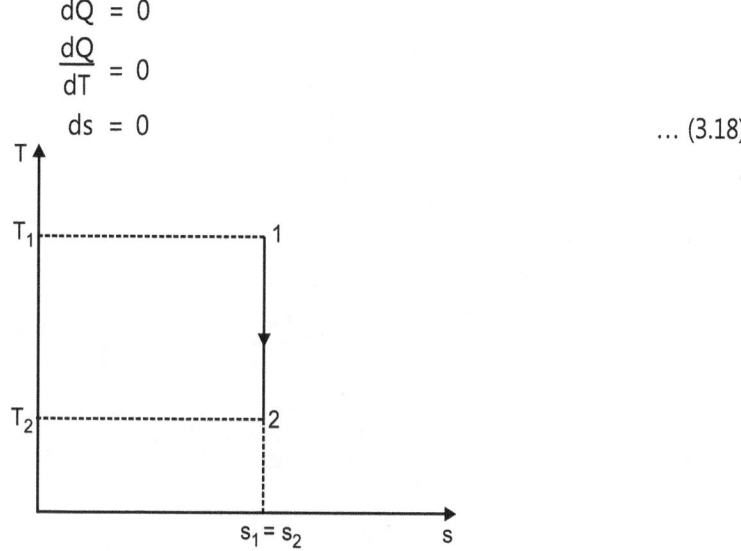

Fig. 3.10: T-s diagram: Adiabatic process

This shows that there is no change in entropy and hence it is known as isentropic process. Fig. 3.10 represents an adiabatic process. It is a vertical line (1-2) and therefore area under this line is nil; hence heat supplied or rejected and entropy change is zero.

(d) Polytropic Process

Refer Fig. 3.11.

The expression for 'entropy change' in polytropic process (pV^n = constant) can be obtained from equation given below.

i.e.
$$s_2 - s_1 = c_v \log_e \frac{T_2}{T_1} + R \log_e \frac{V_2}{V_1}$$

Fig. 3.11: T-s diagram: Polytropic process

Also $\quad p_1 V_1^n = p_2 V_2^n$

or $\quad \dfrac{p_1}{p_2} = \left(\dfrac{V_2}{V_1}\right)^n$ ... (i)

Again, as $\quad \dfrac{p_1 V_1}{T_1} = \dfrac{p_2 V_2}{T_2}$

or $\quad \dfrac{p_1}{p_2} = \dfrac{V_2}{V_1} \times \dfrac{T_1}{T_2}$ ... (ii)

From equations (i) and (ii), we get

$$\left(\dfrac{V_2}{V_1}\right)^n = \dfrac{V_2}{V_1} \times \dfrac{T_1}{T_2}$$

or $\quad \left(\dfrac{V_2}{V_1}\right)^{n-1} = \dfrac{T_1}{T_2}$

or $\quad \dfrac{V_2}{V_1} = \left(\dfrac{T_1}{T_2}\right)^{\frac{1}{n-1}}$

$= c_v \log_e \dfrac{T_2}{T_1} - R\left(\dfrac{1}{n-1}\right) \log_e \dfrac{T_2}{T_1}$

$= c_v \log_e \dfrac{T_2}{T_1} - (c_p - c_v) \times \left(\dfrac{1}{n-1}\right) \log_e \dfrac{T_2}{T_1}$ $\quad [\because R = c_p - c_v]$

$= c_v \log_e \dfrac{T_2}{T_1} - (\gamma \cdot c_v - c_v) \times \left(\dfrac{1}{n-1}\right) \log_e \dfrac{T_2}{T_1}$ $\quad [\because c_p = \gamma \cdot c_v]$

$= c_v \left[1 - \left(\dfrac{\gamma - 1}{n - 1}\right)\right] \log_e \dfrac{T_2}{T_1} = c_v \left[\dfrac{(n-1) - (\gamma - 1)}{(n-1)}\right] \log_e \dfrac{T_2}{T_1}$

$= c_v \left(\dfrac{n - 1 - \gamma + 1}{n - 1}\right) \log_e \dfrac{T_2}{T_1}$

$= c_v \left(\dfrac{n - \gamma}{n - 1}\right) \log_e \dfrac{T_2}{T_1}$ per kg of gas

$\therefore \quad s_2 - s_1 = c_v \left(\dfrac{n - \gamma}{n - 1}\right) \log_e \dfrac{T_2}{T_1}$ per kg of gas ... (3.19)

(e) Approximation for Heat Absorbed

The curve AB shown in Fig. 3.12 is obtained by heating 1 kg of gas from initial state A to final state B. Let temperature during heating increase from T_1 to T_2. Then heat absorbed by the gas will be given by the area (shown shaded) under curve AB.

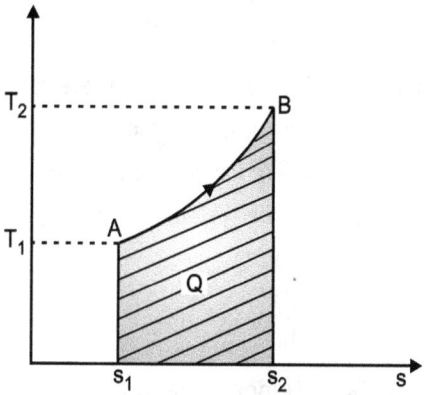

Fig. 3.12

As the curve on T-s diagram which represents the heating of the gas, usually has very slight curvature, it can be assumed a straight line for a small temperature range. Then,

$$\text{Heat absorbed} = \text{Area under the curve AB}$$
$$= (s_2 - s_1)\left(\frac{T_1 + T_2}{2}\right) \qquad \ldots (3.20)$$

In other words, heat absorbed approximately equals the product of change of entropy and means absolute temperature.

Table 3.1: Summary of Formulae

Sr. No.	Process	Change of Entropy (per kg)
1.	General case	(i) $c_v \log_e \frac{T_2}{T_1} + R \log_e \frac{V_2}{V_1}$ (in terms of T and V)
		(ii) $c_v \log_e \frac{p_2}{p_1} + c_v \log_e \frac{V_2}{V_1}$ (in terms of p and V)
		(iii) $c_p \log_e \frac{T_2}{T_1} - R \log_e \frac{p_2}{p_1}$ (in terms of T and p)
2.	Constant volume	$c_v \log_e \frac{T_2}{T_1}$
3.	Constant pressure	$c_p \log_e \frac{T_2}{T_1}$
4.	Isothermal	$R \log_e \frac{V_2}{V_1}$
5.	Adiabatic	Zero
6.	Polytropic	$c_v \left(\frac{n - \gamma}{n - 1}\right) \log_e \frac{T_2}{T_1}$

3.4.3 Entropy Changes for an Open System

In an open system, as compared with closed system, there is additional change of entropy due to the mass crossing the boundaries of the system. *The net change of entropy of a system due to mass transport is equal to the difference between the product of the mass and its specific entropy at the inlet and at the outlet of the system.* Therefore, the total change of entropy of the system during a small interval is given by,

$$ds \geq \frac{dQ}{T_0} + \Sigma s_i \cdot dm_i - \Sigma s_o \cdot dm_o$$

where,
T_0 = Temperature of the surroundings, in K
s_i = Specific entropy at the inlet, J/kg·K
s_o = Specific entropy at the outlet, J/kg·K
dm_i = Mass entering the system, kg/sec
dm_o = Mass leaving the system, kg/sec

(Subscripts i and o refer to inlet and outlet conditions.)

The above equation in general form can be written as,

$$ds \geq \frac{dQ}{T_0} + \Sigma s \cdot dm \qquad \ldots (3.21)$$

In equation (3.20), entropy flow into the system is considered positive and entropy outflow is considered negative. The equality sign is applicable to reversible process in which the heat interactions and mass transport to and from the system is accomplished reversibly. The inequality sign is applicable to irreversible processes.

If equation (3.20) is divided by dt, then it becomes a rate equation and is written as,

$$\frac{ds}{dt} \geq \frac{1}{T_0} \cdot \frac{dQ}{dt} + \Sigma s \cdot \frac{dm}{dt} \qquad \ldots (3.22)$$

In a steady-state, steady flow process, the rate of change of entropy of the system $\left(\frac{ds}{dt}\right)$ becomes zero.

∴

$$0 \geq \frac{1}{T_0}\frac{dQ}{dt} + \Sigma s \cdot \frac{dm}{dt}$$

or

$$\frac{1}{T_0} + \Sigma s \cdot \leq 0 \qquad \ldots (3.23)$$

where

$$= \frac{dQ}{dt} \quad \text{and}$$

$$= \frac{dm}{dt}$$

For adiabatic steady flow process,

$$= 0$$

$$\Sigma \dot{s} \leq 0 \qquad \ldots (3.24)$$

If the process is reversible and adiabatic, then,

$$\Sigma \dot{s} = 0 \qquad \ldots (3.25)$$

3.4.4 The Entropy Change of Solids and Liquids

The Tds equation is,

$$Tds = du + pdV \qquad \ldots (3.26)$$

or

$$ds = \frac{du}{T} + \frac{pdV}{T}$$

The solids and liquids are idealized as incompressible substances since their volumes remain essentially constant during a process.

Thus, change in volume, $dV = 0$ for solids and liquids.

Equation (3.29) reduces to

$$ds = \frac{du}{T} = c\frac{dT}{T} \qquad \ldots (3.27)$$

As $c_p = c_v = c$ for incompressible substances and $du = c\,dT$, the entropy change for a process is determined by integration.

$$s_2 - s_1 = \int_1^2 c(T)\frac{dT}{T} \text{ kJ/kg·K} \qquad \ldots (3.28)$$

The specific heat 'c' of liquids and solids depend on temperature. We need a relation for 'c' as a function of temperature to perform the integration. In many cases 'c' may be taken as average value.

$$\therefore \quad s_2 - s_1 = c_{av} \cdot \ln\left(\frac{T_2}{T_1}\right) \text{ kJ/kg·K} \qquad \ldots (3.29)$$

3.5 Availability

It comes to our mind why an engineer has to understand the availability. The answer is to save energy, to consume energy in an optimal way, to reduce energy wastage etc. To achieve these, the engineers have to take a closer look at all the energy conversion devices (e.g. prime movers and energy consuming devices) and to develop new techniques to better utilize the existing limited resources. The first law of thermodynamics deals with conversion of energy from one form to another and tells that energy cannot be created or destroyed. It tells only the conversion of one form of energy to another however, it does not quantify the energy that changes from one form to another. First law is not a sufficient tool to quantify the process inefficiency or thermodynamic irreversibility which are inherently present in all real processes. For Problem, as per first law, throttling process is a constant enthalpy process. The energy content of the fluid before throttling and after throttling remains constant. Throttling is a real expansion process. The real process is always accompanied with process irreversibility. It is the limitation of first law that it could not quantify such process irreversibilities.

The second law of thermodynamics deals with the quality of energy. Second law is concerned with the degradation of energy during a process. It quantifies the process irreversibility and offers an opportunity to obtain maximum work output from a stream while bringing it from high temperature and pressure conditions to the reference temperature and pressure conditions. Therefore, at this stage, it becomes necessary to study available and unavailable energy of a system undergoing through a process.

3.6 Available and Unavailable Energy

'Available energy' is the maximum portion of the energy which could be converted into useful work and which reduces the system to a 'dead state'. The dead state is one at which the system reaches thermodynamic equilibrium with the surrounding.

When a system is at high pressure than atmospheric pressure, then there is an opportunity to obtain useful work while reducing it to ambient pressure through an expansion device. Similarly, any system which is at higher temperature than ambient temperature, then also there is an opportunity to obtain useful work while reducing its temperature to ambient temperature through a thermodynamic cycle.

Therefore, available energy can be further defined as "the theoretical maximum useful work that can be obtained from a system while changing its state (p_1 and T_1) to reference state (p_0 and T_0) through a reversible process".

To obtain a maximum useful work from a system, its state (p_1 and T_1) has to be reduced to reference state (p_0 and T_0) through a reversible process. However, in reality, the end state of the system will not be at reference state but little above that state. It means say the system reaches to a state (p_2 and T_2) which is in between the initial state (p_1 and T_1) and reference state (p_0 and T_0). Therefore, the actual work obtained is less than that of maximum possible work (available energy). The portion of the available energy which is not converted to useful work is known as **unavailable energy.**

3.7 Available Energy Referred to a Cycle

The maximum work output obtainable from a certain heat input in a cyclic heat engine (reversible engine) is called the available energy (AE). The minimum energy that has to be rejected to the sink as per the second law is called the unavailable energy (UE) or the unavailable part of supplied energy.

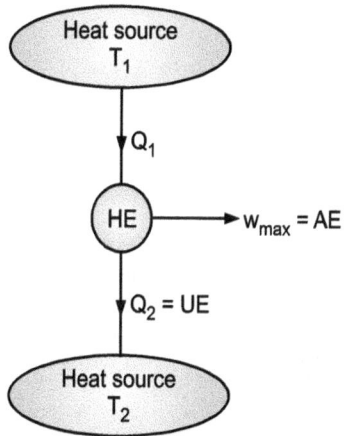
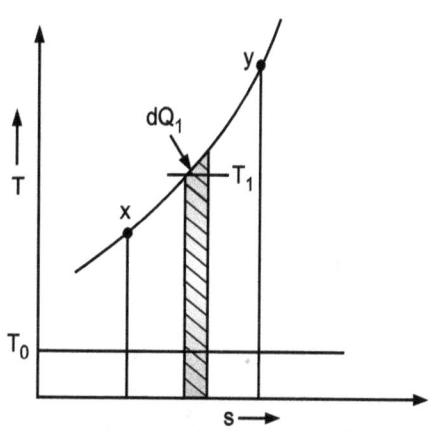

Fig. 3.13: Available and unavailable energy in a cycle   **Fig. 3.14: Availability of energy**

Let Q_1 be the heat energy supplied, which consists of two parts (AE and UE).

Therefore,
$$Q_1 = AE + UE \quad \ldots (3.30)$$
$$W_{max} = AE = Q_1 - UE$$

For the heat engine working between T_1 and T_2,
$$\eta_{rev} = 1 - \frac{T_2}{T_1}$$

For a given source temperature T_1, η_{rev} will increase with decrease of sink temperature T_2. The lowest possible temperature at which heat rejection would take place is the temperature of the surroundings, T_0.

$$\eta_{max} = 1 - \frac{T_0}{T_1}$$
$$W_{max} = \left(1 - \frac{T_0}{T_1}\right) Q_1$$

Let us consider a process x-y, during which heat is supplied reversibly to a heat engine as shown in Fig. 5.2. Assuming an elementary cycle, dQ_1 is the heat supplied to a reversible heat engine at T_1, then

$$dW_{max} = \eta_{rev} \times dQ_1$$
$$= \left(\frac{T_1 - T_0}{T_1}\right) \cdot dQ_1$$
$$= dQ_1 - \frac{T_0}{T_1} dQ_1 = AE$$

The heat engine receiving heat for the whole process x-y and rejecting heat at T_0

$$\int_x^y dW_{max} = \int_x^y dQ_1 - \int_x^y \frac{T_0}{T_1} \cdot dQ_1$$

$$\therefore \quad W_{max} = AE = Q_{xy} - T_0 (S_y - S_x) \quad \ldots (3.31)$$

Unavailable energy, $UE = Q_{xy} - W_{max}$
$$= T_0 (S_y - S_x)$$

The unavailable energy is nothing but the product of the lowest temperature of heat sink (T_0) and the change of entropy of the system during the process, which is as shown in Fig. 3.15.

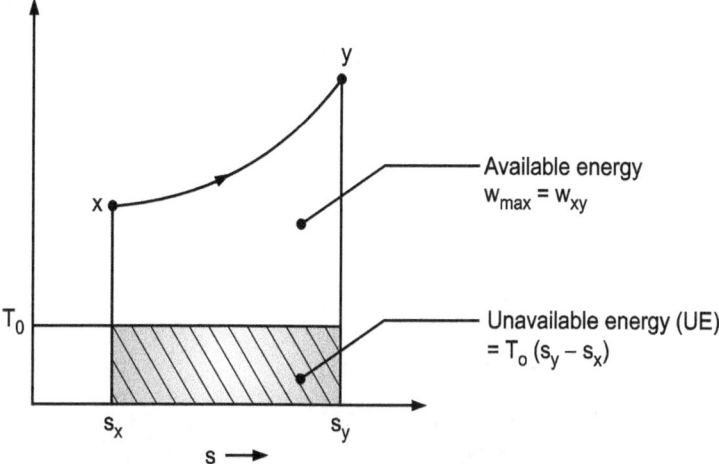

Fig. 3.15: Unavailable energy according to second law

The available energy is also known as **exergy** and the unavailable energy as **anergy.** It may please be note here that exergy and anergy are the correct words.

3.8 Decrease in Available Energy in a Heat Transfer Process Through a Finite Temperature Difference

In order to transfer heat from one system to another, a finite temperature difference is needed. To achieve this, there is a decrease in the availability of energy. This can be shown as given below.

Consider a reversible heat engine (Carnot engine) operating between the temperature limits T_1 and T_0 as shown in Fig. 5.4.

$$\text{Heat supplied, } Q_1 = T \cdot \Delta s$$
$$\text{Heat rejected, } Q_2 = T_0 \cdot \Delta s$$
$$\text{Max. work done, } w = A.E = [T_1 - T_0] \Delta s$$

Assume heat Q_1 is transferred through a finite temperature difference (ΔT) from the source at T_1 to the engine absorbing heat at T_1', lower than T_1 (See Fig. 5.5). The availability of Q_1 as received by the engine at T_1' can be found by allowing the engine to operate reversibly in a cycle between T_1' and T_0 receiving Q_1 and rejecting Q_2'. Now, the heat supply Q_1 takes place at lower temperature.

The heat, $\quad Q_1 = T_1 \Delta s = T_1' \Delta s'$

Since $\quad T_1 > T_1'$

∴ $\quad \Delta s' = \Delta s$

The heat rejected, $\quad Q_2 = T_0 \Delta s$

$\quad Q_2' = T_0 \Delta s'$

∴ $\quad \Delta s' > \Delta s$

∴ $\quad Q_2' > Q_2$

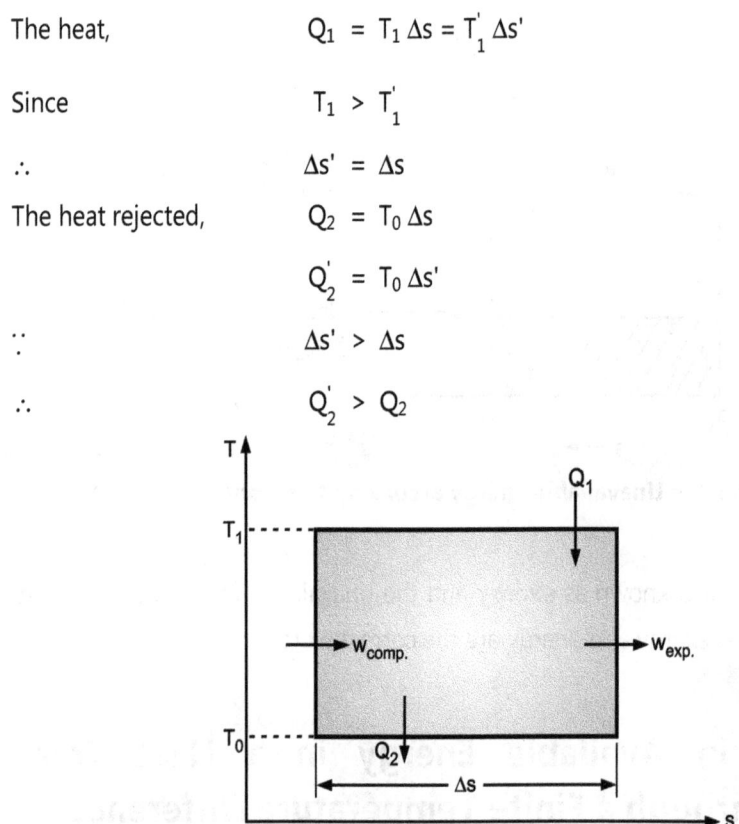

Fig. 3.16: Reversible (Carnot) engine on T-s diagram

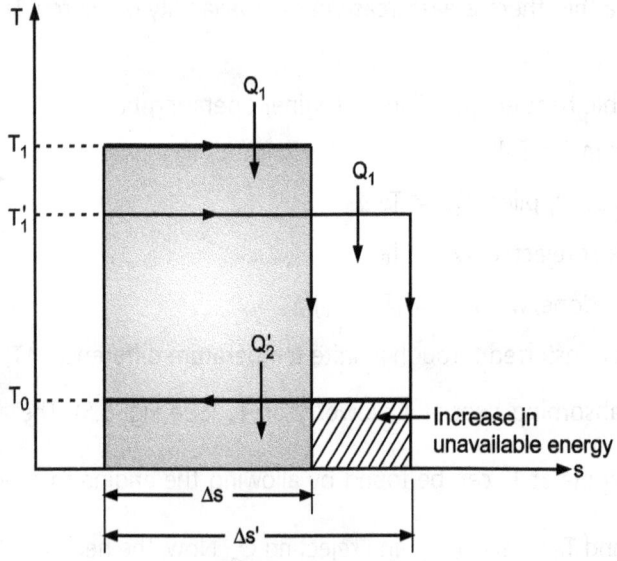

Fig. 3.17: Increase in unavailable energy due to heat transfer through a finite temperature difference

Now, work done in new cycle (with ΔT at source).

$$w' = Q_1 - Q_2' = T_1' \Delta s' - T_0 \Delta s'$$

and with no ΔT

$$w = Q_1 - Q_2 = T_1 \Delta s - T_0 \Delta s$$

$\therefore$

$$w' < w, \text{ because } Q_2' > Q_2$$

The loss of available energy due to irreversible heat transfer through finite temperature difference between the source and the working fluid during the heat addition process is given as,

$$w - w' = Q_2' - Q_2$$

$$= T_0 (\Delta s' - \Delta s)$$

i.e. decrease in available energy, A.E.

$$= T_0 (\Delta s' - \Delta s) \qquad \ldots (3.32)$$

Hence, the decrease in AE is the product of the lowest feasible temperature of heat rejection (T_0) and the additional entropy change in the system while receiving heat irreversibly, compared to the case of reversible heat transfer from the same source. The greater is the temperature difference ($T_1 - T_1'$), the greater is the heat rejection Q_2' and the greater will be the unavailable part of the energy supplied which is shown in Fig. 3.17.

Energy is said to be degraded each time it flows through a finite temperature difference (ΔT). That is, why the second law of thermodynamics is sometimes called the law of degradation of energy.

EXERCISE

1. Suppose you have to explain entropy production to a child, how will you explain it?
2. Think a process of a closed system for which the entropy of both the system and its surroundings increase.
3. Is it possible for the entropy of both a closed system and its surroundings to decrease during a process?
4. Discuss the transfer of entropy into or out of a closed system.

5. How will you calculate the entropy production in a nuclear reactor?
6. How will you calculate the entropy production during a storm?
7. All state of an adiabatic and internally reversible process of a closed system have the same entropy, but is a process between two states having same entropy necessarily adiabatic and internally reversible?
8. Define Clausius inequality and prove it.
9. Define entropy and show that it is a property of the system.
10. Give a physical explanation of entropy.
11. Why is the Carnot cycle on T-s plot a rectangle?
12. What do you understand by entropy principle?
13. Show that the entropy of an isolated system increases in all real process and is conserved in reversible process.
14. Why is the entropy increase of an isolated system a measure of the extent of irreversibility of the process undergone by the system?
15. State the summary given by Rudolf Clausius about first and second laws of thermodynamics.
16. Show that the transfer of heat through a finite temperature difference is irreversible.
17. Show that the adiabatic mixing of two fluids is irreversible.
18. What causes an increase in entropy?
19. Why is the second law called a directional law of nature?
20. Derive the expression for entropy generation (production) in a closed system.
21. Derive the expression for entropy generation in a open system (control volume).
22. What do you mean by absolute value of entropy?

Unit IV

POWER CYCLES

4.1 Introduction

Analysis of engine cycle is an important tool to design and study the internal combustion engines. A thermodynamic cycle consists of a series of processes through which the working fluid progresses (passes). In other words, a thermodynamic cycle implies a closed system with no exchange of matter with surroundings. Truly speaking internal combustion engine element operate on a thermodynamic cycle as it consists of an open system wherein a new fluid continuously enters the engine at one set of conditions and leaves at another condition. This is shown in Fig. 4.1.

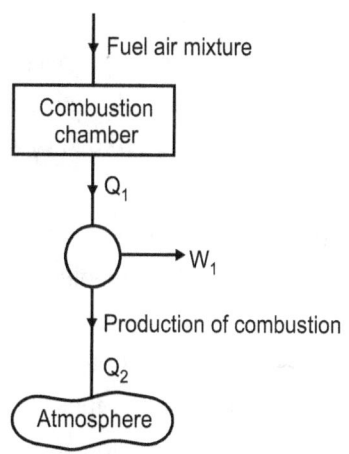

Fig. 4.1: Internal combustion engine: A block diagram

An accurate analysis of an internal combustion engine is very difficult due to the complex chemical reactions that take place when fuel burns. Not only it involves friction between piston and cylinder walls, but also heat transfer between the gases and cylinder walls. Hence, it is an usual practice to analyse the cycle making some simplifying assumptions.

The two commonly employed approximation of an actual engine in order of their increasing accuracy are:
(i) Ideal or air standard cycle analysis.
(ii) Fuel-air cycles analysis.

These two cycles are theoretical cycles.

Numerical result obtained by the above theoretical analysis are different from actual results due to above approximations. The results so obtained are not only for academic interests but have a great practical importance. The analysis of the theoretical cycle indicates the upper limit of the performance of an engine.

4.2 Ideal or Air Standard Cycle

Air standard cycles are defined as cycles using a perfect gas (ideal gas) as the working substance. Air is almost invariably used as the working fluid in internal combustion engines (I.C. engines). Air is assumed to behave as a perfect gas. The **following assumptions are made in the analysis of standard cycles**:

(1) The working substance is a *perfect* gas, i.e. it follows the characteristic gas equation, pv = mRT.
(2) The working substance (fluid) is a fixed mass of air contained in a closed system.
(3) The physical constants of the working medium (substance) such as c_p = 1.005 kJ/kg·K, c_v = 0.718 kJ/kg·K and γ = 1.4 are taken in the calculations, for air.
(4) The specific heats of working substance are assumed constant.
(5) The working medium does not undergo chemical changes.
(6) Heat is supplied and rejected in a reversible manner and if necessary, can be supplied and rejected instantaneously. (In actual engine, energy is supplied by combustion of fuel and rejected by exhaust gases).
(7) The compression and expansion processes are reversible adiabatic (isentropic).
(8) The operation of the engine is frictionless.
(9) Kinetic and potential energies are neglected.

The work output, peak pressure, peak temperature and *thermal efficiency* based on ideal cycle are higher than those of actual engine.

Thermal efficiency is the ratio of work output to the heat supplied to the engine.

Mathematically, $$\eta_{th} = \frac{\text{Work output}}{\text{Heat supplied}}$$

Thermal efficiency is referred as **Air standard efficiency** for the cycle which uses air as the working substance.

4.3 Carnot Cycle (Reversible Cycle)

It is also called as **reversible cycle** because all the processes are reversible one. It works between two different temperature reservoirs. It consists of two reversible adiabatic and two reversible isothermal processes.

Carnot engine working between two thermal reservoirs is shown in Fig. 4.2.

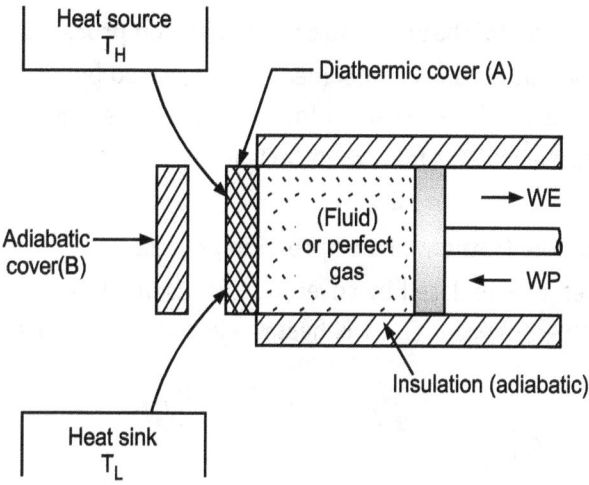

Fig. 4.2.: Carnot heat engine

Carnot cycle is represented on p-V plane [Fig. 4.3 (a)] and on T-s plane [Fig. 4.3 (b)].

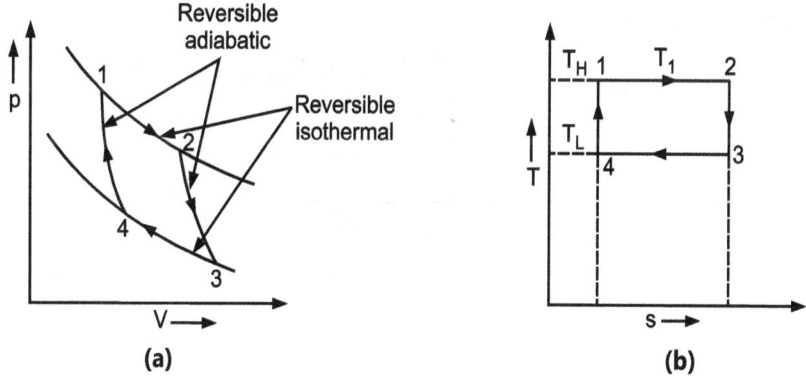

Fig. 4.3: p-V and T-s diagrams

Process 1 - 2 : Reversible Isothermal Expansion process:

The hot body at temperature T_H is brought in contact with working fluid (diathermic cover A is in contact with cylinder head), so that heat is transferred isothermally.

∴ According to the first law of thermodynamics,

$$Q_{1-2} = \Delta U + W_{1-2} \qquad (\because \Delta U = 0)$$

∴
$$Q_{1-2} = W_{1-2} = m \cdot R \cdot T_H \ln\left(\frac{V_2}{V_1}\right)$$

$$= T_1 (s_2 - s_1) \text{ kJ} \qquad \ldots (i)$$

Process 2 - 3: Reversible Adiabatic (Isentropic) Expansion process :

In this process, diathermic cover 'A' is assumed to be replaced by the adiabatic cover 'B'. No heat transfer occurs. Work W_E is obtained from the system; at the cost of internal energy. Therefore, temperature decreases from T_H to T_L (T_2 to T_3).

$$\therefore \quad Q_{2-3} = 0$$

Process 3 - 4: Reversible Isothermal Compression process :

Again adiabatic cover 'B' is replaced by cover 'A'. It is assumed that the fluid is brought into contact with low temperature sink (T_L). The heat is rejected isothermally from the fluid to sink.

$$Q_{3-4} = W_{3-4} = -mRT_L \cdot \ln\left(\frac{V_4}{V_3}\right)$$

$$= mRT_L \ln\left(\frac{V_3}{V_4}\right)$$

$$= T_3 (s_3 - s_4) \text{ kJ} \qquad \ldots \text{(ii)}$$

Process 4 - 1: Reversible Adiabatic (Isentropic) Compression process :

This compression process is continued till the fluid reaches initial state at point 1. The work is done on the fluid in this process and therefore internal energy increases. So temperature increases from T_L to T_H.

$$\text{Thermal efficiency} = \frac{\text{Heat supplied} - \text{Heat rejected}}{\text{Heat supplied}}$$

$$= \frac{mRT_H \ln\left(\frac{V_2}{V_1}\right) - mRT_L \ln\left(\frac{V_3}{V_4}\right)}{mRT_H \ln\left(\frac{V_2}{V_1}\right)}$$

$$\frac{V_3}{V_2} = \frac{V_4}{V_1} \quad \text{or} \quad \frac{V_2}{V_1} = \frac{V_3}{V_4}$$

$$\eta_{th} = \frac{T_H - T_L}{T_H} \quad \text{or} \quad \frac{T_1 - T_3}{T_1} \qquad \ldots \text{(iii)}$$

$$= 1 - \frac{T_L}{T_H}$$

If T_L is constant (i.e. the temperature of heat sink such as atmosphere, lake water etc.) and source temperature T_H increases, the thermal efficiency of the cycle increases.

The relative work outputs of various piston engine cycles are given by mean effective pressure (m_{ep} or p_m). The **mean effective pressure** is defined as the constant pressure producing the same net work output while causing the piston to move through the same swept volume as in the actual cycle (See Fig. 4.4).

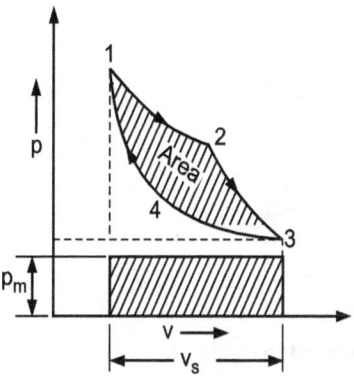

Fig. 4.4: Mean effective pressure

Let p_m = mean effective pressure, N/m²
V_s = swept volume, m³
W = net work output per cycle, N-m

Then, $p_m = \dfrac{\text{Work done per cycle}}{\text{Stroke volume}}$

$$= \dfrac{W}{V_s} = \dfrac{\int pdV}{V_s} \quad \ldots \text{(iv)}$$

∴ $p_m = \dfrac{\text{Area of indicator diagram}}{\text{Stroke volume}}$

4.4 Otto Cycle

It is also known as constant volume cycle. It consists of two constant volume processes and two reversible adiabatic processes.

This Otto cycle is the theoretical cycle for the spark - ignition engine.

The cycle is represented on p-v and T-s planes [Fig. 4.5 (a) and (b)].

In the air cycle analysis, the induction and exhaust processes, represented by lines 0 – 1 and 1 – 0 respectively are neglected. The work done during both the processes is equal and opposite and hence cancel each other.

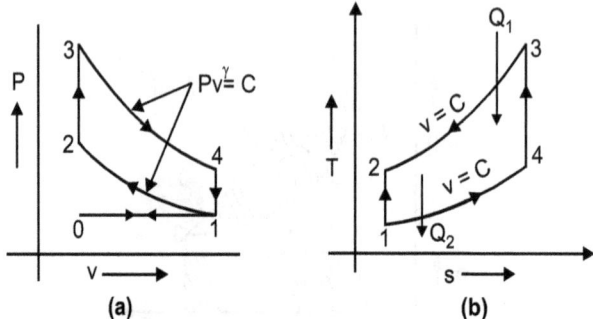

Fig. 4.5: Otto Cycle on P-v and T-s diagram

Process 1-2:
Reversible adiabatic compression of the air. The piston moves from Bottom Dead Centre (BDC) position to the Top Dead Centre (TDC) position. No heat transfer takes place during the process.

Process 2-3:
Heat is added at constant volume so that the state of air changes from point 2 to 3.
For unit mass of air, heat supplied,
$$Q = c_v (T_3 - T_2) \qquad \ldots (i)$$

Process 3-4:
Isentropic (reversible adiabatic) expansion of the air takes place. During this process, piston moves from TDC position to BDC position. No heat transfer occurs during the process.

Process 4-1:
The heat is rejected at constant volume. It is assumed that the heat rejection occurs instantaneously.

For unit mass of air, heat rejected,
$$Q_2 = c_v (T_4 - T_1) \qquad \ldots (ii)$$

$\therefore \quad$ Work done = Heat added − Heat rejected
$$= c_v (T_3 - T_2) - c_v (T_4 - T_1)$$

$$\text{Thermal efficiency} = \frac{\text{Work done}}{\text{Heat supplied}}$$

$$= \frac{c_v (T_3 - T_2) - c_v (T_4 - T_1)}{c_v (T_3 - T_2)}$$

$$= 1 - \frac{(T_4 - T_1)}{(T_3 - T_2)} \qquad \ldots (iii)$$

Now, Compression ratio $= \dfrac{V_1}{V_2} = r_c$

Expansion ratio $= \dfrac{V_4}{V_3} = r_e$

Here, $r_c = r_e = r$

For ideal gas, $pv = RT$ and $pv^\gamma = C$

$$\dfrac{p_1 v_1}{T_1} = \dfrac{p_2 v_2}{T_2} \qquad\qquad p_1 v_1^\gamma = p_2 v_2^\gamma$$

$$\dfrac{T_2}{T_1} = \dfrac{p_2 v_2}{p_1 v_1} \qquad\qquad \dfrac{p_2}{p_1} = \left(\dfrac{v_1}{v_2}\right)^\gamma$$

$$= \left(\dfrac{v_1}{v_2}\right)^\gamma \cdot \dfrac{v_2}{v_1}$$

$\therefore \qquad \dfrac{T_2}{T_1} = \left(\dfrac{v_1}{v_2}\right)^{\gamma-1}$

$$= \left(\dfrac{v_4}{v_3}\right)^{\gamma-1} = \dfrac{T_3}{T_4} = r^{\gamma-1}$$

$\therefore \qquad T_3 = T_4 \cdot r^{\gamma-1}$ and $T_2 = T_1 \cdot r^{\gamma-1}$

Put these values of T_3 and T_2 in equation (iv).

$\therefore \qquad$ Thermal efficiency $= 1 - \dfrac{(T_4 - T_1)}{(T_4 - T_1) \, r^{\gamma-1}}$

$$\eta_{thermal} = 1 - \dfrac{1}{r^{\gamma-1}} \qquad\qquad\qquad ...(iv)$$

Mean effective pressure (MEP) of Otto cycle:

See Fig. 4.6.

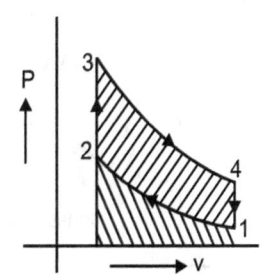

Fig. 4.6: Otto Cycle on P-v Plot

Let clearance volume,

$v_2 = v_3 = 1$

and $\qquad v_1 = v_4 = r$

Also

$$\dfrac{p_3}{p_2} = \dfrac{p_4}{p_1} = \alpha$$

$$\dfrac{p_2}{p_1} = \dfrac{p_3}{p_4} = r^\gamma$$

Work done $=$ Area of the P-v diagram

$$= \dfrac{P_3 v_3 - P_4 v_4}{\gamma - 1} - \dfrac{P_2 v_2 - P_1 v_1}{\gamma - 1}$$

$$= \dfrac{1}{\gamma - 1}\left[P_4 v_4 \left(\dfrac{P_3}{P_4} \cdot \dfrac{v_3}{v_4} - 1\right) - P_1 v_1 \left(\dfrac{P_2 v_2}{P_1 v_1} - 1\right)\right]$$

$v_4 = r$, because $v_4 = v_1 = r$

$$= \frac{1}{\gamma-1}\left[P_4 \cdot r\left(\frac{P_3}{P_4 \cdot r}-1\right) - P_1 r\left(\frac{P_2}{P_1 r}-1\right)\right]$$

$\dfrac{P_3}{P_4} = r^\gamma$ and $\dfrac{P_2}{P_1} = r^\gamma$

$$= \frac{r}{\gamma-1}\left[P_4(r^{\gamma-1}-1) - P_1(r^{\gamma-1}-1)\right]$$

$$= \frac{r}{\gamma-1}(r^{\gamma-1}-1) \cdot (P_4 - P_1), \frac{P_4}{P_1} = \alpha$$

$$= \frac{r}{\gamma-1} \cdot P_1(\alpha-1)(r^{\gamma-1}-1)$$

Length of the diagram = $r - 1$

$$\therefore \quad \text{mep} = \frac{\text{Area of the P-v diagram}}{\text{Length of diagram}}$$

$$= \frac{P_1 \cdot r(\alpha-1)(r^{\gamma-1}-1)}{(\gamma-1)(r-1)} \quad \ldots (v)$$

4.5 The Diesel Cycle

It is the thermal cycle for compression-ignition (CI) or diesel engine. The main difference between Otto and Diesel cycles is that heat addition is at constant pressure in Diesel cycle. While the same is at constant volume in Otto cycle. The heat rejection process takes place at constant volume in both the cycles. The Diesel cycle is shown in P-v and T-s diagram in Fig. 4.7.

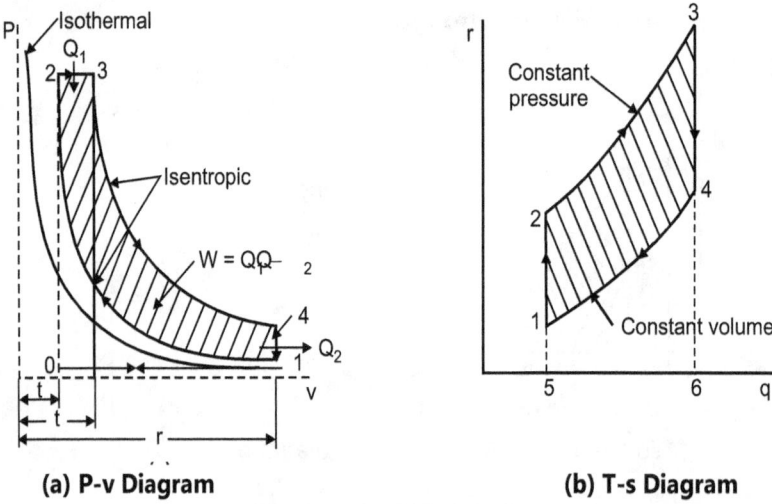

(a) P-v Diagram   (b) T-s Diagram

Fig. 4.7: The Diesel Cycle

Process 1-2: It is an isentropic compression (reversible adiabatic compression) of air through the compression ratio $r = \dfrac{V_1}{V_2}$.

The piston moves from bottom dead center (bdc) position to top dead center (tdc) position. No heat transfer takes place during the process.

Process 2-3: Heat is added at constant pressure so that state of air changes from point 2 to 3. For unit mass of air,

$$\text{Heat supplied, } Q_s = C_p (T_3 - T_2) \qquad \text{... (ii)}$$

Process 3-4: Isentropic expansion of air takes place. No heat transfer occurs during the process.

Process 4-1: Heat is rejected at constant volume. It is assumed that heat rejection takes place instantaneously. For unit mass of air, heat rejected, Q_r.

$$Q_r = C_v \cdot (T_4 - T_1) \qquad \text{... (iii)}$$

$$\therefore \quad \text{Work done} = Q_s - Q_r$$

$$= C_p (T_3 - T_2) - C_v (T_4 - T_1) \qquad \text{... (iv)}$$

The thermal efficiency of the Ideal Diesel cycle is given by,

$$\eta = \frac{\text{Heat added} - \text{Heat rejected}}{\text{Head added}}$$

$$= \frac{C_p (T_3 - T_2) - C_v (T_4 - T_1)}{C_v (T_3 - T_2)}$$

$$= 1 - \frac{1}{\gamma} \left(\frac{T_4 - T_1}{T_4 - T_2} \right)$$

$$= 1 - \frac{T_1}{\gamma T_2} \left(\frac{T_4/T_1 - 1}{T_3/T_2 - 1} \right) \qquad \text{... (v)}$$

For isentropic compression and expansion processes:

$$\frac{T_1}{T_2} = \left(\frac{V_2}{V_1}\right)^{\gamma-1} \text{ and } \frac{T_4}{T_3} = \left(\frac{r_3}{V_4}\right)^{\gamma-1}$$

For constant pressure heat addition 2-3,

$$\frac{T_3}{T_2} = \frac{V_3}{V_2}$$

Also $\quad V_4 = V_1$

Thus, $\quad \dfrac{T_4}{T_1} = \dfrac{T_3}{T_2} \left(\dfrac{V_3/V_4}{V_2/V_1}\right)^{\gamma-1} = \dfrac{V_3}{V_2} \left(\dfrac{V_3}{V_2}\right)^{\gamma-1} = \left(\dfrac{V_3}{V_2}\right)^{\gamma}$

Substituting these values in equation (v), we get,

$$\eta = 1 - \frac{1}{\gamma (V_1/V_2)^{\gamma-1}} \left[\frac{(V_3/V_2)^{\gamma} - 1}{(V_3/V_2) - 1} \right]$$

$$= 1 - \frac{1}{r^{\gamma-1}} \left[\frac{\rho^{\gamma} - 1}{\gamma (\rho - 1)} \right] \qquad \text{... (vi)}$$

Note that the efficiency of the Diesel cycle differs from that of the Otto cycle only by the bracketed term, which is always greater than unity (except when $\rho = 1$ and there is no heat addition). Thus, the Diesel cycle always has lower efficiency than Otto cycle for the same compression ratio.

4.5.1 MEP of Diesel Cycle

To derive an equation for mean effective pressure for Diesel cycle, refer Fig. 4.8.
Let clearance volume be unity.

$$\text{Work done} = \text{Area of P-v diagram}$$

$$= P_2(v_3 - v_2) + \frac{P_3 v_3 - P_4 v_4}{\gamma - 1} - \frac{P_2 v_2 - P_1 v_1}{\gamma - 1}$$

$$= P_2(\rho - 1) + \frac{P_2\rho - P_4 r - (P_2 - P_1 r)}{\gamma - 1}$$

$$= \frac{P_2(\rho - 1)(\gamma - 1) + P_2(\rho - \rho^\gamma r^{1-\gamma}) - P_2(1 - r^{1-\gamma})}{\gamma - 1}$$

$$-\frac{P_2}{\gamma - 1}[\gamma(\rho - 1) - r^{1-\gamma}(\rho^\gamma - 1)]$$

$$\text{mep} = \frac{\text{Area of the indicator diagram}}{\text{Length of the indicator diagram}}$$

$$= \frac{P_2[(\rho - 1) - r^{1-\gamma}(\rho^\gamma - 1)]}{(\gamma - 1)(r - 1)}$$

$$= \frac{P_1 r^\gamma [\gamma(\rho - 1) - r^{1-\gamma}(\rho^\gamma - 1)]}{(\gamma - 1)(r - 1)} \quad \ldots \text{(vii)}$$

4.5.2 Effect of Compression Ratio on Diesel Cycle Efficiency

The Diesel cycle always has a lower efficiency than the Otto cycle for the same compression ratio which is shown in Fig. 4.8.

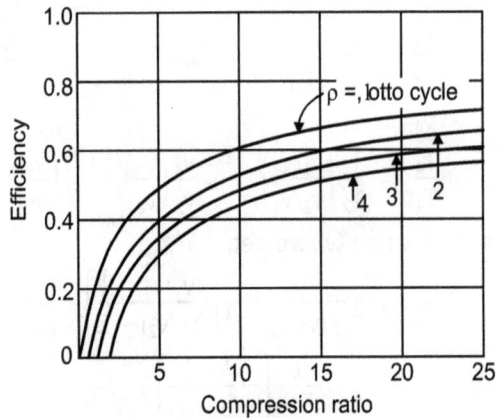

Fig. 4.8: Efficiency of the Diesel Cycle for Various Cut-off and Compression Ratios

In Diesel engine the cut-off ratio ($\rho = V_3/V_2$) depends on the load on the engine. It is maximum for maximum load.

The air standard efficiency of Diesel cycle depends on load and increases as the load is decreased and equals as that off Otto cycle efficiency at the limiting condition of zero load.

Diesel engine has normal compression ratio between 15 to 22 and Otto engine has this ratio between 6 to 10. The actual η of Diesel engine is higher than that of Otto engine (Petrol engine).

4.6 The Dual Cycle of Limited Pressure Cycle

(The Dual Combustion Cycle)

High speed diesel engines normally work according to the dual cycle (the dual combustion cycle is shown in Fig. 4.9).

In this cycle, port of head addition is at constant volume and remaining at constant pressure.

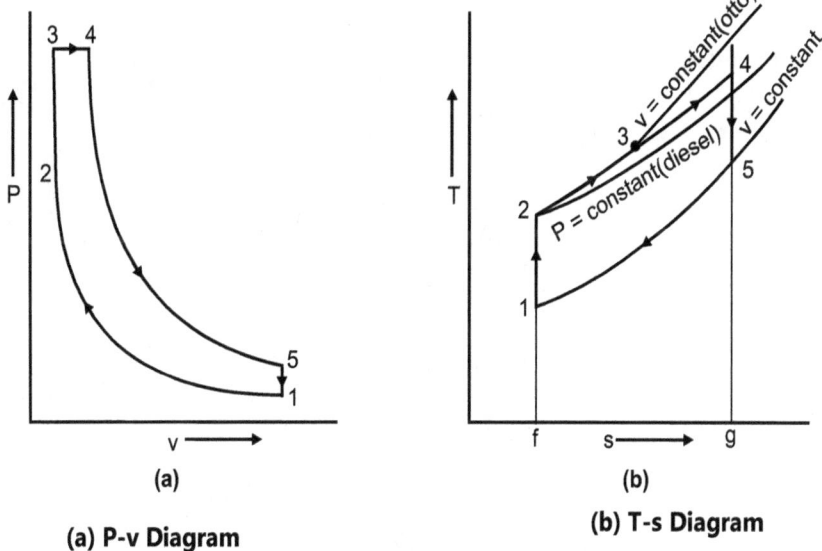

(a) P-v Diagram

(b) T-s Diagram

Fig. 4.9: Dual or Mixed or Limited Pressure Cycle

The various processes of the cycle are as given below:

Process 1-2: It is an isentropic compression of air through the compression ratio $r = \dfrac{V_1}{V_2}$. The piston moves from bdc position to tdc position. No heat exchange takes place during the process.

Process 2-3: Partial heat addition at constant volume per unit mass of air,

$$Q_{s1} = C_v (T_3 - T_2) \qquad \ldots (i)$$

Process 3-4: Partial heat, addition at constant pressure per unit mass of air,
$$Q_{s2} = C_p (T_4 - T_3) \qquad \ldots \text{(ii)}$$
Process 4-5: Isentropic expansion of air takes place.
No heat exchange takes place during the process.
Process 5-1: Heat is rejected at constant volume per unit mass of air,
$$Q_R = C_v (T_5 - T_1) \qquad \ldots \text{(iii)}$$
The efficiency of the cycle may be written as,

$$\eta = \frac{\text{Heat supplied} - \text{Heat rejected}}{\text{Heat supplied}}$$

$$= \frac{C_v (T_3 - T_2) + C_v (T_4 - T_3) - C_v (T_5 - T_1)}{C_v (T_3 - T_2) + C_v (T_4 - T_2)}$$

$$= 1 - \frac{T_5 - T_1}{(T_3 - T_2) + \gamma (T_4 - T_3)} \qquad \ldots \text{(iv)}$$

Now, $T_2 = T_1 \left(\dfrac{V_1}{V_2}\right)^{\gamma - 1} = T_1 r^{\gamma - 1}$, $T_3 = T_2 \dfrac{P_3}{P_2} = T_1 r^{\gamma - 1} \alpha$

where, α is the pressure ratio $\dfrac{P_3}{P_2}$.

$$T_4 = T_3 \frac{V_4}{V_3} T_1 r^{\gamma - 1} \times \rho$$

and $\quad T_5 = T_4 \left(\dfrac{V_4}{V_5}\right)^{\gamma - 1} = T_1 r^{\gamma - 1} \cdot \alpha\rho \left(\dfrac{V_4}{V_5}\right)^{\gamma - 1}$

Now, $\quad \dfrac{V_4}{V_5} = \dfrac{V_4}{V_1} = \dfrac{V_4 V_3}{V_3 V_1} = \dfrac{V_4 V_2}{V_3 V_1}$, etc. since $v_2 = v_3$.

$\therefore \quad \dfrac{V_4}{V_5} = \dfrac{\rho}{r}$ and hence $T_1 = T_1 \alpha \rho^{\gamma}$

Substituting for T_2, T_3, T_4 and T_5 into equation (iv), we obtain

$$\eta = 1 - \frac{1}{r^{\gamma - 1}} \left[\frac{\alpha \rho^{\gamma} - 1}{(\alpha - 1) + \alpha \gamma (\rho - 1)} \right] \qquad \ldots \text{(v)}$$

If $\alpha > 1$ in the equation (v), gives higher value of efficiency for the given value of ρ and γ.
Thus, the efficiency of dual cycle is intermediate between those of Otto cycle and Diesel cycle having the same compression ratio.
If one substitutes $\rho = 1$ in equation (v), it becomes Otto cycle and with $\alpha = 1$ it becomes diesel cycle.
The name dual combustion is derived due to the incorporation of features of both Otto cycle and Diesel cycle in dual cycle. Many a times, the world dual cycle can be avoided as it may cause confusion with dual fuel cycle. The heat addition at constant volume increases the cycle efficiency while heat addition at constant pressure limits the maximum pressure in the cycle. Therefore, the dual cycle is usually referred as limited pressure cycle.

4.6.1 Mean Effective Pressure of Limited Pressure Cycle

Referring to Fig. 4.10, one can write

$$\text{Work done} = \text{Area of P-v diagram}$$

$$= P_3 (V_4 - V_2) + \frac{P_4 V_4 - P_5 V_5}{\gamma - 1} - \frac{P_2 V_2 - P_1 V_1}{\gamma - 1}$$

$$= P_3 (\rho - 1) + \frac{P_3 \rho - P_5 r - P_2 + P_1 r}{\gamma - 1}$$

$$= P_3 (\rho - 1) + \frac{P_3 (\rho - \rho^\gamma r^{1-\gamma}) - P_2 (1 - r^{1-\gamma})}{\gamma - 1}$$

$$= \frac{P_3 [(\rho - 1)(\gamma - 1) + \rho - \rho^\gamma r^1 - \gamma - 1/\alpha (1 - r^{1-\gamma})]}{\gamma - 1}$$

$$= \frac{P_3 [\rho^\gamma - \rho - \gamma + 1 + \rho - \rho^\gamma r^{1-\gamma} - 1/x (1 - r^1 - \gamma)]}{\gamma - 1}$$

$$= \frac{P_3 [\alpha \gamma (\rho - 1) + \alpha - \alpha \rho^\gamma r^{1-\gamma} - (1 - r^{1-\gamma})]}{\alpha (\gamma - 1)}$$

$$= \frac{P_3 [\alpha \gamma (\rho - 1) + (\alpha - 1) - r^{1-\gamma}(\alpha \rho^\gamma - 1)]}{\alpha (\gamma - 1)}$$

$$\text{mep} = \frac{\text{Area of the indicator diagram}}{\text{Length of the indicator diagram}}$$

$$= \frac{P_2 [\alpha \gamma (C - 1) + (\alpha - 1) - r^{1-\gamma}(\alpha \rho^\gamma - \alpha \rho^\gamma 1)]}{\alpha (r - 1)(\gamma - 1)}$$

$$= \frac{P_1 r^\gamma [\alpha \gamma (\rho - 1) + (\alpha - 1) - r^{1-\gamma}(\alpha \rho^\gamma - 1)]}{(\gamma - 1)(r - 1)} \quad \ldots \text{(vi)}$$

4.7 Brayton Cycle

The constant pressure or open cycle gas turbine works on Brayton cycle.

- This cycle consists of four reversible processes.
- Two processes are reversible constant pressure and two are isentropic.
- As compressor requires about 70% of turbine output, overall efficiency of cycle is very less.
- Therefore this cycle is not generally used in practice.
- It is used in aeroplanes.

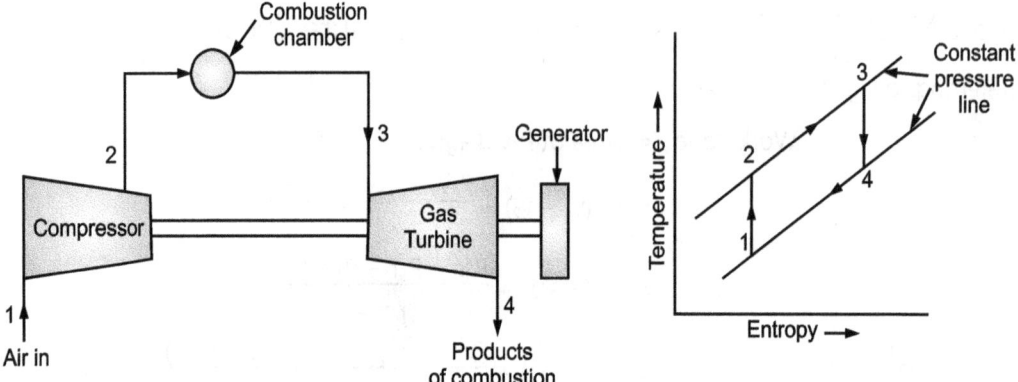

Fig. 4.10: Constant pressure gas turbine   **Fig. 4.11: Constant pressure cycle**

(Joule or Brayton cycle)

The constant pressure gas turbine works on Joule or Brayton cycle.

Process 1 – 2 : Fresh atmospheric air is drawn into compressor. The compressor is of axial flow type. The air is compressed to 2 to 4 bar. The compression is assumed to be isentropic.

Process 2 – 3 : The compressed air enters the combustion chamber. Here the fuel is injected and ignited by spark plug. The combustion takes place at constant pressure. The temperature rises to @ 2000°C. The turbine blades cannot withstand such a high temperature, hence products of combustion are cooled by the arrangement shown in Fig. 4.6.

The air passing in the annular space cools the products of combustion and reduces its temperature.

The permissible temperature for turbine blade material is in the range of 730°C to 930°C.

Process 3 – 4 : This is an isentropic expansion process. The products of combustion at high temperature and pressure expand isentropically. The pressure energy is converted into kinetic energy.

Process 4 – 1 : The products of combustion after expansion are let off to atmosphere at constant pressure.

The turbine is coupled to the generator and compressor. The compressor absorbs about 60-70% of the turbine output. The remaining power is used to drive the generator.

4.7.1 Assumptions for Ideal Cycle Analysis

It is assumed that working fluid in the turbine plant is an ideal gas and following assumptions are made for ideal cycle analysis.

(i) Compression and expansion are reversible and adiabatic.
(ii) There are no pressure losses in combustion chamber, inlet ducting, exhaust ducting, heat exchangers etc.
(iii) The mass flow of gas is constant throughout the cycle.
(iv) The composition of working fluid does not change throughout the cycle and working fluid is a perfect gas.
(v) Frictional losses at bearings and windage losses are neglected.
(vi) Between inlet and outlet of each component, change of kinetic energy of working fluid is neglected.

With these assumptions, we will calculate thermal efficiency of the Brayton or Joule cycle.

4.7.2 Thermal Efficiency and Work Ratio

Referring to Fig. 4.11, for 1 kg of working fluid,

The heat is supplied during constant pressure process 2 – 3.

$$\text{Heat supplied} = Q_s = h_3 - h_2 = C_p (T_3 - T_2)$$

The heat is rejected during constant pressure process 4 – 1.

$$\text{Heat rejected} = h_4 - h_1 = C_p (T_4 - T_1)$$

$$\text{Net work} = \text{Heat supplied} - \text{Heat rejected}$$

$$= C_p [(T_3 - T_2) - (T_4 - T_1)]$$

This net work can also be found from turbine and compressor work

$$\text{Work done by the turbine} = W_t = h_3 - h_4$$

$$= C_p (T_3 - T_4)$$

$$\left[\begin{array}{c}\text{Work consumed by the}\\ \text{compressor which is supplied}\\ \text{by the turbine}\end{array}\right] = W_c = h_2 - h_1$$

$$= C_p (T_2 - T_1)$$

$$\text{Net work} = W_T - W_C$$

$$= C_p [(T_3 - T_2) - (T_4 - T_1)]$$

$$\text{Thermal efficiency} = \frac{\text{Net work}}{\text{Heat supplied}} = \frac{W_T - W_C}{Q_s}$$

$$= \frac{C_p [(T_3 - T_2) - (T_4 - T_1)]}{C_p (T_3 - T_2)}$$

$$= 1 - \frac{T_4 - T_1}{T_3 - T_2} \qquad \ldots \text{(i)}$$

Normally in gas turbine, initial and final pressures are known, hence this equation will be expressed in terms of P_1, P_2, etc.

Now 1 – 2 and 3 – 4 are isentropic processes.

Hence
$$\frac{T_2}{T_1} = \left(\frac{P_2}{P_1}\right)^{\frac{\gamma-1}{\gamma}}$$

and
$$\frac{T_3}{T_4} = \left(\frac{P_3}{P_4}\right)^{\frac{\gamma-1}{\gamma}}$$

However, as $P_2 = P_3$ and $P_1 = P_4$,

$$\therefore \quad \frac{T_2}{T_1} = \frac{T_3}{T_4} = \left(\frac{P_2}{P_1}\right)^{\frac{\gamma-1}{\gamma}} = (r_p)^m$$

where $m = \dfrac{\gamma-1}{\gamma}$ and r_p = pressure ratio = $\dfrac{P_2}{P_1} = \dfrac{P_3}{P_4}$

$$\therefore \quad \frac{T_1}{T_2} = \frac{T_4}{T_3} = \frac{T_4 - T_1}{T_3 - T_2} \quad \ldots \text{(ii)}$$

But thermal efficiency $= 1 - \dfrac{T_4 - T_1}{T_3 - T_2} = 1 - \dfrac{T_1}{T_2}$

$$\therefore \quad \text{Thermal efficiency} = 1 - \frac{1}{(r_p)^{\frac{\gamma-1}{\gamma}}} \quad \ldots \text{(iii)}$$

From the above equation we observe that the thermal efficiency of the Brayton or Joule's cycle is function of r_p, the pressure ratio.

As pressure ratio increases, thermal efficiency increases. However, pressure ratio cannot increase beyond a certain value. As pressure ratio increases, temperature T_2 increases which in turn increase T_3. The value of T_3 is limited by metallurgical considerations. Normally, a pressure ratio of 2 to 4 is used.

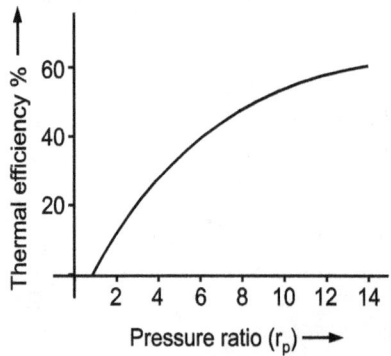

Fig. 4.12: Pressure ratio Vs thermal efficiency

Another term normally used is work ratio.

Work ratio is defined as the ratio of the net work to the work developed by the turbine.

$$\text{Work ratio} = r_w = \frac{W_T - W_C}{W_T}$$

Now, $\quad W_T - W_C = C_p(T_3 - T_4) - C_p(T_2 - T_1)$

$$\therefore \quad W_T - W_C = W_n = C_p T_3\left(1 - \frac{T_4}{T_3}\right) - C_p T_1\left(\frac{T_2}{T_1} - 1\right)$$

where, $\quad W_n = $ Network

$$\therefore \quad W_n = C_p T_3\left(1 - \frac{1}{r_p^m}\right) - C_p T_1\left(r_p^m - 1\right) \quad \ldots \text{(iv)}$$

Now,
$$r_w = \text{Work ratio} = \frac{W_T - W_C}{W_T} = 1 - \frac{W_C}{W_T}$$

$$= 1 - \frac{C_p(T_2 - T_1)}{C_p(T_3 - T_4)}$$

$$= 1 - \frac{C_p T_1\left[\frac{T_2}{T_1} - 1\right]}{C_p T_3\left(1 - \frac{T_4}{T_3}\right)}$$

$$= 1 - \frac{C_p T_1\left(r_p^m - 1\right)}{C_p T_3\left(1 - \frac{1}{r_p^m}\right)}$$

$$= 1 - \frac{T_1\left(r_p^m - 1\right)}{T_3\left(r_p^m - 1\right)} \cdot \infty \, r_p^m$$

$$= 1 - \frac{T_1}{T_3} \cdot r_p^m \quad \ldots \text{(v)}$$

The work ratio is maximum when $\frac{T_1}{T_3} = r_p^m$ is minimum.

This is when T_1 is minimum and T_3 is maximum for the same r_p.

Remarks:

(i) T_3 is decided by metallurgical considerations and is limited to @ 1000 K.

(ii) T_1 is atmospheric temperature which is usually 15°C or 288 K.

(iii) $r_w = $ work ratio $= 1 - \frac{T_1}{T_3} \cdot r_p^m$ is a function of temperature ratio and pressure ratio.

(iv) Thermal efficiency $= 1 - \frac{1}{r_p^{\frac{\gamma-1}{\gamma}}}$ is function of pressure ratio only.

4.8 Atkinson Cycle

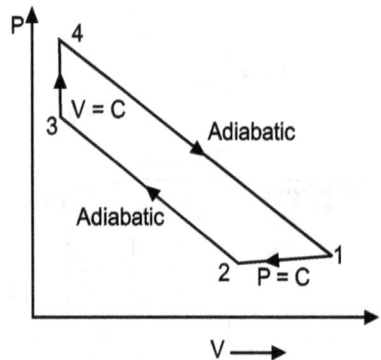

Fig. 4.13

The Atkinson Cycle consists of:
- Two adiabatic process.
- One constant volume process.
- One constant pressure process.

The cycle consists of the following four operations:
Process 1-2, Constant pressure heat rejection.
Process 2-3, Adiabatic compression.
Process 3-4, Heat addition at constant volume.
Process 4-1, Adiabatic expansion.

Four unit mass of air,
$$\text{Compression ratio, } r = \frac{V_2}{V_3}$$
$$\text{Expansion ratio, } \alpha = \frac{V_1}{V_4}$$

Heat supplied at constant volume,
$$Q_{3-4} = C_p (T_4 - T_3)$$

Heat rejected at constant pressure
$$Q_{1-2} = C_p (T_1 - T_2)$$

Work done = Heat supplied − Heat rejected

$$\eta = \frac{C_v (T_4 - T_3) - C_p (T_1 - T_2)}{C_v (T_4 - T_3)}$$

$$= 1 - \frac{\gamma (T_1 - T_2)}{(T_4 - T_3)} \quad \ldots (1)$$

For adiabatic compression 2-3,
$$\frac{T_3}{T_2} = \left(\frac{V_2}{V_3}\right)^{\gamma-1} = (r)^{\gamma-1} \qquad \ldots (2)$$

For constant pressure process 1-2,
$$\frac{V_1}{T_1} = \frac{V_2}{T_2}$$
$$\frac{T_2}{T_1} = \frac{V_2}{V_1} = \frac{\gamma}{\alpha} \qquad \left[\frac{V_2}{V_1} = \frac{V_2}{V_3} \times \frac{V_3}{V_1} = \frac{V_2}{V_3} \times \frac{V_4}{V_1} = \frac{\gamma}{\alpha}\right] \ldots (3)$$

$$\frac{T_4}{T_1} = \left(\frac{V_1}{V_4}\right)^{\gamma-1} = (\alpha)^{\gamma-1}$$

$$T_1 = \frac{T_4}{(\alpha)^{\gamma-1}} \qquad \ldots (4)$$

Putting T_1 in equation (3),
$$T_2 = T_1 \times \frac{\gamma}{\alpha}$$
$$= \frac{T_4}{(\alpha)^{\gamma-1}} \times \frac{\gamma}{\alpha}$$
$$T_2 = \frac{\gamma T_4}{\alpha^k} \qquad \ldots (5)$$

Substituting T_2 in equation (2),
$$T_3 = \frac{\gamma}{\alpha^\gamma}(r)^{\gamma-1} = \left(\frac{\gamma}{\alpha}\right)^\gamma T_4$$

Finally, substituting T_1, T_2 and T_3 in equation (1),
$$\eta = 1 - \gamma \left[\frac{\frac{T_4}{\alpha^{\gamma-1}} - \frac{2T_4}{\alpha^\gamma}}{T_4 - \left(\frac{\gamma}{\alpha}\right)^\gamma T_4}\right]$$

4.9 Ericsson Cycle

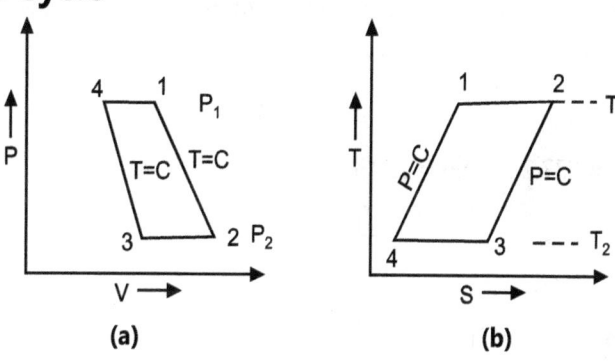

Fig. 4.14

The Ericsson Cycle is made up of

- two reversible isotherms and two reversible isobars.

For unit mass of gas,

$$Q_{1-2} = W_{1-2} = RT_1 \ln \frac{P_1}{P_2}$$

$$Q_{2-3} = C_p (T_2 - T_1)$$

$$W_{2-3} = P_2 (V_3 - V_2) = R (T_2 - T_1)$$

$$Q_{3-4} = W_{3-4} = -RT_2 \ln \frac{P_1}{P_2}$$

$$Q_{4-1} = C_p (T_1 - T_4)$$

$$W_{4-1} = P_1 (V_1 - V_4) = R (T_1 - T_2)$$

Efficiency of Ericsson Cycle,

$$\eta = 1 - \frac{Q_2}{Q_1} = 1 - \frac{RT_2 \ln P_1/P_2}{RT_1 \ln P_1/P_2}$$

$$\eta = 1 - \frac{T_2}{T_1}$$

As the part of heat transferred at constant pressure and part at constant temperature the efficiency of Ericsson cycle is less.

SOLVED PROBLEMS

Problem 4.1: A Carnot engine which rejects heat to a cooling pond at 27°C has an efficiency of 30 percent. If the cooling pond receives 837.2 kJ/min, what is the power developed by the cycle? Find the temperature of the source.

Solution: $T_L = 27 + 273 = 300$ K

$\eta_{th} = 30\ \%$, $Q_L = 837.2$ kJ/min $= 139.5$ kW

$$\eta_{carnot} = \frac{T_H - T_L}{T_H}$$

$$0.3 = \frac{T_H - (300)}{T_H}$$

∴ $T_H = \mathbf{428.5\ K}$

For reversible engine,

$$\frac{Q_L}{Q_H} = \frac{T_L}{T_H}$$

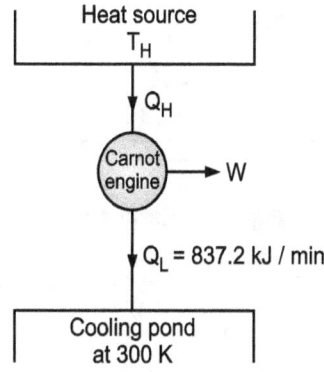

Fig. 4.15: Heat engine

$$Q_H = \frac{Q_L}{T_L} \cdot T_H$$

$$= \frac{837.2 \times 428.5}{300} = \mathbf{1196\ kJ/min.}$$

Power developed, $W = Q_H - Q_L$

$$= 1196 - 837.2 = 358.6\ kJ/min = \mathbf{5.97\ kW} \qquad \text{... Ans.}$$

Problem 4.2: The working substance in a Carnot engine is 0.05 kg of air. The maximum cycle temperature is 900 K and maximum pressure is 8.5 MPa. The heat added per cycle is 5 kJ. Determine the maximum cylinder volume if the minimum temperature during the cycle is 300 K.

Solution: Given : $m = 0.05$ kg, $T_H = 900$ K
Maximum pressure = $p_1 = 8.5 \times 10^6$ N/m²

The maximum temperature and pressure corresponds to a point 1 on p-V diagram (See Fig. 1.77) and maximum volume at state 3.
We apply gas equation to find the volume V_1.

$$p_1 V_1 = mRT_1 \qquad \therefore V_1 = \frac{mRT_1}{p_1} = \frac{0.05 \times 0.287 \times 900}{8.5 \times 10^3} = 1.52 \times 10^{-3}\ m^3$$

Heat supplied, $Q = p_1 V_1 \ln V_2/V_1$

$$5 \times 10^3 = 8.5 \times 10^6 \times 1.52 \times 10^{-3} \ln \frac{V_2}{V_1}$$

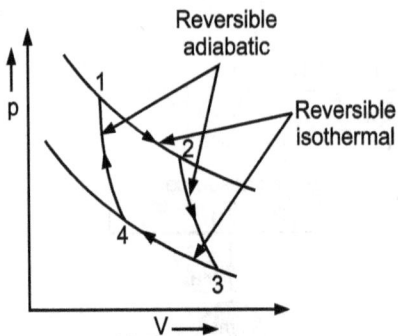

Fig. 4.16: Carnot cycle

$\therefore \quad \log \dfrac{V_2}{V_1} = 0.387 \quad \therefore \dfrac{V_2}{V_1} = 1.4727$

$\therefore \quad V_2 = 1.52 \times 10^{-3} \times 1.4727 = 2.23 \times 10^{-3} \text{ m}^3$

But $\dfrac{V_3}{V_2} = \left(\dfrac{T_2}{T_3}\right)^{1/\gamma - 1}$

$\therefore \quad V_3 = V_2 \left(\dfrac{T_2}{T_3}\right)^{1/\gamma - 1} = 2.23 \times 10^{-3} \left(\dfrac{900}{300}\right)^{1/1.4 - 1}$

$= 0.0347 \text{ m}^3$

$\therefore$ Maximum cylinder volume = **0.0347 m³** ... **Ans.**

Problem 4.3 (Air Standard Efficiency of Otto Cycle): The bore and stroke of an engine working on the Otto cycle are 17 cm and 30 cm respectively. The clearance volume is 0.002025 m³. Calculate the air standard efficiency.

Solution: d = 17 × 10⁻² m, L = 0.3 m, v_c = 0.002025 m³.

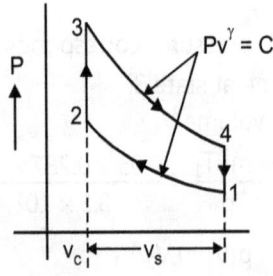

Fig. 4.17

$$\text{Swept volume} = \left(\frac{\pi}{4}\right) d^2 \cdot L = \left(\frac{\pi}{4}\right) (0.17)^2 \times 0.3$$

$$V_s = 6.8094 \times 10^{-3} \text{ m}^3$$

$$\text{Clearance volume} = v_c = 0.002025 \text{ m}^3$$

$$\text{Total cylinder volume} = v_1 = v_c + v_s$$

$$= 8.8344 \times 10^{-3} \text{ m}^3$$

$$\text{Compression ratio} = r = \frac{v_1}{v_c} = 4.36$$

$$\text{Air standard efficiency} = 1 - \frac{1}{r^{\gamma-1}} = 1 - \frac{1}{(4.36)^{1.4-1}}$$

$$= 0.445 \text{ or } 44.5 \% \quad \text{... Ans.}$$

Problem 4.4 (Otto Cycle: P, v, T at Salient Points): In an ideal Otto cycle, the compression ratio is 6. The initial pressure and temperature of the air are 1 bar and 373 K. The maximum pressure in the cycle is 35 bar. For 1 kg of air flow, calculate the values of pressure, temperature at the four salient points of the cycle. What is the ratio of heat supplied to the heat rejected?

Assume, for air, R = 0.287 kJ/kg·K, γ = 1.4.

Solution: Given: r = 6, P_1 = 1 bar, T_1 = 373 K, P_3 = 35 bar

(i) Point 1:

(i) To calculate v_1

$$P_1 v_1 = m R T_1, \ m = 1$$

$$\therefore \quad v_1 = \frac{287 \times 373}{1 \times 10^5} = 1.0705 \text{ m}^3$$

$$P_1 = 1 \text{ bar}, \ v_1 = 1.0705 \text{ m}^3, \ T_1 = 373 \text{ K}$$

(ii) Point 2:

$$P_1 v_1^\gamma = P_2 v_2^\gamma$$

$$p_2 = p_1 \left(\frac{v_1}{v_2}\right)^\gamma = 1 \times (6)^{1.4} = \mathbf{12.28 \text{ bar}}$$

$$v_2 = \frac{v_1}{6} = \frac{1.0705}{6} = \mathbf{0.1784 \text{ m}^3}$$

$$\frac{P_1 v_1}{T_1} = \frac{P_2 v_2}{T_2} \quad \therefore T_2 = \frac{P_2 v_2}{P_1 v_1} \cdot T_1$$

$$\therefore \quad T_2 = \frac{12.28 \times 0.1784}{1 \times 1.0705} \times 373 = \mathbf{763.4 \text{ K}}$$

$$p_2 = 12.28 \text{ bar}, \ v_2 = 0.1784 \text{ m}^3, \ T_2 = 763.4 \text{ K}$$

(iii) Point 3:

$$V_3 = V_2 = 0.1784 \text{ m}^3$$

$$\frac{P_3}{T_3} = \frac{P_2}{T_2}$$

$$T_3 = \frac{P_3}{P_2} \cdot T_2 = \frac{35}{12.28} \times 763.4 = \mathbf{2175.8 \text{ K}}$$

∴ $P_3 = 35$ bar, $v_3 = 0.1784$ m³, $T_3 = 2175.8$ K

(iv) Point 4:

$$P_3 v_3^\gamma = P_4 v_4^\gamma$$

∴ $$P_4 = P_3 \left(\frac{V_3}{V_4}\right)^\gamma = 35 \left(\frac{1}{6}\right)^{1.4} = \mathbf{2.85 \text{ bar}}$$

$$V_4 = V_1 = 1.0705 \text{ m}^3$$

$$\frac{P_4}{T_4} = \frac{P_1}{T_1} \quad \therefore T_4 = \frac{P_4}{P_1} \cdot T_1 = \mathbf{1062.5 \text{ K}}$$

∴ $P_4 = 2.85$ bar, $v_4 = 1.0705$ m³, $T_4 = 1062.5$ K

$$\text{Heat supplied} = C_V (T_3 - T_2)$$

$$= \frac{R}{\gamma - 1}(T_3 - T_2) \text{ where, } C_V = \frac{R}{\gamma - 1} = \mathbf{0.7175}$$

$$= \frac{0.287}{1.4 - 1}(2175.8 - 763.4) = \mathbf{1013.4 \text{ kJ/kg}}$$

$$\text{Heat rejected} = C_V (T_4 - T_1)$$

$$= 0.7175 (1062.5 - 373) = \mathbf{494.72 \text{ kJ/kg}}$$

$$\frac{\text{Heat supplied}}{\text{Heat rejected}} = \frac{1013.4}{494.7} = \mathbf{2.05} \quad \text{... Ans.}$$

Problem 4.5: In an ideal Otto cycle, if T_3 and T_1 represent the maximum and minimum temperatures respectively, show that for the maximum work to be done in the cycle,

$$T_2 = \sqrt{T_1 T_3}$$

where, T_2 is the temperature after the compression.

Solution:

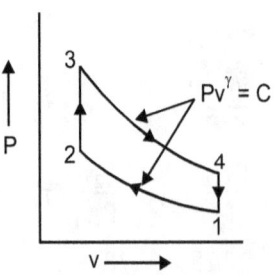

Fig. 4.18

Heat added during the process 2-3 is
$$Q_1 = C_V (T_3 - T_2) \text{ for unit mass} \quad \ldots (I)$$
Heat rejected during the process 4 – 1 is
$$Q_2 = C_V (T_4 - T_1) \text{ for unit mass} \quad \ldots (II)$$
Processes 1-2 and 3-4 are reversible adiabatic processes, no heat transfer takes place.

$$\text{Net work done} = Q_1 - Q_2$$
$$= C_V (T_3 - T_2) - C_V (T_4 - T_1)$$
$$W = C_V [T_3 - T_2 - T_4 + T_1]$$

but $\dfrac{T_2}{T_1} = \dfrac{T_3}{T_4}$, $T_4 = T_3 \cdot \dfrac{T_1}{T_2}$

$$W = C_V \left[T_3 - T_2 - T_3 \cdot \dfrac{T_1}{T_2} + T_1 \right]$$

For maximum work output,
$$\dfrac{dW}{dT_2} = 0, \quad 0 = -1 + \dfrac{T_1 T_3}{T_2^2}$$
$$\therefore \quad T_2 = \sqrt{T_1 T_3}$$

Problem 4.6: Show that the compression ratio for the maximum work to be done per kg of air in an Otto cycle between upper and lower limits of absolute temperatures T_3 and T_1 is given by

$$R_C = \left(\dfrac{T_3}{T_1} \right)^{\dfrac{1}{2(\gamma - 1)}}$$

Solution: Let us consider P-v diagram of an Otto cycle and also T-s diagram.

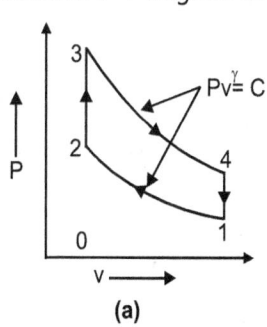 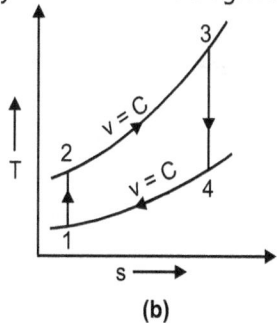

(a)   (b)

Fig. 4.19

Heat added during the process 2-3 is
$$Q_1 = C_V (T_3 - T_2) \text{ for unit mass} \quad \ldots (I)$$
Heat rejected during the process 4-1 is
$$Q_2 = C_V (T_4 - T_1) \text{ for unit mass} \quad \ldots (II)$$
Processes 1-2 and 3-4 are reversible adiabatic processes, hence no heat transfer occurs.

Net work done,
$$W = Q_1 - Q_2$$
$$= C_V (T_3 - T_2) - C_V (T_4 - T_1)$$
$$= C_V (T_3 - T_2 - T_4 + T_1)$$

But, $\dfrac{T_2}{T_1} = \dfrac{T_3}{T_4}$, $T_4 = T_3 \cdot \dfrac{T_1}{T_2}$

$\therefore \quad W = C_V \left(T_3 - T_2 - \dfrac{T_3 \cdot T_1}{T_2} + T_1 \right)$

For maximum work output, $\dfrac{dW}{dT_2} = 0$.

$\therefore \quad 0 = -1 + \dfrac{T_1 T_3}{T_2^2}$

$\therefore \quad \dfrac{T_3}{T_2^2} \cdot T_1 = 1$

Multiply and divide by T_1

$\therefore \quad \dfrac{T_3}{T_2^2} \cdot \dfrac{T_1^2}{T_1} = 1$

$\therefore \quad \dfrac{T_3}{T_1} = \dfrac{T_2^2}{T_1^2}$

$$\boxed{\dfrac{T_2}{T_1} = \left(\dfrac{V_1}{V_2}\right)^{\gamma - 1} = r^{\gamma - 1}}$$

$\dfrac{T_3}{T_1} = (R_c)^{2(\gamma - 1)}$ Let $r = R_c$

$\therefore \quad R_c = \left(\dfrac{T_3}{T_1}\right)^{\dfrac{1}{2(\gamma - 1)}}$ proved.

Problem 4.7: An air-standard diesel cycle has a compression ratio of 14. The pressure at the beginning of the compression stroke is 1 bar and the temperature is 27°C. The maximum temperature is 2500°C. Determine the thermal efficiency and the mean effective pressure.

Solution:

$$T_2 = T_1 \left(\dfrac{V_1}{V_2}\right)^{\gamma - 1} = 300 \times (14)^{0.4} = 300 \times 2.88 = \mathbf{864\ K}$$

$$P_2 = P_1 \left(\dfrac{T_2}{T_1}\right)^{\dfrac{\gamma}{\gamma - 1}} = 1 \left(\dfrac{864}{300}\right)^{3.5} = 1 \times 40.5 = \mathbf{40.5\ bar}$$

Now, $\quad \dfrac{V_3}{V_2} = \dfrac{T_3}{T_2} = \dfrac{2773}{864} = 3.21$

and $\quad \dfrac{T_3}{T_4} = \left(\dfrac{V_4}{V_3}\right)^{\gamma - 1} = \left(\dfrac{V_4}{V_2} \times \dfrac{V_2}{V_3}\right)^{\gamma - 1} = \left(\dfrac{14}{3.21}\right)^{0.4} = (4.36)^{0.4} = \mathbf{1.8}$

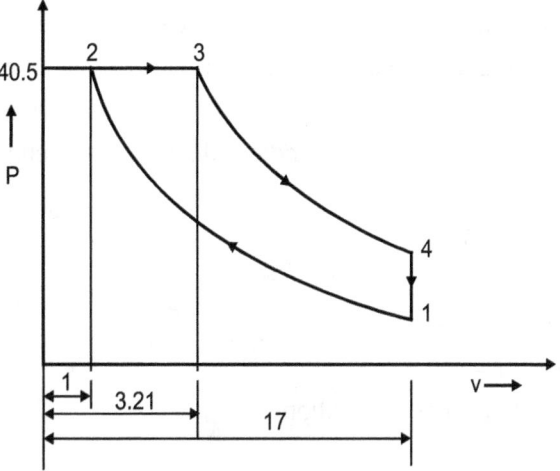

Fig. 4.20

$$\therefore \quad T_4 = \frac{T_3}{1.8} = \frac{2773}{1.8} = \mathbf{1540\ K}$$

$$\eta = \frac{C_v(T_3 - T_2) - C_v(T_4 - T_1)}{C_p(T_3 - T_2)}$$

$$= 1 - \frac{T_4 - T_1}{\gamma(T_3 - T_2)} = 1 - \frac{1540 - 300}{1.4(2773 - 864)}$$

$$\eta = 1 - 0.464 = 0.536 = \mathbf{53.62\%}$$

$$V_1 \text{ for 1 kg} = \frac{RT_1}{P_1} = \frac{0.287 \times 300}{1 \times 10^2} = \mathbf{0.861\ m^3/kg}$$

$$\text{Stroke volume} > V_1 - V_2 = V_1\left(1 - \frac{1}{14}\right)$$

$$= 0.861\left(1 - \frac{1}{14}\right)$$

$$= 0.800\ m^3/kg$$

$$\text{Mean effective pressure} = \frac{\text{Net work/Cycle}}{\text{Stroke volume}}$$

$$= \frac{C_p(T_3 - T_2) - C_v(T_4 - T_1)}{0.8}$$

$$P_m = \frac{1.005 \times 1909 - 0.718 \times 1240}{0.8}$$

$$P_m = 10.282\ \text{bar} \qquad \ldots \mathbf{Ans.}$$

Problem 4.8: Overall compression ratio of an ideal diesel engine is 18. Constant pressure heat addition ceases at 10% of stroke. Intake conditions are 1 bar and 20°C. The air consumption is 100 m³/hr. Determine (a) Maximum temperature and pressure in the cycle, (b) Thermal efficiency of the engine and (c) Indicated power of the engine. Assume $\gamma = 1.4$.

Solution:

Let clearance volume = 1.
Swept volume = 18 − 1 = 17.
10% of the swept volume
$= 17 \times 0.1 = 1.7$

∴ Constant pressure energy addition ceases at $1 + 1.7 = 2.7$

$$\frac{V_3}{V_2} = \rho = \frac{2.71}{1} = 2.7$$

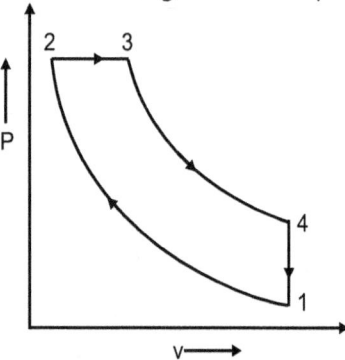

Fig. 4.21: Diesel Cycle

Thermal efficiency

$$\eta_{th} = 1 - \frac{1}{r^{\gamma-1}} \left[\frac{\rho^{\gamma}-1}{r(\rho-1)} \right]$$

$$= 1 - \frac{1}{(18)^{1.4}-1} \left[\frac{(2.7)^{1.4}-1}{1.4(2.7-1)} \right]$$

$\eta_{th} = 1 - 0.4 = 0.6$ or 60% ... **Ans.**

$T_1 = 20 + 273 = 293$ K, $P_1 = 1$ bar

$$P_2 = P_1 \times \left(\frac{V_1}{V_2}\right)^{\gamma} = 1 \times (18)^{1.4} = \mathbf{53.6 \text{ bar}}$$

$P_3 = P_2 = 53.6$ bar

$$T_2 = T_1 \times \left(\frac{V_1}{V_2}\right)^{\gamma-1} = 293 \times (18)^{1.4-1}$$

$= 293 \times 3.175 = \mathbf{930 \text{ K}}$

$$\frac{P_2 V_2}{T_2} = \frac{P_3 V_3}{T_3}$$

$T_3 = T_2 \frac{V_3}{V_2} = 930 \times 2.7 = 2510$ K or **2237°C** ... **Ans.**

The maximum temperature and pressure of the cycle are 2237°C and 153.6 bar respectively.

(a) Let us consider the cycle for 100 m³ for air

∴ $V_1 - V_2 = 100$ m³, $V_1 = 18 V_2$ (∵ r = 18)

$18 V_2 - V_2 = 100$

or $\quad V_2 = \dfrac{100}{17} = 6.13 \text{ m}^3$

$V_1 = 100 + 6.13 = \mathbf{106.13 \text{ m}^3}$

$V_3 = 2.7\, V_2 = 2.7 \times 6.13 = \mathbf{15.9 \text{ m}^3}$

$V_4 = V_2 = \mathbf{106.13 \text{ m}^3}$

$P_4 = P_3 \left(\dfrac{V_3}{V_4}\right)^\gamma = 53.6 \left(\dfrac{15.9}{106.13}\right)^{1.4}$

$\quad = 53.6 \dfrac{1}{14.6} = 3.67 \text{ bar}$

Work done $= P_2 (V_3 - V_2) + \dfrac{(P_3 V_3 - P_4 V_4) - (P_2 V_2 - P_1 V_1)}{(\gamma - 1)}$

$= 53.6 (15.9 - 6.13) +$

$\quad \dfrac{(53.6 \times 15.9 - 3.67 \times 106.13) - (53.6 \times 6.13 - 1 \times 106.13)}{1.4 - 1}$

$= 524 + 602.6 = 1126.5 \times 10^2 \text{ kJ}$

Indicated power $= \dfrac{1126.5 \times 10^2}{60 \times 60} = \mathbf{30.67 \text{ kW}}$

Problem 4.9: An ideal diesel engine has a diameter of 12 cm and stroke 18 cm. The clearance volume is 10% of the swept volume. Determine the compression ratio and the air standard efficiency of the engine if the cut-off takes place at 6% of the stroke.

Solution:

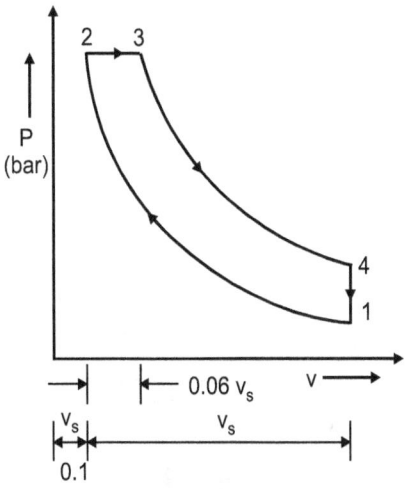

Fig. 4.22

Stroke volume, $V = \dfrac{\pi}{4} \times d^2 \times L = \dfrac{\pi}{4} (12)^2 \times 18$

$\quad = \mathbf{2035 \text{ cm}^3}$

Clearance volume, V_c = $0.1 \times V_a = 0.1 \times 2035$ = **203.5 cm³**

Total volume, V_1 = $V_c + V_a = 203.5 + 2035$ = **2239 cm³**

∴ Compression ratio = $\dfrac{V_1}{V_2} = \dfrac{V_1}{V_c} = \dfrac{2239}{203.5} = 11.00$ ... **Ans.**

Cut-off ratio, $\rho = \dfrac{V_3}{V_2} = \dfrac{V_2 + (V_3 - V_2)}{V_2}$

$= \dfrac{203.5 + 0.06 \times 203.5}{203.5}$

$= 1.6$

∴ The air standard efficiency of the cycle

$\eta = 1 - \dfrac{1}{r^{\gamma-1}}\left[\dfrac{\rho^\gamma - 1}{\gamma(\rho - 1)}\right]$

$= 1 - \dfrac{1}{(11)^{0.4}}\left[\dfrac{(1.6)^{1.4} - 1}{1.4(1.6 - 1)}\right]$

$\eta = 0.57$ or 57% ... **Ans.**

Problem 4.10: A dual combustion cycle has an adiabatic compression volume ratio of 15 : 1. The conditions at the beginning of compression are 1 bar, 25°C and 0.15 m³. The maximum pressure of the cycle is 66 bar and the maximum temperature of the cycle is 1500°C. If C_v = 0.71 kJ/kg·K and γ = 1.4. Calculate the pressure, volume and temperature at the corners of the cycle and the thermal efficiency of the cycle.

Solution:

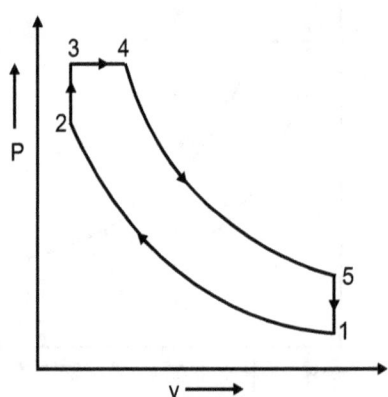

Fig. 4.23

$P_1 = 1$ bar, $T_1 = 25 + 273 = 298$ K, $V_1 = 0.1$ m³

$V_2 = \left(\dfrac{0.1}{15}\right) = 0.01$ m³

$$P_2 = P_1 \times \left(\frac{V_1}{V_2}\right)^\gamma = P_1 \left(\frac{V_1}{V_2}\right)^\gamma$$
$$= 1 \times (15)^\gamma$$
$$= 44.2 \text{ bar}$$

$$T_2 = T_1 \cdot \left(\frac{V_1}{V_2}\right)^{\gamma-1} = 298 \left(\frac{1}{15}\right)^{1.4-1}$$
$$= 882 \text{ K}$$

$P_3 = 63 \text{ bar}$

$$T_3 = T_2 \cdot \left(\frac{P_3}{P_2}\right)$$
$$= 882 \times 65 (44.2)$$
$$= 1297 \text{ K}$$

$V_3 = V_2 = 0.01 \text{ m}^3$

$$V_4 = V_3 \left(\frac{T_4}{T_2}\right) = 0.01 \times \frac{(1500+273)}{1297} = 0.066 \times \frac{1773}{1297}$$
$$= 0.0136 \text{ m}^3$$

$P_4 = P_3 = 65 \text{ bar}$
$V_5 = V_1 = 0.1 \text{ m}^3$

$$P_5 = P_4 \left(\frac{V_4}{V_5}\right)^\gamma = 16 \times \left(\frac{0.0136}{0.1}\right)^{1.4}$$

$P_5 = 0.061 \text{ bar}$

$$T_5 = T_4 \left(\frac{V_4}{V_5}\right)^{\gamma-1} = 1773 \left(\frac{0.0136}{0.1}\right)^{1.4-1} = \frac{1773}{2.62}$$
$$= 798 \text{ K or } 525°C$$

	Pressure (bar)	Volume (m³)	Temperature (°C)
Point 1	1	0.15	25
Point 2	44.2	0.01	882
Point 3	65	0.01	1297
Point 4	63	0.0136	1500
Point 5	0.061	0.15	525

Thermal efficiency,

$$\eta_{th} = 1 - \frac{T_5 - T_1}{T_3 - T_2 + \gamma(T_4 - T_3)}$$
$$= 1 - \frac{525 - 25}{(1297 - 882) + 1.4(1500 - 1297)}$$
$$= 1 - \frac{500}{415 + 1.4 \times 203}$$
$$= 0.284 \qquad \text{... Ans.}$$

Problem 4.11: A high speed diesel engine working on ideal dual combustion cycle takes in air at a pressure of 1 bar and temperature of 50°C and compresses it adiabatically to 1/15 of its original volume. At the end of the compression the heat is added in such a manner that during the first stage the pressure increases at constant volume to twice the pressure of the adiabatic compression and during the second stage following the constant volume addition, the volume is increased twice the clearance volume at constant pressure. The air is then allowed to expand adiabatically to the end of the stroke where it is exhausted heat being rejected at constant volume. Calculate (a) The temperature at the key points of the cycle and (b) In the ideal thermal efficiency.

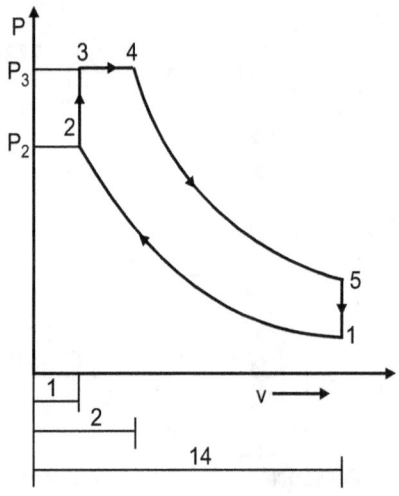

Fig. 4.24

Solution:

(a)
$$T_2 = T_1 (r)^{\gamma-1} = 323 (14)^{0.4} = \mathbf{930\ K}$$

$$P_2 = P_1 \left(\frac{V_1}{V_2}\right)^{\gamma} = 1 (15)^{1.4} = \mathbf{44.3\ bar}$$

$$P_2 = 2 \times 44.3 = 88.6\ \text{bar}$$

$$T_3 = T_2 \left(\frac{P_3}{P_2}\right) = 930 \times \frac{88.6}{44.3} = \mathbf{1860\ K} \quad \text{... Ans.}$$

$$T_4 = T_3 \left(\frac{V_4}{V_3}\right) = 1860 \times 2 = \mathbf{3720\ K} \quad \text{... Ans.}$$

Now expansion ratio $= \dfrac{V_5}{V_4} = \dfrac{15}{2} = 7.5$

$\therefore \quad T_5 = \dfrac{T_4}{\left(\dfrac{V_5}{V_4}\right)^{\gamma-1}} = \dfrac{3720}{(7.5)^{0.4}} = \mathbf{1661.5\ K}$ ... **Ans.**

(b) Heat added $= C_v(T_3 - T_2) + C_p(T_4 - T_3)$

$= 0.718(1860 - 930) + 1.005(3720 - 1860)$

$= 2537\ kJ/kg$

Heat rejected $= C_v(T_5 - T_1) = 0.718(1661.5 - 323)$

$= \mathbf{961.0\ kJ/kg}$

Air standard efficiency $= \dfrac{2537 - 961}{2537} = 0.621$ or **62.1%**

EXERCISE

1. What are the assumptions made in air standard cycle analysis?
2. What is use of air standard cycle analysis?
3. Define mean effective pressure. What does this criterion indicate for reciprocating engines?
4. Obtain an expression for the air standard efficiency on a volume basis of an engine working on the Otto cycle.
   Hence show that the efficiency of the Otto cycle is lower than that of Carnot cycle.
5. Show by graphs how the efficiency of the Otto cycle varies with compression ratio and the ratio of specific heats of working medium.
6. Derive an expression for the mean effective pressure of the Otto cycle?
7. What is the difference between Otto and Diesel cycle? Derive the formula for the efficiency of the Diesel cycle. Hence show that the efficiency of Diesel Cycle is always lower than the efficiency of the Otto cycle for the same compression ratio.
8. Explain why the higher efficiency of the Otto cycle compared to Diesel cycle for the same compression ratio is not a result of practical importance.
9. Derive an expression for the mean effective pressure of Diesel cycle.
10. Explain the dual combustion cycle? Why this cycle is also called limited pressure cycle? Derive an expression for the air standard efficiency of dual cycle.

11. Compare the Otto, Diesel and limited pressure cycles for the same compressor ratio and same heat input.
12. Compare the Otto and Diesel cycles for:
    (a) Same constant maximum pressure and same heat input.
    (b) Same maximum pressure and temperature.
    (c) Same maximum pressure and output.

Unit V

Chapter 5: PROPERTIES OF STEAM OR PURE SUBSTANCES

5.1 Introduction

Steam is a pure substance. A pure substance is defined as a homogeneous and chemically stable substance eventhough it undergoes a change of phase.

Steam is used in many engineering and chemical industries. It is used as a working substance for steam power plants and is used as a medium for heating in chemical, sugar and textile industries. Therefore, it is essential to study the properties of steam at different conditions.

Substances may exist in different phases. At atmospheric pressure and temperature conditions, copper is a solid, mercury is a liquid and nitrogen is a gas. Under different conditions, each may appear in different phase. So let us discuss the phase transformation of water at constant pressure.

5.2 Phase Transformation of Water AT Constant Pressure

1. Assume 1 kg mass of ice at –20°C and 1 atm. pressure in a frictionless piston cylinder arrangement. Weight W is kept on the piston to maintain a pressure of 1 atm. on the ice.

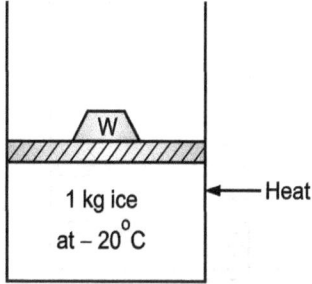

Fig. 5.1: At 1 atm. pressure and – 20°C, water exists in the solid phase

2. As we add heat, the temperature of ice will go on increasing till it reaches 0°C. At this stage, ice starts melting and there will be no rise in temperature till all the ice melts. (Process a – b in Fig. 5.7)

3. The addition of heat will be utilised to increase the temperature of water from 0°C to 100°C (Process c - d in Fig. 5.7).

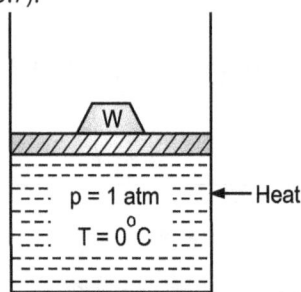

Fig. 5.2: At 1 atm. pressure and at 0°C, water exists in the liquid state (compressed liquid)

4. Now on further heating, water starts boiling and gets converted into vapour.

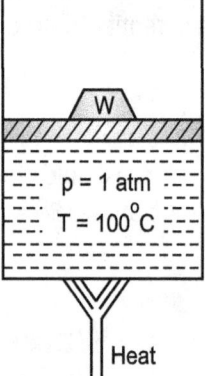

Fig. 5.3: At 1 atm. pressure and 100°C, water exists as a liquid which is ready to vaporise (saturated liquid)

5. Part of the water is evaporated. Therefore, there is a mixture of water and vapour.

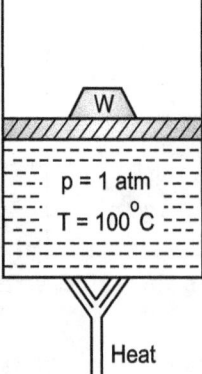

Fig. 5.4: As more heat is added, part of saturated liquid vaporizes (saturated liquid–vapour mixture)

6. See point 'd' in Fig. 5.7. The entire cylinder is filled with vapour. Any heat loss from this vapour will cause some of the vapour to condense.

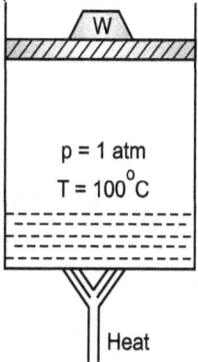

Fig. 5.5: At 1 atm. pressure, the temperature remains constant at 100°c until the last drop of liquid is vaporised (saturated vapour).

7. Further addition of heat will increase the temperature of steam. So, it is called as superheated steam.

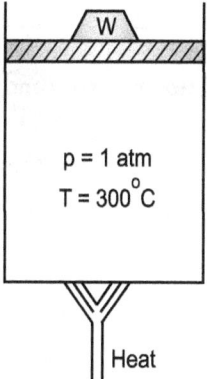

Fig. 5.6: As more heat is added, the temperature of the vapour starts rising (superheated vapour)

All the above steps are represented in Fig. 5.7.

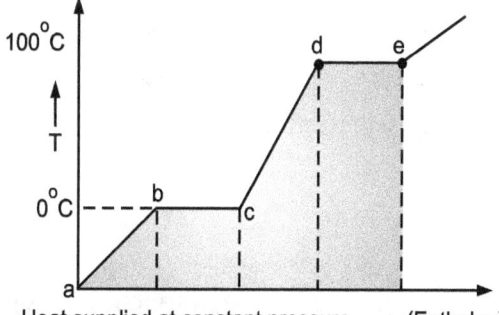

Fig. 5.7: Temperature - Heat supplied

In Fig. 5.7, a – b → Sensible heating of ice
              b – c → Melting of ice
              c – d → Sensible heating of liquid
              d – e → Saturated mixture of liquid and vapour
From point e – onwards, superheating of steam.

5.3 Effect of Pressure on Boiling Point

The boiling temperature of water increases with increasing pressure. The 'Boiling Temperature' of water at a particular pressure is known as "saturation temperature" and corresponding pressure is known as 'saturation pressure.'

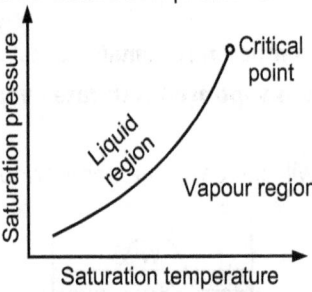

Fig. 5.8: Relation between saturation pressure and saturation temperature of water

The critical temperature of steam is defined as the temperature above which it is impossible to liquify the steam by pressure alone, irrespective of the intensity of temperature. At critical point "the change of volume falls to zero".

For water, the properties are:

$$\text{Critical pressure } (p_c) = 221.2 \text{ bar}$$
$$\text{Critical temperature } (T_c) = 647.3 \text{ K}$$
$$\text{Critical volume, } (v_c) = 0.00317 \text{ m}^3/\text{kg}$$

5.4 Property Diagrams

5.4.1 p–v Diagram of Water

The p-v diagram of a pure substance is shown in Fig. 5.9.

From Fig. 5.9, it is clear that as the saturation temperature is increased, the volume of saturated liquid increases.

Volume of the saturated liquid is very small compared with the volume of saturated vapour. As the pressure goes on increasing, the volume of vapour goes on decreasing upto critical point.

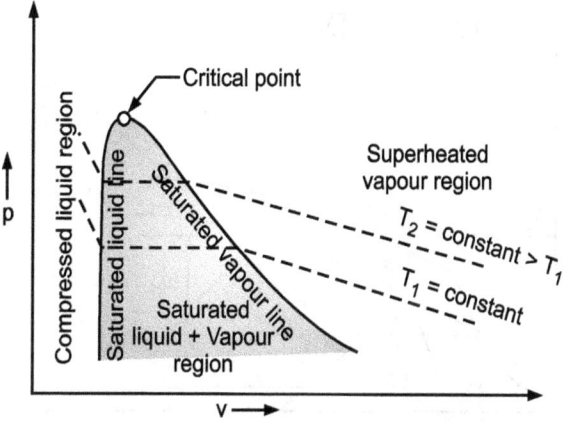

Fig. 5.9: p-v Diagram of a Pure Substance

5.4.2 Temperature Specific Volume Diagram of Water

The phase change diagram of water at 1 atm. pressure is described in Article 5.2. The process is repeated for different pressures to draw T-v diagram as shown in Fig. 5.10.

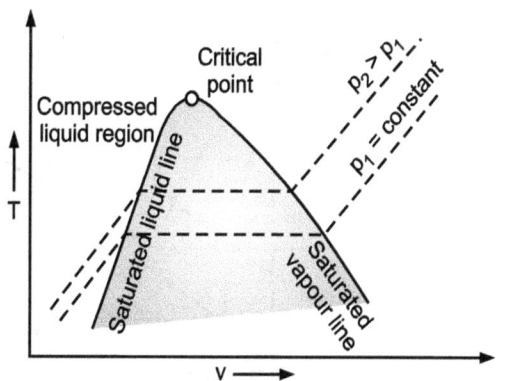

Fig. 5.10: T-v diagram for Pure Substance

From Fig. 5.10, we can draw the following conclusions:

1. Water starts boiling at a much higher temperature corresponding to higher pressures.
2. The specific volume of the saturated liquid is larger and the specific volume of saturated vapour is smaller than the corresponding values at 1 atm. pressure. It means, the horizontal line that connects the saturated liquid and saturated vapour states is much shorter.

5.4.3 Enthalpy – Entropy (h–s) Diagram of Water

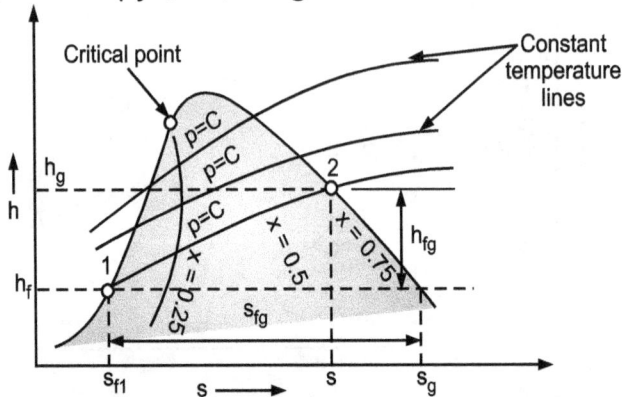

Fig. 5.11: Enthalpy-Entropy diagram of water (Mollier diagram)

Fig. 5.11 is the h-s or Mollier diagram indicating only the liquid and vapour phases. As the pressure increases, saturation temperature increases and also slope of the isobar increases. On this diagram, constant volume lines diverging in vapour region, is also shown. As the pressure increases, h_{fg} decreases and reduces to zero ($h_{fg} = 0$) at critical point.

5.4.4 T-s Diagram for Water

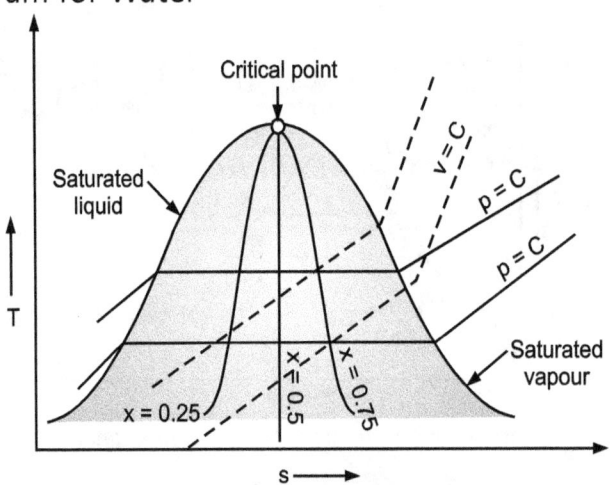

Fig. 5.12: Temperature-Entropy diagram for water

For reversible process, the change in entropy is given as:

$$ds = \frac{\partial Q}{T} = \int Tds = \int dQ$$

The area under the curve (T-s) for a process gives the heat transfer.

Fig. 5.12 shows T-s diagram for water. Constant pressure, constant specific volume and constant quality lines are also shown.

5.5 Properties of Steam

(a) Sensible Heat of Water or Enthalpy of Water: The quantity of heat absorbed by one kg of water to raise its temperature from the freezing point to the boiling point is known as sensible heat.

It is denoted by h_f and calculated as

$$h_f = c_p \Delta T \text{ for unit mass} \quad \ldots (5.1)$$

where, c_p = Specific heat of water at constant pressure, kJ/kg·K
ΔT = Temperature rise, °C
h_f = Sensible heat, kJ/kg

The error resulted in the value of h_f, calculated by this formula increases as the temperature rises. Therefore, generally h_f is taken from Steam Table.

(b) Latent Heat (Enthalpy of Evaporation) (h_{fg}): It is the amount of heat required to convert one kg of water at a given saturated temperature T_s and pressure 'P' into steam at the same temperature and pressure conditions. This varies with pressure.

For given temperature or pressure, it can be obtained from steam table.

Ex. (i) Find the enthalpy of evaporation at 3.5 kPa pressure.
Ans. Referring the steam table based on pressure, h_{fg} = 1753.7 kJ/kg at 3.5 kPa.
(ii) Find enthalpy of evaporation at 150°C.
Ans. h_{fg} = 2114.3 kJ/kg at 150°C.

(c) Enthalpy or Total Heat: It is the amount of heat required to raise the temperature of one kg of water from freezing point to the boiling temperature, (corresponding to given pressure) and then to convert it into dry saturated steam at the same temperature and pressure.

It is denoted by h_g.

$$h_g = h_f + h_{fg} \quad \ldots (5.2)$$

where, h_f = Sensible heat, kJ/kg and
h_{fg} = Latent heat, kJ/kg

(d) Wet Steam: It is a homogeneous mixture of vapour and fine water particles. This exists in the steam space of boiler.

The quality of wet steam depends on the amount of water particles present in the mixture. The quality of wet steam is defined by the dryness fraction.

The dryness fraction (x) is expressed by the ratio of mass of dry vapour (steam) to the total mass of the mixture of water and steam.

$$\therefore \quad x = \frac{m_s}{m_w + m_s} \qquad \ldots (5.3)$$

where, x = Dryness fraction or quality of steam
m_s = Mass of dry steam, kg
m_w = Mass of liquid water in the mixture, kg

If dryness fraction of wet steam (x) = 0.8, then one kg of steam contains 0.2 kg of water (moisture) and 0.8 kg of dry steam.

(i) Enthalpy of evaporation or Latent heat of 1 kg of wet steam
$$= x \cdot h_{fg} \text{ kJ/kg} \qquad \ldots (5.4)$$

(ii) Total heat or enthalpy of one kg of wet steam is equal to the sum of the enthalpy of saturated water + enthalpy of evaporation i.e.
$$h_g = h_f + x h_{fg} \text{ kJ/kg} \qquad \ldots (5.5)$$
$$= h_f + x (h_g - h_f)$$

(iii) Specific volume: Let us consider 1 kg of water heated at constant pressure (1.01325 bar). This heating process is shown in T-v diagram of Fig. 5.13.

Let point A be on the line 2–3 in vapour region having dryness fraction x. Therefore, each of mixture at 'A' contains x kg of vapour and (1 – x) kg of liquid water. At point 2, the water is at saturated liquid state completely (x = 0). At state point 3, the mixture is completely saturated steam (dry saturated state), therefore, x = 1.

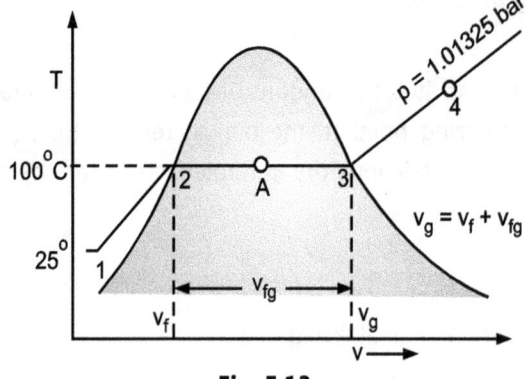

Fig. 5.13

If v_A is the specific volume at point A, then,
$$v_A = (1 - x) v_f + x \cdot v_g \qquad \ldots (5.6)$$
But $\quad v_g = v_f + v_{fg}$
Put in equation (5.6) and simplify
$$v_A = v_f + x \cdot v_{fg} \text{ ...... m}^3/\text{kg} \qquad \ldots (5.7)$$
This is the specific volume of wet steam having dryness fraction x.

(e) The specific volume of superheated steam at superheat temperature T_{sup} is calculated by using Charle's law.

$$\frac{V_g}{T_s} = \frac{V_{sup}}{T_{sup}}$$

$$\therefore \quad V_{sup} = \frac{V_g}{T_s} \cdot T_{sup} \qquad \ldots (5.8)$$

where, V_g = Specific volume of dry saturated steam
T_s = Temperature of dry saturated steam, K
V_{sup} = Specific volume of superheated steam

(f) Superheated steam: When steam is heated out of contact with water, it will result in increase of temperature. Superheating of the steam occurs at constant pressure. The amount of superheating is measured by the rise in temperature of the steam above its saturation temperature (t_s). Greater superheating of the steam will help to acquire the properties of perfect gas.

Enthalpy of superheat
$$= c_p (T_{sup} - T_{sat}) \text{ kJ/kg} \qquad \ldots (5.9)$$

where, c_p = Mean specific heat of superheated steam at constant temperature

The term $(T_{sup} - T_{sat})$ is known as degree of superheat.

The value of c_p ranges from 2 kJ/kg·K to 2.5 kJ/kg·K

The enthalpy (total heat) of one kg of superheated steam (H_{sup}) is

$$h_{sup} = h_f + h_{fg} + c_p (T_{sup} - T_{sat}) \text{ kJ/kg} \qquad \ldots (5.10)$$
$$= h_g + c_p (T_{sup} - T_{sat}) \qquad \ldots (5.11)$$

(g) Internal energy: We know that change in enthalpy is

$$dh = du + d(pv)$$
$$h_2 - h_1 = u_2 - u_1 + (p_2 v_2 - p_1 v_1) \text{ for unit mass}$$
$$\therefore \quad u_2 - u_1 = (h_2 - h_1) - (p_2 v_2 - p_1 v_1) \text{ for m = 1} \qquad \ldots (5.12)$$

(i) For wet steam,
Let x_2 and x_1 be dryness fractions at conditions 2 and 1 respectively.

$$\therefore \quad h_2 = h_{f_2} + x_2 \cdot h_{fg_2}$$
and $\quad v_2 = x_2 v_{g_2}$
$$h_1 = h_{f_1} + x_1 \cdot h_{fg_1}$$
and $\quad v_1 = x_1 \cdot v_{g_1}$

Then, change in internal energy,

$$(u_2 - u_1) = [(h_{f_2} + x_2 h_{fg_2}) - (h_{f_1} + x_1 h_{fg_1})]$$
$$- (p_2 \cdot x_2 \cdot v_{g_2} - p_1 x_1 \cdot v_{g_1}) \qquad \ldots (5.13)$$

(ii) Internal energy of superheated steam.
$$h_2 = h_{sup_2} = h_{g_2} + c_p(T_{sup_2} - T_{sat_1})$$
and
$$v_2 = v_{sup_2} = \frac{v_{sat_2}}{T_{sat_2}} \times T_{sup_2}$$
$$\therefore \quad u_2 - u_1 = (h_{sup_2} - h_1) - (p_2 v_{sup_2} - p_1 v_1) \quad \ldots (5.14)$$

(h) Entropy (s): Entropy of a dry saturated steam can be obtained from steam table corresponding to a pressure or temperature of steam.

(i) Entropy of wet steam
$$s = (1-x)s_f + x \cdot s_g$$
or
$$s = s_f + x \, s_{fg}$$
$$= s_f + x(s_g - s_f)$$
$$= s_f + x \, s_g \quad \ldots (5.15)$$
because xs_f is very small.

(ii) Entropy of superheated steam,
$$s_{sup} = s_g + \text{Entropy of superheat kJ/kg·K}$$
$$\text{Entropy of superheat} = c_p \ln \frac{T_{sup}}{T_{sat}}$$
$$\therefore \quad s_{sup} = s_g + c_p \ln \frac{T_{sup}}{T_{sat}} \text{ kJ/kg·K for unit mass} \quad \ldots (5.16)$$

SOLVED PROBLEMS

Problem 5.1: Obtain all the properties of steam in the following cases:
 (i) Steam is dry saturated at 11 bar.
 (ii) Steam has a pressure of 8 bar and dryness fraction 0.9.
 (iii) Steam is superheated having pressure 15 bar and temperature 250°C. Assume c_p for superheated steam.

Solution: (i) Dry saturated steam at 11 bar
$$T_{sat} = 184.1°C \text{ from steam table}$$
$$v_g = 0.17739 \text{ m}^3/\text{kg}$$
$$v_f = 0.001133 \text{ m}^3/\text{kg}$$
$$h_f = 781.1 \text{ kJ/kg}$$
$$h_{fg} = 1998.6 \text{ kJ/kg}$$
$$h_g = h_f + h_{fg} = 2779.7 \text{ kJ/kg}$$
$$s_f = 2.179 \text{ kJ/kg·K}$$

$$s_{fg} = \frac{h_{fg}}{T_{sat}} = 4.371 \text{ kJ/kg·K}$$

$$s_g = s_f + s_{fg}$$
$$= 6.55 \text{ kJ/kg·K}$$

(ii) Steam at 8 bar and 0.9 dryness fraction

→ Wet steam

T_{sat} at 8 bar = 170.4°C from steam table

v_f = 0.0011150 m³/kg

$v_x = (1-x) v_f + x \cdot v_g$
$= (1-0.9) \times 0.001115 + 0.9 \times 0.24026$
$= \mathbf{0.21635 \text{ m}^3/\text{kg}}$

$h_x = h_f + x h_{fg}$
$= 720.9 + 0.9 \times 2046.5$
$= \mathbf{2562.75 \text{ kJ/kg}}$

s_f = 2.046 kJ/kg·K

$s_x = s_f + x \cdot s_{fg}$
$= 2.046 + 0.9 \times 4.614$
$= \mathbf{6.1986 \text{ kJ/kg·K}}$

(iii) Superheated steam at 15 bar and 250°C from steam table, T_{sat} = 198.3°C at 15 bar.

$$v_{sup} = \frac{T_{sup}}{T_{sat}} \cdot v_g$$

$$= \left(\frac{250 + 273}{198.3 + 273}\right) \times 0.13167$$

$= 0.14611 \text{ m}^3/\text{kg}$

$h_{sup} = h_g + c_p (T_{sup} - T_{sat})$
$= 2789.9 + 2.1 (250 - 198.3)$
$= \mathbf{2898.47 \text{ kJ/kg}}$

$$s_{sup} = s_g + c_p \cdot \ln\left(\frac{T_{sup}}{T_{sat}}\right)$$

$$= 6.441 + 2.1 \ln\left(\frac{250 + 273}{198.3 + 273}\right)$$

$= \mathbf{6.6596 \text{ kJ/kg}}$

Problem 5.2: Estimate the condition of the steam in the following cases.

(i) p = 20 bar, h = 2797.2 kJ/kg

(ii) p = 14 bar, v = 0.13 m³/kg

(iii) p = 12 bar, s = 6.70 kJ/kg·K

Solution:
(i) For p = 20 bar, h_g = 2797.2 kJ/kg from steam table. Therefore, h_g = h.

∴ **Steam is dry and saturated.**

(**Note:** If h < h_g, it would be wet and if h > h_g, it would be superheated).

(ii) p = 14 bar, v = 0.13 m³/kg,

From steam table, at p = 14 bar, v_g = 0.14073 m³/kg

Comparison of v and v_g:

v < v_g (0.13 < 0.14073)

∴ **Steam is wet.**

∴ $$v = v_x = x \, v_g$$

∴ $$x = \frac{v_x}{v_g} = \frac{0.13}{0.14073} = \mathbf{0.9237}$$

Note: The steam would have been dry saturated if v = v_g and would be superheated if v > v_g.

(iii) p = 12 bar, s = 6.7 kJ/kg·K

Now s_g = 6.519 kJ/kg·K for dry saturated steam (from steam table).

Comparison of s and s_g:

s > s_g. Therefore steam is superheated.

(**Note:** It would be dry saturated if s = s_g and wet if s < s_g)

∴ $$s_{sup} = s_g + c_p \ln\left(\frac{T_{sup}}{T_{sat}}\right)$$

$$6.7 = 6.519 + 2.1 \ln\left(\frac{T_{sup}}{188 + 273}\right)$$

∴ T_{sup} = **229.496°C**

5.6 Thermodynamic Processes

The general energy equations applicable to perfect gases are also applicable to vapours and the procedure for finding the change in internal energy is also same as was adopted in case of gases.

The different processes of expansion and compression of gases are also applicable to vapours but the results obtained may be different.

The equations for the work done by vapour are the same as those used for perfect gases.

5.6.1 Constant Volume Heating or Cooling

The process can be represented on p-v and T-s planes (See Fig. 5.14).

It is assumed that wet steam (state 1) is heated at constant volume, till it reaches a superheat condition (state 2).

$$v_1 = v_2 \text{ for constant volume}$$
$$x_1 \cdot v_{g_1} = v_{sup_2}$$
$$x_1 v_{g_1} = \frac{T_{sup_2}}{T_{sup_2}} \cdot v_{sat_2} \qquad \ldots (5.17)$$

(a) Work done,
$$W_{1-2} = \int_1^2 p\, dv = 0, \text{ as } dv = 0$$

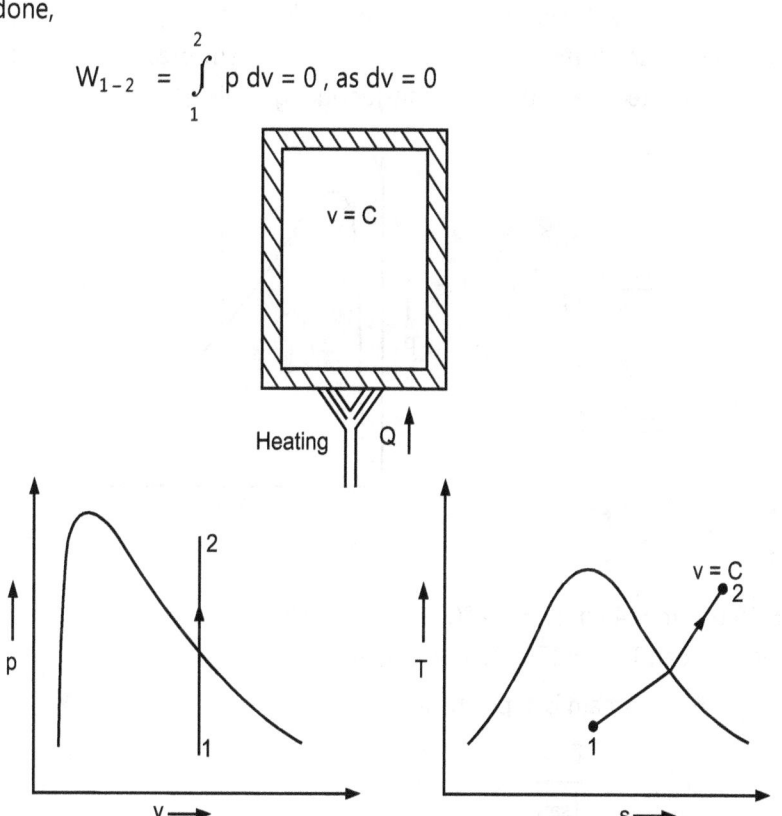

Fig. 5.14: Heating of vapour at constant volume (assuming state 2 superheated)

(b) Heat transferred by first law,
$$\delta Q = du + pdx$$
$$Q_{1-2} = (u_2 - u_1) \text{ as } pdv = 0$$
$$= (h_2 - p_2 v_2) - (h_1 - p_1 v_1) \qquad \ldots (5.18)$$

where, $h_2 = h_{sup_2}$
$$= h_g + c_p (T_{sup_2} - T_{sat_2}) \text{ kJ/kg}$$

p_2 = Pressure at 2 kPa,

$v_2 = v_{sup_2}$, m³/kg

$h_1 = h_{x_1} = h_{f_1} + x \cdot h_{fg_1}$ kJ/kg

p_1 = Pressure at 1, kPa

$$v_1 = vx_1$$
$$= v_{f_1} + x \cdot v_{fg_1} \text{ m}^3/\text{kg}$$

Similar equations are considered if the condition of steam at state 2 is wet.

SOLVED PROBLEMS

Problem 5.3: Constant volume: A vessel contains 4 kg of steam at 10 bar and 220°C. Find the volume of the vessel. If the vessel is cooled till the steam pressure drops to 3 bar, find the final condition of steam and the heat transfer during cooling.

Solution:

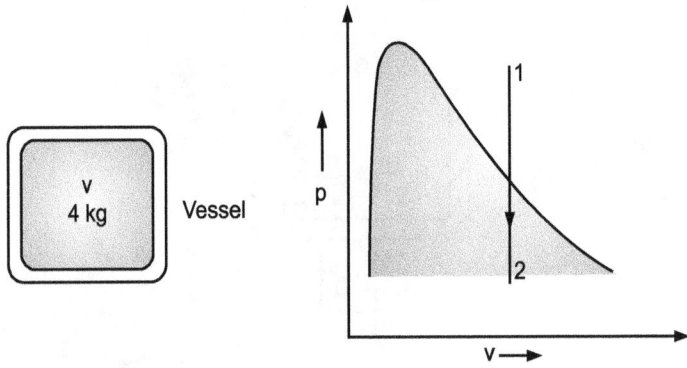

Fig. 5.15

Given: $p_1 = 10$ bar, $m = 4$ kg, $T_1 = 220°C$ and $p_2 = 3$ bar.

For $p_1 = 10$ bar, $T_{sat_1} = 179.9°C$ from steam table.

$T_1 > T_{sat_1}$, hence steam is super-heated.

$$v_{sup_1} = \frac{T_{sup_1}}{T_{sat_1}} \times v_{g_1} \text{ m}^3/\text{kg}$$

$$= \frac{(220 + 273)}{(179.9 + 273)} \times 0.1943$$

$$= 0.2115 \text{ m}^3/\text{kg}$$

∴ Volume of vessel,

$$V = m \times v_{sup\ 1}$$
$$= 4 \times 0.2115$$
$$= \mathbf{0.846 \text{ m}^3}$$

The steam undergoes a non-flow constant volume cooling process. If V_2 is the final specific volume of steam,

Volume of vessel $= v = m \cdot v_2$

∴ $$V_2 = \frac{v}{m} = \frac{0.846}{4} = 0.2115 \text{ m}^3/\text{kg}$$

Final condition of steam is found by comparing v_2 with v_{g_2} at 3 bar.

$\therefore \quad v_{g_2} = 0.60553$ m³/kg from steam table

$\quad v_2 < v_{g_2}$, the steam is wet having dryness fraction x_2

$\quad v_2 = x_2 \cdot v_{g_2}$

$\quad 0.2115 = x_2 \times 0.60553$

$\therefore \quad x_2 = \mathbf{0.3493}$

The heat transferred during the non-flow constant volume process can be found from the following equation

$$Q = \Delta u + W_{1-2}$$

$$W_{1-2} = \int_1^2 pdv = 0, \text{ Since } dv = 0$$

$$Q = \Delta u$$
$$= m(u_2 - u_1)$$
$$= m\left[(h_2 - p_2v_2) - (h_1 - p_1v_1)\right] \text{ kJ}$$
$$= m\left[(h_2 - h_1) - v_1(p_2 - p_1)\right] \text{ kJ}$$

$\therefore \quad h_2 = h_{f_2} + x_2 \cdot h_{fg_2}$

$\quad = 561.4 + 0.3493 \times 2163.2$

$\quad = \mathbf{1316.96}$ **kJ/kg**

$h_1 = h_{g_1} + c_p(T_{sup_1} - T_{sat_1})$

$\quad = 2776.2 + 2.1(220 - 179.9)$

$\quad = \mathbf{2860.4}$ **kJ/kg**

$\therefore \quad Q = $ Heat transfer

$\quad = 4\left[(1316.96 - 2860.4) - 0.2115(3 - 10) \times 100\right]$

$\quad = \mathbf{-5581.58}$ **kJ rejected.**

Problem 5.4: A closed vessel of 0.75 m³ capacity contains dry saturated steam at 0.35 MPa. The vessel is cooled until the pressure is reduced to 0.2 MPa. Calculate

(i) Mass of steam in the vessel.

(ii) The final dryness fraction of steam.

(iii) The amount of heat transferred during the cooling process.

Extract from steam table

Pressure in MPa	T_s °C	v_f m³/kg	v_g m³/kg	h_f kJ/kg	h_{fg} kJ/kg	h_g kJ/kg
0.18	116.9	0.001057	0.978	491	2211	2702
0.20	120.2	0.001061	0.886	505	2202	2702
0.3	133.5	0.001073	0.605	561	2163	2724
0.35	138.9	0.001078	0.524	584	2148	2732
0.40	143.6	0.001084	0.462	605	2134	2739

Solution: Given: Volume of vessel, $V = 0.75$ m³, $p_1 = 0.35$ MPa.

At this pressure, specific volume, $v_{g_1} = 0.524$ m³/kg.

(i) Mass of steam in the vessel

$$= \frac{V}{v_{g_1}} = \frac{0.75}{0.524} = \mathbf{1.431 \text{ kg}}$$

(ii) The volume of vessel, $V = m \cdot v_2$

$$v_2 = \frac{V}{m} = \frac{0.75}{1.431} = \mathbf{0.524 \text{ m}^3/\text{kg}}$$

At pressure $p_2 = 0.2$ MPa, volume of steam (dry saturated) $= v_{g_2} = 0.8860$.

$v_2 < v_{g_2}$. Therefore it is a wet steam.

∴ $\quad x_2 v_{g_2} = v_2$

∴ $\quad x_2 = \dfrac{v_2}{v_{g_2}} = \dfrac{0.524}{0.886} = 0.589$

(iii) Heat Transfer,

$$Q = \Delta u + \int_1^2 p\,dv \text{ where } \int_1^2 p\,dv = 0$$

∴ $Q = \Delta u$

$\quad = m[(h_2 - p_2 v_2) - (h_1 - p_1 v_1)]$

$h_2 = h_{f_2} + x \cdot h_{fg_2}$

$\quad = 505 + 0.589 \times 2202 = \mathbf{1801.9 \text{ kJ/kg}}$

$V_2 = x \cdot v_{g_2} = 0.589 \times 0.886$

$\quad = \mathbf{0.524 \text{ m}^3/\text{kg}}$

$p_2 = 0.2$ MPa $= 200$ kPa

$h_1 = h_{g_1} = 2732$ kJ/kg

$p_1 = \mathbf{350 \text{ kPa}}$

$v_1 = v_{g_1} = 0.524$

$Q = 1.431[(1801.9 - 200 \times 0.524) - (2732 - 350 \times 0.524)]$

$\quad = 1.431[1697.1 - 2548.6]$

$\quad = \mathbf{-1218.5 \text{ kJ}}$

5.6.2 Constant Pressure Process

The process is represented on p-v and T-s planes (See Fig. 5.16).

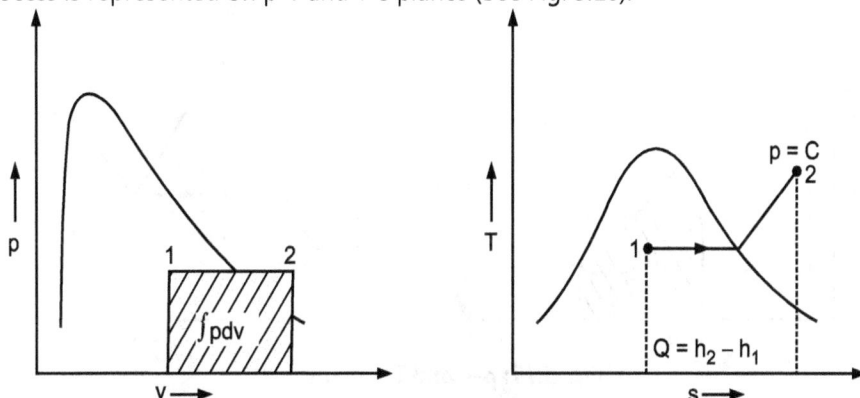

Fig. 5.16: Constant pressure process on p–v and T–s planes

(a) Work done:
$$W_{1-2} = \int pdv = p \int dv$$
$$= p(v_2 - v_1) \text{ kJ/kg} \quad \ldots (5.19)$$

p is in kN/m² and v in m³/kg

$$v_2 = v_{sup_2}$$
$$= \frac{T_{sup}}{T_{sat}} \times v_g \quad \ldots (5.20)$$

$v_1 = x_1 \cdot v_{g_1}$ at pressure p_1 and dryness fraction x_1

(b) Heat transfer:
$$Q_{1-2} = (u_2 - u_1) + \int_1^2 pdv$$
$$= (u_2 - u_1) + p(v_2 - v_1) \text{ kJ/kg}$$

where p is in kN/m² and v in m³/kg

$$p = p_1 = p_2$$
$$\therefore Q_{1-2} = h_2 - h_1 \quad \ldots (5.21)$$

(c) Change in internal energy:
$$u_2 - u_1 = (h_2 - h_1) - (pv_2 - pv_1) \text{ kJ/kg} \quad \ldots (5.22)$$
$$= (h_2 - h_1) - p(v_2 - v_1) \text{ kJ/kg} \quad \ldots (5.23)$$

v_2 and v_1 are to be determined depending upon the condition.

Problem 5.5: Constant Pressure Process: Steam at 10 bar and 230°C is cooled under constant pressure until the quality of steam becomes 80% dry. Find (a) the work done, (b) change in enthalpy and heat transfer, if the process is non-flow.

Solution:

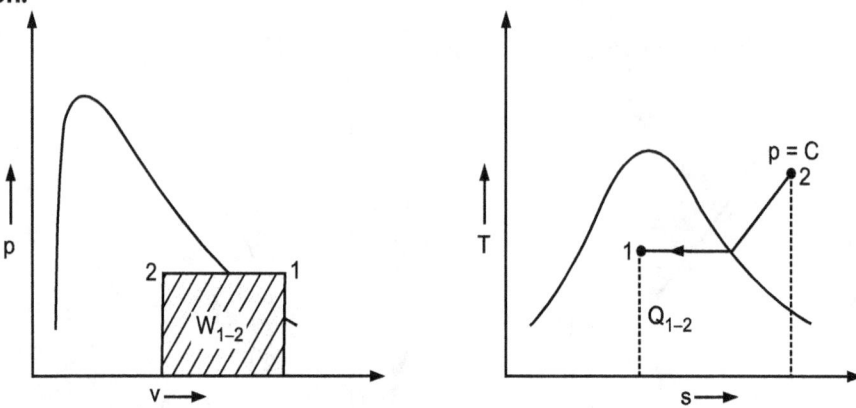

Fig. 5.17: p-v and T-s diagrams

For 10 bar pressure,
$T_s = 179.9°C$, $v_f = 0.001127$ m³/kg, $v_g = 0.194$,
$h_f = 763$ kJ/kg, $h_{fg} = 2015$ kJ/kg

(i) Work done, $\quad W_{1-2} = \int_1^2 pdv$

$$W_{1-2} = p(v_2 - v_1) \text{ for } m = 1$$

As $T_s = 179.9°C$, but given temperature at state 1 is 230°C. Therefore steam is superheated at state 1.

$$\therefore \quad v_{sup_1} = \frac{v_{sup_1}}{v_{sat_1}} \times v_{sat_1}$$

$$= \frac{(230 + 273)}{(179.9 + 273)} \times 0.194$$

$$= \mathbf{0.2154 \text{ m}^3/\text{kg}}$$

Therefore, steam is in wet condition at state 2.
Therefore $\quad v_2 = x_2 \cdot v_{g_2}$

$$= 0.8 \times 0.198$$

$$= \mathbf{0.1584 \text{ m}^3/\text{kg}}$$

$$W_{1-2} = \frac{10 \times 10^5}{10^5} \times (0.1584 - 0.2154)$$

$$= \mathbf{-57 \text{ kJ/kg}}$$

Negative sign indicates that work is done on the steam.

(ii) Change in enthalpy = Heat transfer
$$= h_2 - h_1$$
$$= \left(h_{f_2} + x_2 h_{fg_2}\right) - \left(h_{f_1} + h_{fg_1} + C_p (T_{sup_1} - T_{sat_1})\right)$$

But $h_{f_2} = h_{f_1}$

∴ Change in enthalpy $= (x_2 - 1) h_{fg_1} + c_p (T_{sup_1} - T_{sat_1})$

$= (0.8 - 1) \times 2015 + 2.1 (230 - 179.9)$
$= -297.8$ **kJ/kg**

Negative sign indicates that heat is lost by the steam (system).

5.6.3 Constant Temperature (Isothermal) Process

For wet steam, a constant temperature process is also a constant pressure process. As soon as the steam becomes superheated, it behaves as a perfect gas and follows isothermal process. This is shown on p-V and T-s planes (See Fig. 5.18).

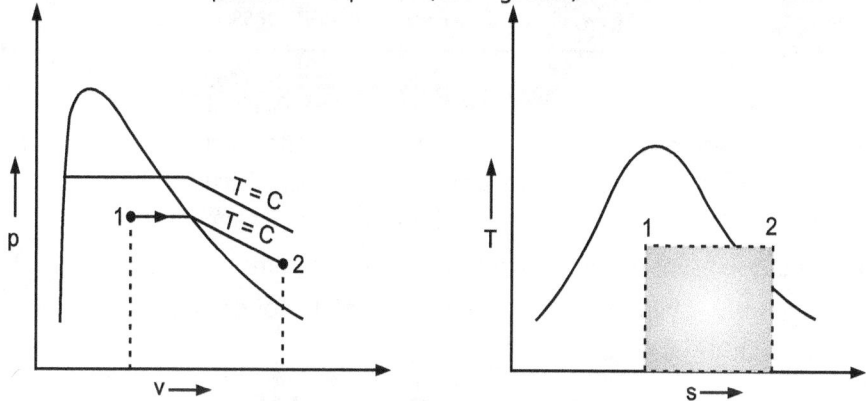

Fig. 5.18: Isothermal process

(a) Isothermal law can be applied to the process 1-2 as,

$$p_1 V_1 = p_2 V_2$$

i.e. $p_1 \cdot (x_1 v_{g_1}) = p_2 (v_{sup_2})$ ... (5.24)

because of the condition that steam is wet at state 1 and it is superheated at state 2 (See Fig. 5.18).

∴ From above equation, x_1 is determined. The state 2 may not be necessarily superheated, but may be wet also.

It follows that,

$h_1 = h_{f_1} + x_1 h_{fg_1}$

$h_2 = h_{f_2} + x_2 h_{fg_2}$ if final condition of steam is wet.

$h_2 = h_{f_2} + h_{fg_1} + k_p (T_{sup_2} - T_{sat_2})$ if steam is superheated at point 2.

(c) Work done: By first law

$$Q_{1-2} = \Delta u + W_{1-2}$$

∴ $W_{1-2} = Q_{1-2} - \Delta u$

$$= Q_{1-2} - (u_2 - u_1)$$
$$= Q_{1-2} - (u_1 - u_2) \quad \text{for unit mass} \ldots (5.25)$$

This W_{1-2} can also be obtained by

$$W_{1-2} = p_1 v_1 \ln \frac{v_2}{v_1}$$

$$\therefore \quad \frac{v_2}{v_1} = r = \frac{p_1}{p_2}$$

$$= p_1 \left(x_1 \cdot V_{g_1}\right) \ln r \quad \ldots (5.26)$$

(b) Heat transfer

$$Q_{1-2} = W_{1-2} + (u_2 - u_1)$$
$$= p_1 \cdot x_1 V_{g_1} \log_e r + (u_2 - u_1) \text{ per unit mass.} \quad \ldots (5.27)$$

SOLVED PROBLEMS

Problem 5.6: A reciprocating steam engine receives dry saturated steam at 14 bar. Expansion takes place hyperbolically to a pressure of 4 bar. Calculate the final condition of steam at the end of expansion and the work done per kg of steam during expansion.

Solution: Let us represent the process on p-v and T-s diagrams.

The expansion is being hyperbolic, $p_1 v_1 = p_2 v_2$. The volume of dry saturated steam at 14 bar pressure is $v_{g_1} = 0.1633$ m³/kg.

The specific volume of dry saturated steam at pressure of 4 bar is $v_{g_2} = 0.4625$ m³.

$$\therefore \quad p_1 v_1 = p_2 v_2$$

$$v_2 = \frac{p_1 v_1}{p_2} = \frac{14}{4} \times 0.1633 = \mathbf{0.49 \text{ m}^3/\text{kg}}$$

$$\therefore \quad v_2 > v_{g_2}$$

∴ Steam is superheated state at point 2.

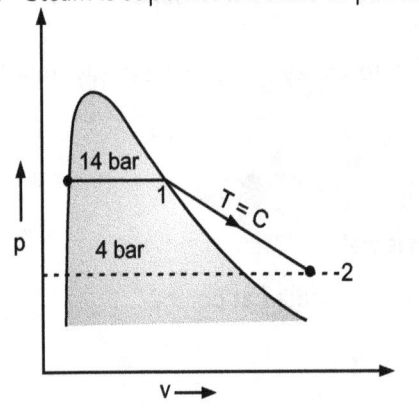 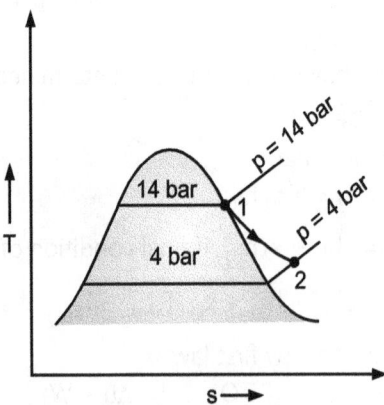

Fig. 5.19: p-v and T-s diagrams

Work done, $W_{1-2} = p_1 v_{g_1} \ln \dfrac{v_2}{v_1} = p_1 v_{g_1} \ln \dfrac{p_1}{p_2}$

$= \dfrac{14 \times 10^5}{1000} \times 0.1633 \times \log \dfrac{12}{4}$

$= \mathbf{251.1 \ kJ/kg}$

5.6.4 Polytropic Process

This process is stated by the law $pv^n = c$, where n = polytropic index. For different values of 'n', each process discussed earlier can be obtained. But for vapour, $pv = RT$ does not apply. The process is shown in Fig. 5.20.

In Fig. 5.20, state 1 is assumed as superheated state and state 2 as wet condition.

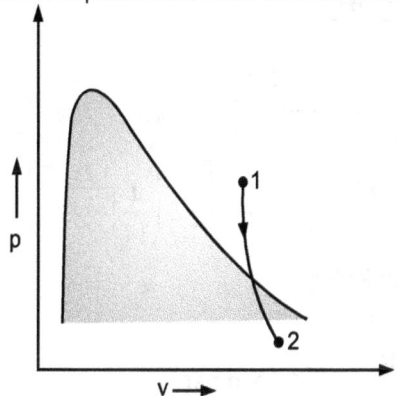

Fig. 5.20: Polytropic process on p-v plane

(a) Work done for non-flow process,

$$W_{1-2} = \int_1^2 pdv = \dfrac{p_1 v_1 - p_2 v_2}{n-1} \qquad \ldots (5.28)$$

(b) Heat transfer during the non-flow process.

$$Q_{1-2} = (u_2 - u_1) + \dfrac{p_1 v_1 - p_2 v_2}{n-1}$$

v_1 and v_2 are calculated for the steam depending upon its state.

SOLVED PROBLEM

Problem 5.7: Steam at a pressure of 14 bar with 50°C superheat expands according to $pv^{1.25} = C$ to a pressure of 4 bar in a cylinder-piston arrangement. Determine (1) work done per kg of steam, (2) heat transferred.

Solution: At pressure of 14 bar, the properties of dry saturated steam are: $T_{sat} = 195.04°C$, $v_{g_1} = 0.14072 \ m^3/kg$, $h_{f_1} = 830 \ kJ/kg$, $h_{fg_1} = 1957.7 \ kJ/kg$, $h_{g_1} = 2787.8 \ kJ/kg$.

Similarly, at 4 bar pressure,
v_{g_2} = 0.46222 m³/kg, h_{f_2} = 604.67 m³/kg, h_{fg_2} = 2133 kJ/kg, h_{f_2} = 2737.6 kJ/kg.

T_1 = 195.04 + 50 = 244.04°C.

As the steam is superheated by 50°C,

$$v_{sup_1} = \frac{T_{sup_1}}{T_{sat_1}} \times v_{sat_1}$$

$$= \frac{(244.04 + 273)}{(195.04 + 273)} \times 0.14072$$

$$= 0.15545 \text{ m}^3/\text{kg}$$

(a) $\quad W_{1-2} = \frac{p_1 v_1 - p_2 v_2}{n - 1}$

$$= \frac{p_1 v_1}{n - 1}\left[1 - \left(\frac{P_2}{P_1}\right)^{\frac{n-1}{n}}\right]$$

$$= \frac{14 \times 10^5}{1000} \times \frac{0.15545}{(1.25 - 1)}\left[1 - \left(\frac{4}{14}\right)^{\frac{1.25-1}{1.25}}\right]$$

$$= \textbf{192.9 kJ/kg}$$

The work done can also be calculated as

$$W_{1-2} = 100\frac{p_1 v_1 - p_2 v_2}{n - 1}; \text{ p in bar}$$

$$192.9 = 100 \times \frac{(14 \times 0.15545 - 4 \times v_2)}{1.25 - 1}$$

$$v_2 = 0.423 \text{ m}^3/\text{kg}$$

but $\quad v_{g_2}$ = 0.4622

∴ $\quad v_{g_1} > v_2$ ∴ Steam is wet.

Dryness fraction x_2 = ?

$$p_1 v_1^{\frac{1}{n}} = p_2 v_2^n$$

$$14 \times (0.15545) = 4 \times (x_2 \cdot v_{g_2})^n$$

∴ $\quad (x_2)^n = \frac{14}{4} \times \left(\frac{0.15545}{0.4622}\right)^n$

$$x_2 = \left(\frac{14}{4}\right)^{\frac{1}{n}} \times \frac{0.15545}{0.4622} = \textbf{0.916}$$

(b) Heat transferred,

$$Q_{1-2} = (u_2 - u_1) + W_{1-2}$$

$$u_1 = h_1 - 100\, p_1 v_1 \text{ at 14 bar, } p_1 \text{ in bar}$$

$$h_1 = h_{g_1} + c_p \log\left(\frac{T_{sup_1}}{T_{sat_1}}\right)$$

$$= 2787.8 + 2.1 \log(50)$$

$$= \mathbf{2796 \text{ kJ/kg}}$$

$$u_1 = 2796 - 100 \times 14 \times 0.15545$$

$$= \mathbf{2578.3 \text{ kJ/kg}}$$

$$u_2 = (h_2 - 100\, p_2 v_2)$$

$$u_2 = h_{f_2} + x_2 \cdot h_{f_2} - 100 \times p_2 v_2$$

where $v_2 = x_2 \cdot v_{g_2}$

∴ $u_2 = (604.04 + 0.916 \times 2133) - 100 \times 4 \times (0.916 \times 0.4622)$

$u_2 = 2388.8$ kJ/kg

$W_{1-2} = 192.9$

∴ $Q_{1-2} = (2388.8 - 2578.3) + 192.9$

$= \mathbf{2.97 \text{ kJ/kg}}$

5.6.5 Adiabatic Process

Reversible adiabatic process is an isentropic process. The process is stated by the law $pV^\gamma = c$, where γ = adiabatic index. This is represented on T-s and h-s planes.

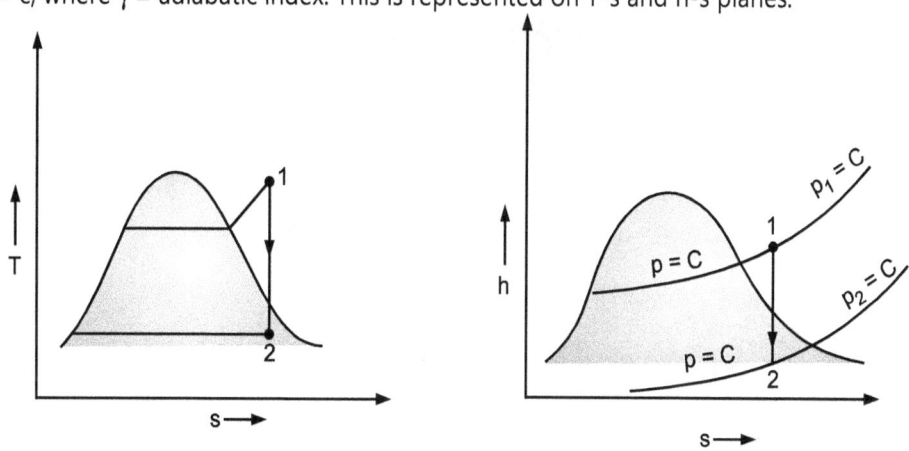

Fig. 5.21: Adiabatic process on T-s and h-s planes

(a) Work done $\quad Q_{1-2} = u_2 - u_1 + W_{1-2}$

For reversible adiabatic process, heat transfer

$Q_{1-2} = 0$

∴ $W_{1-2} = -(u_2 - u_1)$

SOLVED PROBLEMS

Problem 5.8: Steam initially at 1.5 MPa and 300°C expands reversibly and adiabatically in a steam engine to 40°C. Determine (a) condition of steam after expansion, (b) work done/kg of steam.

Solution: The reversible adiabatic expansion of steam in a turbine is a steady flow isentropic process.

Data: $p_1 = 15$ bar, $T_1 = 300°C$, $T_2 = 40°C$, $p_2 = p_{sat}$ at 40°C and $s_2 = s_1$.

Now,
$$s_1 = s_{g_1} + c_p \ln\left(\frac{T_1}{T_{sat}}\right) \text{ kJ/kg·K}$$

$$= 6.441 + 2.1 \ln\left(\frac{300 + 273}{198.3 + 273}\right)$$

$$= 6.85732 \text{ kJ/kg·K} = s_2 \text{ at } p_2$$

From steam table,

$p_2 = 0.07375$ bar at $T_2 = 40°C$.

and $s_{g_2} = 8.258$ kJ/kg·K at 40°C

$s_2 < s_{g_2}$

Therefore steam after expansion is wet.

$$s_2 = 6.85132$$
$$= s_{x_2}$$
$$= s_{f_2} + x_2 \cdot s_{fg_2}$$
$$6.85732 = 0.572 + x_2 \times 7.686$$

∴ $x_2 = \mathbf{0.81698}$

Adiabatic expansion process is represented on h-s diagram (See Fig. 5.22).

(b) Work done (W_{1-2}):

By first law,

$$Q_{1-2} = u_2 - u_1 + W_{1-2}$$
$$Q_{1-2} = 0 \text{ for adiabatic process}$$

∴ $W_{1-2} = u_1 - u_2$

$$= (h_1 - h_2) - (p_1 v_1 - p_2 v_2) \quad \ldots (1)$$

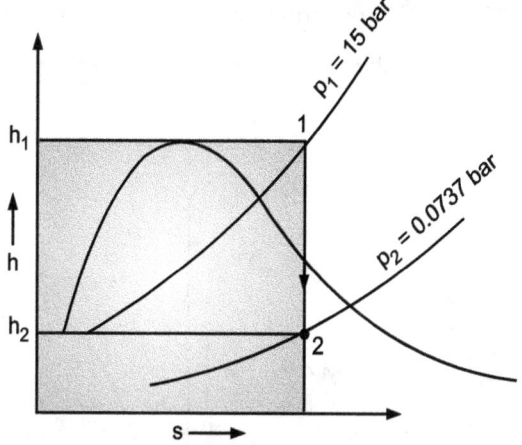

Fig. 5.22: h-s diagram

Now, $\quad h_1 = h_{g_1} + c_p \cdot \ln\left(\dfrac{T_{sup_1}}{T_{sat_1}}\right)$

$= 2789.9 + 2.1 \ln\left(\dfrac{300 + 273}{198.1 + 273}\right)$

$= \mathbf{2790.3 \ kJ/kg}$

$h_2 = h_{f_2} + x_2 h_{fg_2}$

$= 167.45 + 0.81698 \times 2406.9$

$= \mathbf{2133.8 \ kJ/kg}$

$v_1 = v_{sup_1} = \dfrac{T_{sup_1}}{T_{sat_1}} \times v_{sat_1}$

$= \dfrac{(300 + 273)}{(198.1 + 273)} \times 0.13166$

$= \mathbf{0.160 \ m^3/kg}$

$v_2 = v_{x_2} = v_{f_2} + x_2 v_{g_2}$

$= 0.0010078 + 0.81698 \times 19.546$

$= \mathbf{15.9697 \ m^3/kg}$

Put all these in equation (1)

$W_{1-2} = (2790.3 - 2133.8) - (15 \times 100 \times 0.160 - 0.07375 \times 100 \times 15.9697)$

$= \mathbf{533.0 \ kJ/kg}$

∴ **Work is obtained**

5.6.6 Throttling Process

When a fluid passes through small aperture (opening), it is said to be throttled and enthalpy of the fluid remains constant during throttling.

Throttling is a steady flow process, therefore, apply steady flow energy equation.

$Q = \Delta h + \Delta KE + \Delta PE + W$

Since Q = 0, W = 0. If ΔPE and ΔKE are neglected, then $\Delta h = 0$ i.e. $h_1 = h_2$.

It is represented on T-s and h-s planes (See Fig. 5.23). Throttling is an irreversible process. Hence shown by dotted lines.

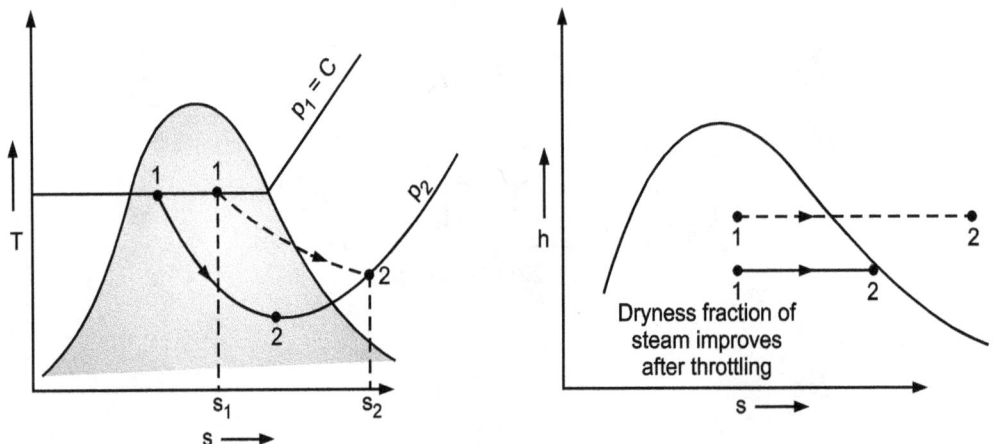

Fig. 5.23: Throttling process

SOLVED PROBLEMS

Problem 5.9: Steam is throttled from 6 bar and 0.98 dryness fraction to a final pressure at 1 bar. Find the final condition of steam.

Solution: Throttling is irreversible and constant enthalpy process,

$$h_1 = h_{x_1} = h_{f_1} + x_1 h_{fg_1}$$

$$= 670.4 + 0.98 \times 2085$$

$$= 2713.7 \text{ kJ/kg}$$

$$= h_2 \text{ kJ/kg}$$

Now $\quad h_{g_2} = 2675.4$ kJ/kg at 1 bar.

$h_2 > h_{g_2}$, hence steam after throttling is superheated

$$h_2 = h_{sup_2} = 2713.7$$

$$h_{sup_2} = h_{g_2} + c_p (T_{sup_2} - T_{sat_2})$$

$$2713.7 = 2675.4 + 2.1 (T_{sup_2} - 99.63)$$

$\therefore \quad T_{sup_2} = \textbf{117.87}$

The final condition of steam after throttling can also be found from Mollier diagram shown below.

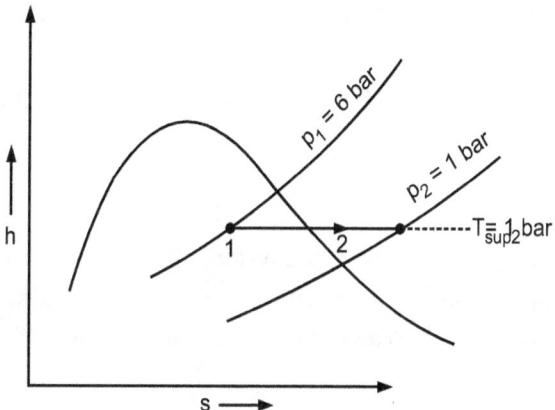

Fig. 5.24: h-s diagram

If the steam is expanded from state 1 (wet condition) to state 2 (wet condition)
∴ $h_{f_1} + x_1 h_{fg_1} = h_{f_2} + x_2 h_{fg_2}$ ... (5.29)

If the steam becomes superheated after throttling as shown by dotted line 1-2, then
$$h_{f_1} + x_1 h_{fg_1} = h_{f_2} + x_2 h_{fg_2} + c_{ps}(T_{sup2} - T_{s_2})$$
$$= h_g + c_{ps}(T_{sup2} - T_{s_2}) \quad ...(5.30)$$

During throttling, the pressure always falls.
∴ $p_2 < p_1$
∴ $h_{f_1} > h_{f_2}$ and $h_{fg_1} < h_{fg_2}$

If the sensible heat difference $(h_{f_1} - h_{f_2}) = h_1$ is greater than $(h_{fg_1} - h_{fg_2}) = h_2$ then the heat $(h_1 - h_2)$ is utilized to dry out the steam or to even superheat which depends upon the initial condition of steam (x_1) and final pressure after throttling. The throttling process is used for:
- determining the dryness fraction of steam,
- controlling the speed of the engine and turbine,
- in refrigeration system to reduce the pressure and temperature of the liquid refrigerant from the condenser condition to the evaporator condition.

5.7 Measurement of Dryness Fraction of Steam

Knowledge of the state of steam is necessary in many applications of the steam. Let the steam be flowing through a pipe. The pressure and temperature of steam through pipe be directly measured with the help of pressure gauge and thermometer. Based on the T and P of the steam, its condition can be determined referring the steam table. If the measured temperature is above the saturation temperature of steam (known from the steam tables as pressure is known), then it is also known that the vapour is in superheated condition. On the other hand, if the measured temperature corresponds to the saturated temperature of steam at the measured pressure, then the steam may be saturated or even it may be in wet condition, state may be anything from saturated liquid to dry and saturated steam.

The quality of steam is designated by the dryness fraction of the steam and it is experimentally measured.

The dryness fraction of the steam is defined as the ratio of the mass of dry steam present in the total mass of steam.

$$\therefore \quad x = \frac{m_s}{m_s + m_w} \quad \ldots (5.31)$$

where, m_s and m_w are the masses of steam and water in the mixture of $(m_s + m_w)$.

The dryness fraction of the steam is measured experimentally with the help of steam calorimeters. There are four types of calorimeters used for measuring the dryness fraction of steam.

5.7.1 Barrel or Tank Calorimeter

1. The dryness fraction of steam can be found with the help of a barrel calorimeter. The arrangement of this calorimeter is known in Fig. 5.25.

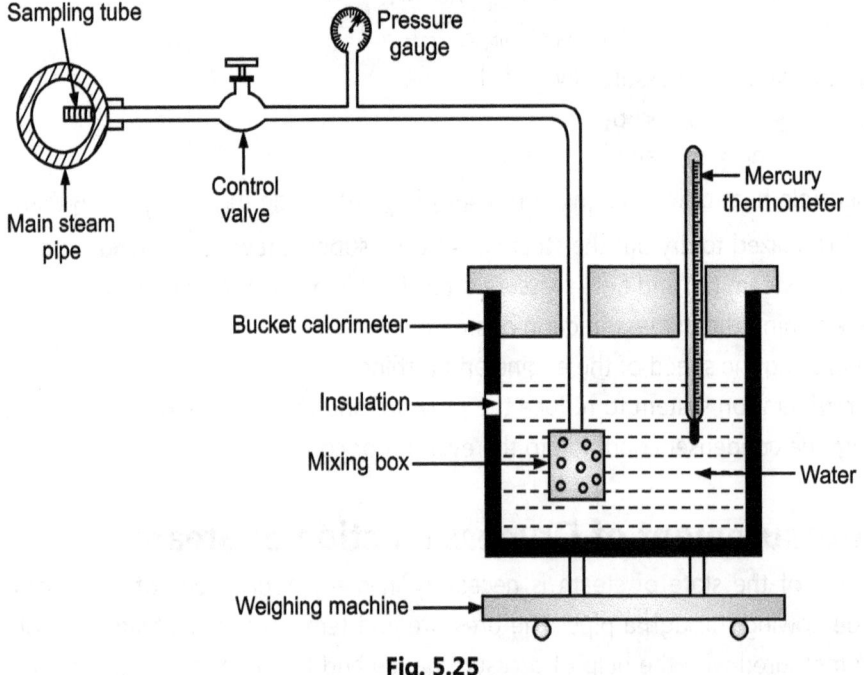

Fig. 5.25

2. A known quantity of steam is passed through a known mass of water and steam is completely condensed.
3. The heat lost by steam is equal to heat gained by the water.

4. The weight of calorimeter with water before mixing the steam and after mixing the steam are obtained by weighing.
5. The temperature of water before and after mixing the steam are measured by mercury thermometer.
6. The pressure of steam passed through the sample tube is measured with the help of pressure gauge.

Let, p_s = Gauge pressure of steam (kPa)
p_a = Atmospheric pressure (kPa)
T_s = Saturation temperature of steam known from the steam table at pressure $(p_s + p_a)$
h_{fg} = Latent heat of steam, kJ/kg
x = Dryness fraction of steam
m_c = Mass of calorimeter in kg
m_1 = Mass of calorimeter and water in kg
$m_w = (m_1 - m_c)$ = Mass of water in calorimeter, kg
m_2 = Mass of calorimeter, water and condensed steam, kg
$m_s = (m_2 - m_1)$ = Mass of steam condensed in calorimeter in kg
T_1 = Temperature of water and calorimeter before mixing the steam in °C
T_2 = Temperature of water and calorimeter after mixing the steam in °C

The heat lost by steam is equal to the heat gained by water and calorimeter, so

$$(m_s)[xh_{fg} + (T_s - T_2)] = (m_w) c_{pw} (T_2 - T_1) + m_c c_{pc} (T_2 - T_1)$$
$$(m_2 - m_1)[xh_{fg} + (T_s - T_2)] = (m_1 - m_c) c_{pw} (T_2 - T_1) + m_c c_{pc} (T_2 - T_1)$$

where, c_{pw} and c_{pc} are the specific heats of water and calorimeter respectively.

$$x = \frac{(c_{pw} m_w + c_{pc} m_c)(T_2 - T_1) - m_s (T_s - T_2)}{m_s h_{fg}} \qquad \ldots (5.32)$$

The $m_c c_{pc}$ is known as water equivalent of calorimeter.

The losses due to convection and radiation are not taken into account. Hence, certain error is involved while determining the dryness fraction. The calculated value of dryness fraction neglecting losses is always less than the actual value of the dryness.

5.7.2 Separating Calorimeter

One important assumption is made here that all the water particles are removed in separating section and the steam entering in the bucket calorimeter is completely dry. The arrangement of the calorimeter is shown in Fig. 5.26.

This calorimeter is used to measure the probable value of dryness fraction of steam when the steam is very wet. The steam is passed through a sample tube as shown in the figure. The moisture is separated mechanically from the steam. Steam is passed through perforated trays and water particles are separated due to inertia of the droplets. The outgoing steam is condensed in the bucket calorimeter as discussed earlier.

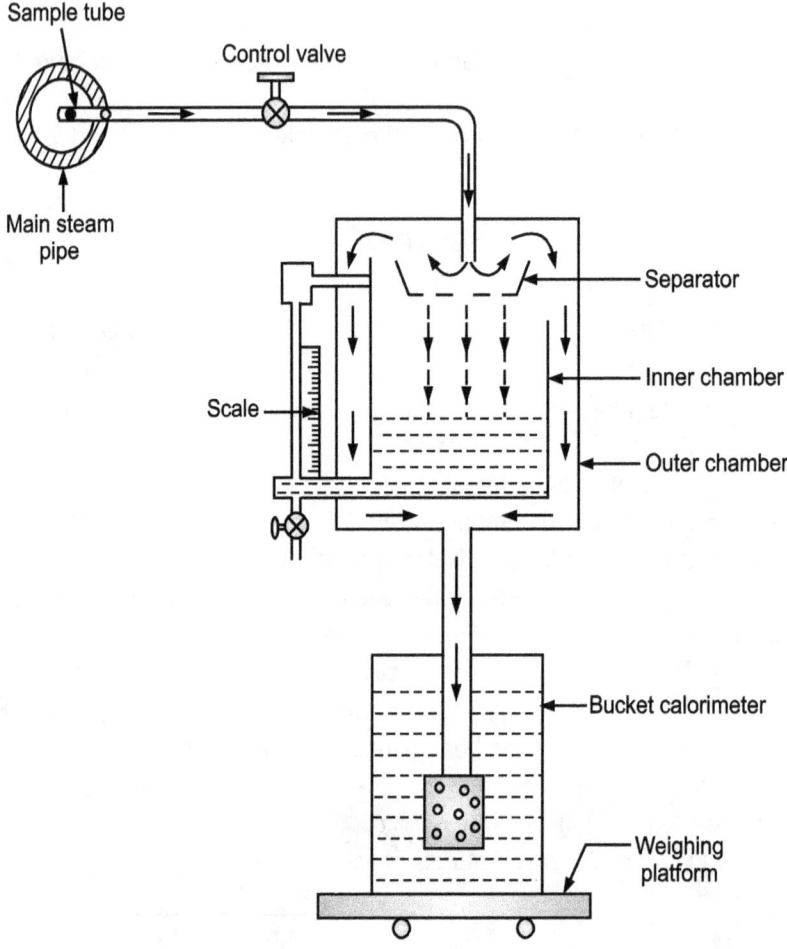

Fig. 5.26: Separating Calorimeter

Let m_w = Mass of water separated from the steam
m_s = Mass of steam condensed in the bucket calorimeter

$$x = \frac{m_s}{m_s + m_w} \qquad \ldots (5.33)$$

The only advantage of this method is the quick determination of the dryness fraction of very wet steam. In practice, it is not possible to remove all the water particles from the steam by this mechanical process and therefore, the dryness fraction obtained by this calorimeter will not be very accurate. The dryness fraction calculated by its method is always greater than the actual. This calorimeter can also be used in combination with throttling calorimeter.

5.7.3 Throttling Calorimeter

The arrangement of this calorimeter is shown in Fig. 5.27.

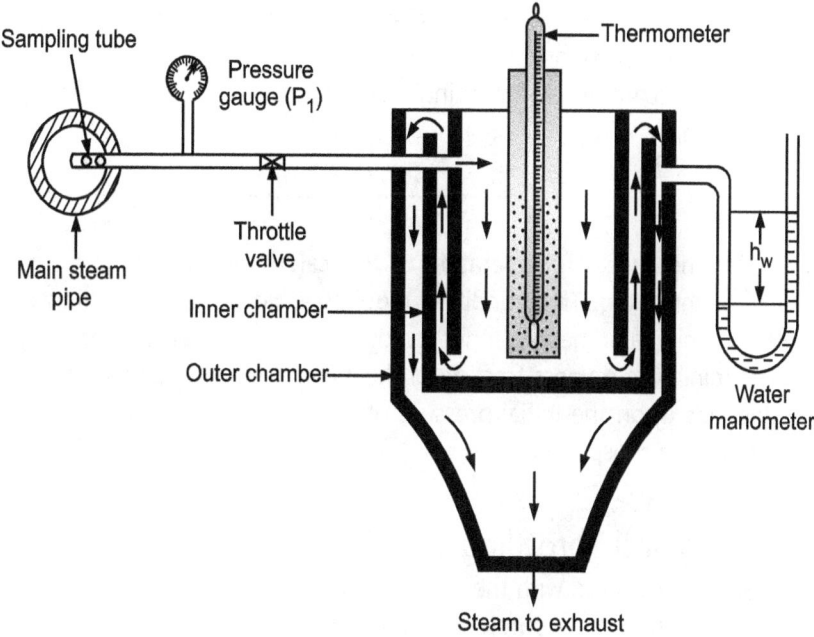

Fig. 5.27: Throttling Calorimeter

- The steam whose dryness fraction is to be determined is taken into the calorimeter through a sample tube and passed through a throttle valve as shown in Fig. 5.27.
- The steam is allowed to throttle down to a lower pressure until it comes out in superheated condition. The pressure and temperature of steam coming out of the throttling valve are measured with the help of a manometer and a thermometer.

Let
p_1 = Gauge pressure of steam in bar
x_1 = Dryness fraction of steam
p_a = Atmospheric pressure in a bar
T_{s1} = Saturation temperature of steam at a pressure of $(p_1 + p_a)$ known from steam tables
h_{fg1} = Latent heat of steam at pressure $(p_1 + p_a)$
h_w = Manometer reading in cm of water above atmospheric pressure

∴ Absolute pressure of steam after throttling

$$p_2 = \left[p_a + \frac{h_w}{13.6} \times \frac{1.03}{76} \right] \text{ bar}$$

T_{s2} = Saturation temperature of steam at pressure p_2
h_{fg2} = Enthalpy of saturated steam at pressure p_2
c_{ps} = Specific heat of superheated steam
T_{sup2} = Temperature of steam after throttling

The enthalpy of steam remains constant during throttling process.

Enthalpy of steam before throttling = Enthalpy of steam after throttling

∴ $h_{f1} + x_1 h_{fg1} = h_{f2} + h_{fg2} + c_{ps}(T_{sup2} - T_{s2}) = h_{g2} + c_{ps}(T_{sup2} - T_{s2})$

∴ $x_1 = \dfrac{[h_{g2} + c_{ps}(T_{sup2} - T_{s2})] - h_{f1}}{h_{fg1}}$ ... (5.34)

The condition for the successful operation of this calorimeter is that the steam must be superheated after throttling. This condition requires a high dryness fraction of the steam before throttling. This calorimeter cannot be used if the dryness fraction of the steam is above 0.96. The minimum dryness fraction of the steam that can be measured by throttling calorimeter depends upon the initial pressure of the steam as the pressure after throttling virtually remains near atmospheric.

5.7.4 Separating and Throttling Calorimeter

The dryness fraction measured with the help of separating calorimeter is always higher than the actual. This is because of incomplete separation of moisture by mechanical means. The arrangement of a separating and throttling calorimeter is shown in Fig. 5.28.

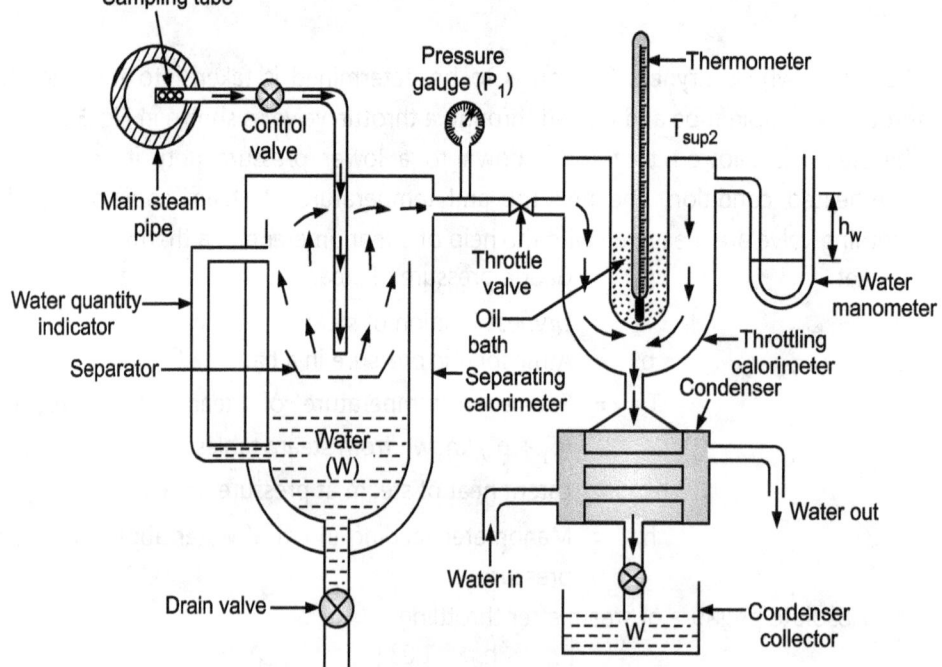

Fig. 5.28: Separating and Throttling Calorimeter

The mass of the water separated in separating calorimeter and the pressure and temperature of the steam leaving the throttle valve are recorded with the help of water manometer and mercury in gall thermometer.

Let
- m_s = Mass of steam condensed and collected from condenser
- m_w = Mass of water collected from separating calorimeter
- x = Actual dryness fraction of steam in main pipe
- x_1 = Apparent dryness fraction of steam measured by separating calorimeter assuming that the steam coming out of separating calorimeter is completely dry
- x_2 = Actual dryness fraction of steam entering into the throttling calorimeter

The apparent dryness fraction is given by $x_1 = \dfrac{m_s}{m_s + m_w}$ ... (5.35)

Amount of water carried by the steam before entering into the calorimeter

$$= (1 - x)(m_s + m_w) \qquad \ldots (5.36)$$

Amount of water separated in separating calorimeter

$$= (1 - x_1)(m_s + m_w) \qquad \ldots (5.37)$$

The amount of water carried by the steam into the throttling calorimeter

$$= (1 - x_2) m_s \qquad \ldots (5.38)$$

The mass of water in the steam given by the equation (5.36) must be equal to the quantities of water given by equations (5.37) and (5.38).

$\therefore \quad (1 - x)(m_s + m_w) = (1 - x_1)(m_s + m_w) + (1 - x_2) m_s$

$\therefore \quad 1 - x = (1 - x_1) + (1 - x_2)\dfrac{m_s}{m_s + m_w}$

But $\dfrac{m_s}{m_s + m_w} = x_1$

Substituting this valve in the above equation,

$$(1 - x) = (1 - x_1) + (1 - x_2) \times x_1 = 1 - x_1 + x_1 - x_1 x_2$$

$$x = x_1 x_2 \qquad \ldots (5.39)$$

This calorimeter gives very accurate value of the dryness fraction of the steam when it is considerably wet and which cannot be measured accurately by any other method discussed earlier.

THERMODYNAMICS-I (SE - Mech. - BAMU) — PROPERTIES OF STEAM OR PURE SUBSTANCES

ADDITIONAL SOLVED PROBLEMS

Problem 5.10: A vessel with a partition in it contains initially 2 kg of dry and saturated steam at 7.0 bar in one compartment and 1 kg of steam with dryness fraction 0.8 at 3.5 bar in the other compartment. After the partition is removed, the pressure of mixture is found to be 5 bar. Neglecting the volume of water, find the dryness fraction of the mixture.

Solution:

Part A	Part B
2 kg	1 kg
dry saturated	0.8 dry
7 bar	3.5 bar
V_A	V_B

Properties from steam tables:

p (bar)	v_g m³/kg	h_f kJ/kg	h_{fg} kJ/kg
3.5	0.52397	584.3	2147.3
5	0.37466	640.1	2107.4
7	0.2727	697.1	2064.9

Volume of compartment A,
$$V_A = m_A \cdot v_{g_A}$$
$$= 2 \times 0.2727$$
$$= \mathbf{0.5454 \ m^3}$$

Volume of compartment B,
$$V_B = m_B \times \left(v_{g_B} \times x_B\right)$$
$$= 1 \times 0.52397 \times 0.8$$
$$= \mathbf{0.419176 \ m^3}$$

Total volume of the vessel = 0.5454 + 0.419176 = **0.9645 m³**

After removal of partition, two steams will mix each other. The pressure of mixture is 5 bar.

∴ Specific volume of mixture at 5 bar is 0.37466 m³/kg.

∴ Total volume of mixture
$$= v_{mix} \times m_{mix}$$
$$= 0.37466 \times 3 = 1.1241 \ m^3$$

∴ Dryness fraction of mixture = $\dfrac{\text{Total volume of vessel}}{\text{Volume of mixture at 5 bar}}$

$= \dfrac{0.9645}{1.1241} = \mathbf{0.8580}$

Problem 5.11: A steam turbine obtains steam from a boiler at a pressure of 15 bar and 0.98 dry. It was observed that steam looses 25 kJ of heat per kg as it flows through the pipe line, while pressure remains constant. Calculate dryness fraction of steam at turbine end of pipe line.

Solution:

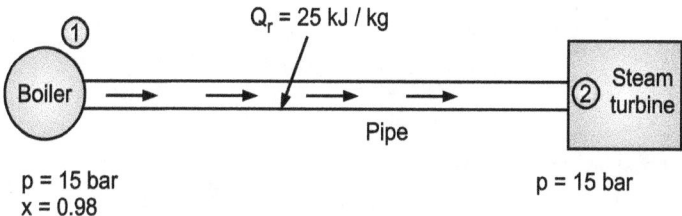

Fig. 5.29: Block diagram

At 15 bar, $h_f = 844.6$ kJ/kg, $h_{fg} = 1945.3$ kJ/kg

Enthalpy of steam at the boiler outlet,

$h_1 = h_{f_1} + x_1 h_{fg_1}$

$= 844.6 + 0.98 \times 1945.3$

$= \mathbf{2750.994 \text{ kJ/kg}}$

Enthalpy of steam at inlet to turbine,

$h_2 = h_{f_2} + x_2 h_{fg_2}$ $h_{f_1} = h_{f_2}, h_{fg_1} = h_{fg_2}$

∴ $h_2 = 844.6 + x_2 \times 1945 - 3$

Equating the enthalpies at point 1 and point 2, considering the heat lost to the surrounding from the pipe,

$2750.994 - 25 = 844.6 + x_2 \times 1945.3$

∴ $x_2 = \mathbf{0.967}$

Problem 5.12: Find enthalpy, internal energy and specific volume in the following cases:

(i) mass = 5 kg, p = 10 bar, quality = 95%

(ii) mass = 2 kg, p = 20 bar, volume = 0.35 m³

Solution: **(i) Given:** For p = 10 bar,

$h_f = 762.6$ kJ/kg

and $h_{f_g} = 2013.6$ kJ/kg

$$v_g = 0.19430 \text{ m}^3/\text{kg}$$
$$h = h_f + x \cdot h_{fg}$$
$$= 762.6 + 0.95 \times 2013.6$$
$$= \mathbf{2675.52 \text{ kJ/kg}}$$

Total enthalpy, $H = m \cdot h$
$$= 5 \times 2675.52$$
$$= \mathbf{13377.6 \text{ kJ}}$$

v_x = specific volume of wet steam
$$= x \cdot v_g$$
$$= 0.95 \times 0.19430$$
$$= \mathbf{0.184585 \text{ m}^3/\text{kg}}$$

Total volume = $m \cdot v_x$
$$V = 5 \times 0.184585$$
$$= \mathbf{0.9223 \text{ m}^3}$$

$$h = u + pv$$
$$u = h - pv$$
$$= 13377.6 - 10 \times 100 \times 0.9223$$

Internal energy = **12454.6 kJ**

(ii) m = 2 kg, at 20 bar, h_f = 908.59 kJ/kg, h_{fg} = 1888.6 kJ/kg, v_g = 0.099536 m³/kg, h_g = 2797.19 kJ/kg.

Given volume is $\quad V = \mathbf{0.35 \text{ m}^3}$

Volume of 2 kg dry saturated steam
$$= 0.099536 \times 2$$
$$= \mathbf{0.19907 \text{ m}^3}$$

∴ Steam is superheated.

$$h = h_g + c_p \log \frac{V_{sup}}{V_{sat}}$$
$$= 2797.19 + 2.1 \log \frac{0.35}{0.19907}$$
$$= \mathbf{2798.3 \text{ kJ/kg}}$$

∴ Total enthalpy $H = 2 \times 2798.3$

∴ $\quad H = \mathbf{5596.75 \text{ kJ}}$

$$H = u + pv$$
$$5596.75 = u + 20 \times 100 \times 0.35$$
$$u = \text{Internal energy} = \mathbf{4896.75 \text{ kJ}}$$

Problem 5.13: Find the condition of steam and determine enthalpy from the following table:

(i) $p = 40$ bar, $v = 0.062$ m³/kg
(ii) $p = 30$ bar, $t = 260°C$
(iii) $p = 40$ bar,   heat added $= 2400$ kJ/kg
(iv) $p = 30$ bar, $v = 0.0666$ m³/kg

Solution:

(i) $p = 40$ bar, $v = 0.062$ m³/kg
From steam table, at 40 bar,
$$v_g = 0.049749 \text{ m}^3/\text{kg}$$
$$T_{sat} = 250.3°C$$
$$h_g = 2800.3$$
As given volume, $v > v_g$, steam is in superheated condition

$$T_{sup} = \frac{T_{sat}}{V_{sat}} \times V_{sup}$$

$$= \frac{(250 + 273)}{0.049749} \times 0.062 = \mathbf{651.7 \text{ K}}$$

∴ Degree of superheat $= 651.7 - (250 + 273)$
$$= \mathbf{128.79 \text{ K}}$$
$$h_{sup} = h_g + C_p (651.7 - 523.3)$$
$$= 2800.3 + 270.45$$
$$= \mathbf{3070.7 \text{ kJ/kg}}$$

(ii) $p = 30$ bar and $t = 260°C$
At 30 bar, $t_{sat} = 233.8°C$
$h = 2802.3$ kJ/kg
$t > t_{sat}$, therefore, steam is superheated.

∴ $$h_{sup} = h_g + C_p \ln \frac{T_{sup}}{T_{sat}}$$

$$= 2802.3 + 2.1 (533 - 506.8)$$
Enthalpy $= \mathbf{2858.3 \text{ kJ/kg}}$

(iii) $p = 40$ bar, $Q = 2400$ kJ/kg, $h_f = 1087.4$ kJ/kg
At 40 bar, $h_g = 2800.4$ kJ/kg, $h_{f_g} = 1712.9$,
$Q = \Delta h = h - h_0$ kJ/kg But $h_0 = 0$
$Q < h_g$ ∴ steam is wet.
$$h = h_f + x \cdot h_{fg}$$
$$2400 = 1087.4 + x \times 1712.9$$
∴ $x =$ dryness fraction $= \mathbf{0.7665}$

$$\text{Enthalpy} = h = h_f + x \cdot h_{fg}$$
$$= 1087.4 + 0.7665 \times 1712.9$$
$$= \textbf{2400 kJ/kg} \text{ already given}$$

(iv) p = 30 bar, v = 0.066 m³/kg

From steam table, v_g = 0.0666 m³/kg at 30 bar.

∴ $v = v_g$ ∴ Steam is dry saturated

Enthalpy = h_g = **2802.3 kJ/kg**

Problem 5.14: Steam at 10 bar and 0.925 dry is contained inside a vessel having a capacity of 1 m³. The delivery valve is opened and the steam is blown-off. The period of blowing is so regulated that pressure drops at 5 bar. The delivery valve is then closed and the vessel is cooled until the pressure becomes 4 bar. Estimate,

(i) Mass of steam blown-off.

(ii) Dryness fraction of steam in the vessel after cooling.

Solution: Extract from steam table

Pressure bar	Specific volume, m³/kg	h_f kJ/kg	h_{f_g} kJ/kg
10	0.1943	762.5	2013.5
5	0.3737	640.1	2107.4
4	0.4622	604.6	2133.0

(i) Initial mass of steam in the vessel

$$= \frac{V}{v_x}$$

$$= \frac{1}{(0.925 \times 0.1943)}$$

$$= \textbf{5.56 kg}$$

Total heat before blowing = Total heat after blowing

$$h_{f_1} + x_1 h_{fg_1} = h_{f_2} + x_2 \cdot h_{fg_2}$$

$$762.5 + 0.925 \times 2013.5 = 640.1 + x_2 \times 2107.4$$

∴ $x_2 = 0.94$

Mass of steam after blowing $= \dfrac{V}{v_{x_2}} = \dfrac{1}{0.94 \times 0.3737}$

$$= \textbf{2.87 kg}$$

Mass of steam blown off = 5.56 – 2.87 = **2.69 kg**

(ii) Dryness fraction after cooling

$$x_3 \, (m \cdot v_{g_3}) = V$$

$$x_3 = \frac{V}{m \cdot v_{g_3}}$$

$$= \frac{1}{2.87 \times 0.4622}$$

$$= \mathbf{0.755}$$

Problem 5.15: 2.5 kg of steam at a pressure of 1 bar and with a dryness fraction of 0.96 is compressed hyperbolically to a pressure of 8.0 bar. Determine:
  (i) The final condition of steam.
  (ii) The heat transferred during compression.

Solution: Given: m = 2.5 kg.
  $p_1 = 1$ bar, $x_1 = 0.96$

(i) Properties of steam at 1 bar are:
$$v_{g_1} = 1.694 \text{ m}^3/\text{kg}$$
$$h_{f_1} = 417 \text{ kJ/kg}$$
$$h_{fg_1} = 2258 \text{ kJ/kg}$$
$$h_{g_1} = 2675 \text{ kJ/kg}$$

∴ $\quad$ Mass of steam $= \dfrac{\text{Volume of steam}}{\text{Specific volume of steam}}$

$$2.5 = \frac{V_1}{1.694 \times 0.96}$$

∴ $\quad V_1 = 4.0656 \text{ m}^3$

∴ Apply hyperbolic law to the compression process.

$$p_1 V_1 = p_2 V_2$$

∴ $\quad V_2 = \dfrac{p_1 V_1}{p_2}$

$$= \frac{1}{8} \times 4.0656 = 0.5082 \text{ m}^3$$

Let x_2 be the dryness fraction after compression.

$$x_2 = \frac{V_2}{m \cdot v_{g_2}}$$

$$= \frac{0.5082}{2.5 \times 0.24030}$$

$$= \mathbf{0.846}$$

$v_{g_2} = 0.24030$ at 8 bar pressure

Properties of dry steam at 8 bar pressure

$$T_{sat_2} = 170.4°C$$
$$V_{g_2} = 0.2403$$
$$h_{f_2} = 721 \text{ kJ/kg}$$
$$h_{fg_2} = 2048$$

(ii) Heat transfer during the compression

$$= h_2 - h_1$$
$$h_1 = m\left(h_{f_1} + x_1 h_{fg_1}\right)$$
$$= 2.5 (417 + 0.96 \times 2258)$$
$$= \mathbf{6461.7 \text{ kJ}}$$
$$h_2 = \text{Total enthalpy at point 2 (after compression)}$$
$$= m\left(h_{f_2} + x_2 h_{fg_2}\right)$$
$$= 2.5 (721 + 0.846 \times 2048)$$
$$= \mathbf{6134 \text{ kJ}}$$

∴
$$Q = h_2 - h_1$$
$$= 6134 - 6461.7$$
$$= -327.68 \text{ kJ is lost by steam during compression.}$$

Problem 5.16: Determine the volume occupied by 1 kg of steam at a pressure of 0.7 MN/m² and having dryness fraction of 0.97.

This is expanded adiabatically to a pressure of 0.12 MN/m², the law of expansion being $pv^{1.13}$ = Constant. Determine

(i) The dryness fraction of steam
(ii) The change of internal energy of the steam during expansion.

P	T_{sat}	kJ/kg			V_g
MN/m²	°C	h_f	h_{fg}	h_g	m³/kg
0.12	104.8	439.4	2244.1	2683.4	1.428
0.70	165	697	2064.9	2762	0.273

Solution: m = 1 kg, p_1 = 0.7 MN/m² = 7 bar, x_1 = 0.97, p_2 = 1.2 bar.

(i) Volume of steam, $V_1 = m \cdot x_1 \cdot v_{g_1}$

$$= 1 \times 0.97 \times 0.273$$
$$= \mathbf{0.2645 \text{ m}^3}$$

$$p_1 v_1^n = p_2 v_2^n$$
$$7 \times (0.2645)^{1.13} = 1.2 \times v_2^{1.13}$$

$$\therefore \quad v_2 = 1.2591 \text{ m}^3/\text{kg}$$

because m = 1

At $p_2 = 1.2$ bar, $v_{g_2} = 1.481 \text{ m}^3/\text{kg}$

$\therefore \quad v_{g_2} > v_2 \therefore$ Steam is wet

$$\text{Dryness fraction, } x_2 = \frac{v_2}{v_{g_2}} = \frac{1.2591}{1.481} = \mathbf{0.88}$$

(ii) Change in internal energy $(\Delta u) = u_2 - u_1$

$$u_1 = h_1 - p_1 v_1$$
$$= \left(h_{f_1} + x_1 h_{fg_1}\right) - 100 \times 7 \times 0.2645$$
$$= (697 + 0.97 \times 2064.9) - 700 \times 0.2645$$
$$= \mathbf{2514 \text{ kJ/kg}}$$

$$u_2 = h_2 - p_2 v_2$$
$$= \left(h_{f_2} + x_2 \cdot h_{fg_2}\right) - 100 \times p_2 \times v_2$$
$$= (489.4 + 0.88 \times 2244.1)$$
$$\quad - 100 \times 1.2 \times (0.88 \times 1.428)$$
$$= 2307.8 \text{ kJ/kg}$$

$\therefore \quad \Delta u = (2307.8 - 2514)$
$$= \mathbf{-206.2 \text{ kJ/kg (decreases)}}$$

Problem 5.17: Dry saturated steam at a pressure of 1.25 MN/m² flows along a steam pipe of 150 mm diameter with velocity of 24 m/sec.

Find:

(i) Volume flow in m³/sec.

(ii) Mass flow in kg/min.

(iii) Final temperature if steam is throttled to 0.12 MN/m².

Take $C_p = 2$ kJ/kg·K

Solution: Given: Dry saturated steam.

$$p_1 = 1.25 \text{ MN/m}^2 = 12.5 \text{ bar}$$
$$D = 150 \text{ mm} = 0.15 \text{ m}$$
$$c = 24 \text{ m/sec}$$

(i) Volume flow rate $= A \times c$

$$= \frac{\pi}{4} D^2 \times c$$
$$= \frac{\pi}{4} (0.15)^2 \times 24$$
$$= \mathbf{0.424 \text{ m}^3/\text{sec.}}$$

(ii) **Mass flow rate:**
At 12.5 bar, from steam table,
$$v_1 = 0.15693 \text{ m}^3/\text{kg}$$
$$\therefore \quad \rho_1 = \frac{1}{v_1} = 6.37 \text{ kg/m}^3$$
$$\therefore \quad \text{Mass flow rate} = \text{Volume flow rate} \times \text{Density}$$
$$= 0.424 \times 6.37$$
$$= 2.7 \text{ kg/sec}$$
$$= 162.11 \text{ kg/min}$$

(iii) **Final temperature after throttling (T_2)**
From steam table, at 12.5 bar,
$$h_1 = h_g = 2784.1 \text{ kJ/kg}$$
For throttling process,
$$h_2 = h_1 = 2784.1 \text{ kJ/kg}$$
From superheated steam table, at $p_2 = 1.2$ bar,
$$h_2 = 2784.1 \text{ kJ/kg}$$

Temperature	h
150	2774.8
y	h_2 = 2784.1
200	2874.4

By interpolation,
$$\frac{200 - 150}{y - 150} = \frac{2874.4 - 2774.8}{2784.1 - 2774.8}$$
$$\therefore \quad y - 150 = 4.6686$$
$$\therefore \quad y = 154.67°C$$
The final temperature of steam after throttling is,
$$T_2 = 154.67°C$$

Problem 5.18: The following data were obtained in a test on a combined separating and throttling calorimeter:

Pressure of steam sample = 15 bar, Pressure of steam at exit = 1 bar, Temperature of steam at the exit = 150°C, Discharge from separating calorimeter = 0.5 kg/min, Discharge from throttling calorimeter = 10 kg/min. Determine the dryness fraction of the sample steam.

Solution: Given data:
Pressure of steam sample, $p_1 = p_2 = 15$ bar
Temperature of steam at the exit, $t_{sup3} = 15°C$
Pressure of steam at the exit, $p_3 = 1$ bar
Discharge from separating calorimeter, $m_w = 0.5$ kg/min

Discharge from throttling calorimeter, m_s = 10 kg/min

From steam tables,

at $p_1 = p_2$ = 15 bar; h_{f_2} = 844.7 kJ/kg, h_{fg2} = 1945.2 kJ/kg

at p_3 = 1 bar and 150°C; h_{sup3} = 2776.4 kJ/kg

Also, $\quad h_2 = h_3$

∴ $\quad h_{f_2} + x_2 h_{fg2} = h_{sup3}$

$844.7 + x_2 \times 1945.2 = 2776.4$

∴ $\quad x_2 = \dfrac{2776.4 - 844.7}{1945.2} = \mathbf{0.993}$

∴ Quality of steam supplied,

$$x_1 = \dfrac{x_2 \cdot m_s}{m_s + m_w} = \dfrac{0.993 \times 10}{10 + 0.5} = \mathbf{0.946}$$

Problem 5.19: Two boilers one with superheater and other without superheater are delivering equal quantities of steam into a common main. The pressure in the boilers and the main is 15 bar. The temperature of the steam from a boiler with a superheater is 300°C and temperature of the steam in the main is 200°C. Determine the quality of steam supplied by the other boiler.

Solution: Boiler B1 = 15 bar and 300°C

Enthalpy, $h_1 = h_{g1} + C_{ps}(T_{sup} - T_s)$

$= 2789.9 + 2.25 (300 - 198.3)$

$= \mathbf{3018.725 \text{ kJ/kg}}$ ... (i)

Boiler B2: 15 bar (temperature not known)

$h_2 = h_{f_2} + x_2 \times h_{fg2}$

$= \mathbf{844.7 + x_2 \times 1945.2}$ ... (ii)

Main: 15 bar, 200°C

Total heat of 2 kg of steam in the steam main

$= 2[h_g + C_{ps}(T_{sup} - T_s)]$

$= 2[2789.9 + 2.25 \times (200 - 198.3)]$

$= \mathbf{5587.45 \text{ kJ}}$ ... (iii)

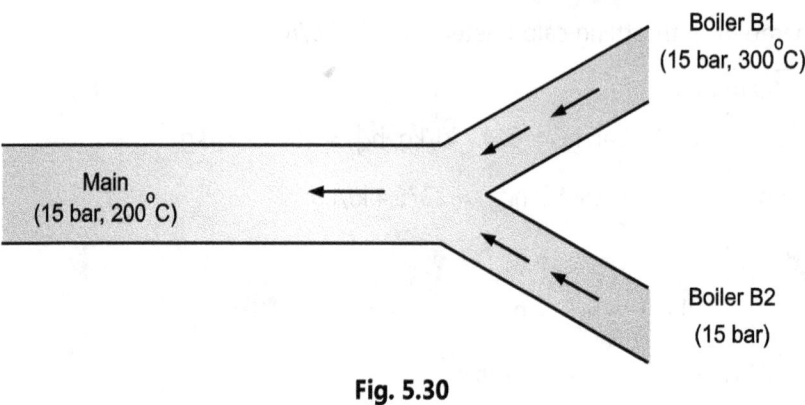

Fig. 5.30

Adding (i) and (ii) and equating with (iii)
$$3018.725 + 844.7 + x_2 \times 1945.2 = 5587.45$$
$$x_2 = \mathbf{0.8863}$$

Hence, quality of steam supplied by the other boiler = 0.8863.

Problem 5.20: A closed vessel of 0.6 m³ capacity contains dry steam at 360 kPa. The vessel is cooled till pressure drops upto 200 kPa. Find out:
 (i) Mass of steam
 (ii) Final dryness of steam

Solution: Given: $V = 0.6 \text{ m}^3$
 Dry steam, $p_1 = 360 \text{ kPa} = 3.6 \text{ bar}$
   $p_2 = 200 \text{ kPa} = 2 \text{ bar}$

Mass of steam:

(i) At 3.6 bar, from steam table,
$$v_1 = v_g = \mathbf{0.51032 \text{ m}^3/\text{kg}}$$

Total volume of vessel,
$$V = m \cdot v_1$$
$$\therefore \quad m = \frac{V}{v_1} = \frac{0.6}{0.51032} = 1.176 \text{ kg}$$
$$\therefore \quad m = \mathbf{1.176 \text{ kg}}$$

(ii) Find dryness fraction of steam:

Volume remains constant,
$$v_1 = v_2 = v_{f2} + x_2 \cdot v_{fg2}$$
$$0.51032 = 0.0010608 + x_2 \times 0.88544$$
$$\therefore \quad x_2 = \mathbf{0.575}$$

EXERCISE

1. Explain phase transformation of water at constant pressure with the help of T-s diagram.
2. What is the effect of pressure on boiling point?
3. Draw p-v, T-v, h-s and T-s diagrams for water.
4. What is meant by sensible heat, latent heat and enthalpy of water?
5. What is dryness fraction? How do you calculate specific volume, enthalpy and entropy of wet steam?
6. How do you find enthalpy and specific volume of superheated steam?
7. What is internal energy? How do you calculate it for a wet steam and superheated steam?
8. Represent the following processes on p-v and T-s diagrams.
   (a) Constant volume
   (b) Constant pressure
   (c) Hyperbolic
   (d) Isentropic

EXAMPLES FOR PRACTICE

1. A closed vessel of 0.75 m³ capacity contains dry saturated steam at 0.35 MPa. The vessel is cooled until the pressure is reduced to 0.2 MPa. Calculate:

   (a) The mass of steam in the vessel.

   (b) The final dryness fraction of steam.

   (c) The amount of heat transferred during the cooling process.

   (Ans. (a) 1.431 kg, (b) 0.591, (c) 927.9 kJ/kg**)**

2. A steam engine obtains steam from a boiler at a pressure of 30 bar and 0.98 dry. It was observed that when steam flows through a pipe, heat lost to the surroundings is 50 kJ/kg and pressure remains constant. Calculate the dryness fraction of steam at engine end of pipe line. **(Ans.** $x = 0.95$**)**

3. A vessel of 1.2 m³ capacity contains steam of 1.0 MPa and 0.92 dryness fraction. Steam is blown off until the pressure drops to 0.5 MPa. The valve is then closed. Determine the mass of steam blown off. **(Ans. 3.31 kg)**

4. A quantity of steam at a pressure of 2.1 MN/m² and 0.9 dry occupies a volume of 0.427 m³. It is expanded according to $pv^{1.25}$ = constant, to a pressure of 0.7 MN/m². Determine:

   (a) Mass of steam

   (b) The work transfer

   (c) The change in internal energy

   (d) The heat exchange between the steam and the surroundings, stating the direction of heat flow. **(Ans. m = 5 kg, Δu = –322.6 kJ/kg, W = 143.4 kJ/kg, dQ = –179.24 kJ/kg)**

✱✱✱

Unit VI

FUELS AND COMBUSTION

6.1 Introduction

Thermal energy is a basic form of energy which is required for heating and power production. It is produced by burning fuels such as wood, coal and fuels from petroleum. Nuclear energy is also used to produce heat. The nuclear fuel does not *'burn'* as such and hence it is outside the scope of oxidation process. This chapter deals with combustion of fuels in air and hence only organic (hydrocarbon) fuels are relevant for discussion in this chapter.

A fuel may be defined as a substance which liberates sufficient thermal energy (also called heat) on oxidation. A fuel mainly consists of the elements: carbon and hydrogen with smaller proportion of sulphur, oxygen, nitrogen and metallic compounds. Carbon, hydrogen and sulphur are called combustibles since they oxidise and produce heat. The metallic compounds are called non-combustibles and produce ash. The combustibles along with nitrogen from air produce products of combustion which are heated to a high temperature during the process. These high temperature gases are used as a source of heat in many apparatus like boilers, furnaces, ovens, I.C. engines, etc. As the temperature of the gases decreases, they transfer less heat and are finally released to the atmosphere. Except carbon dioxide and water vapour in the products of combustion, all other constituents are harmful to the environment and are called pollutants.

6.2 Calorific Value of a Fuel

The amount of thermal energy produced per unit quantity of fuel when completely burned is called its calorific value (CV). For solid and liquid fuels, the unit quantity is kilogram and calorific value is given in *kilojoules per kilogram, abbreviated as kJ/kg in S.I. system.* The unit quantity for gaseous fuels is one cubic metre at a certain pressure and temperature. The calorific value for gaseous fuels is stated in *kilojoules per cubic metre, abbreviated as kJ/m³.*

Higher Calorific Value:

The heat liberated from the fuel is initially used to heat the products of combustion, which give up their heat to the apparatus. If all of the heat of products of combustion is to be realised, they should be cooled down to room temperature. The heating value of the fuel in such a case is called Higher Heating Value (HHV) or Higher Calorific Value (HCV) or sometimes Gross Calorific Value (GCV). The *Higher Calorific Value* is defined as the heat released by burning unit quantity of fuel completely to its final products when the products of combustion are cooled down to the room temperature.

In short, the calorific value is called the higher calorific value when the moisture in the products is in the liquid form.

Lower Calorific Value:

The products of combustion contain water vapour formed due to oxidation of hydrogen fraction of the fuel and also free moisture from the fuel and the air. This moisture evaporates during combustion process and takes away enthalpy of evaporation. When the products of combustion do not cool to room temperature, this hidden heat is not released. The heating value in this case is less than the higher heating value and is called the Lower Heating Value (LHV). It is also called the Lower Calorific Value (LCV) or the Net Calorific Value (NCV). The *Lower Calorific Value* is defined as the amount of heat released by burning the unit quantity of a fuel completely to its final products which leave the apparatus at a higher temperature without condensing the moisture.

It is called lower calorific value when the moisture remains in the vapour form. The HCV and LCV are related by the following formula:

$$LCV = HCV - \left\{\begin{array}{c}\text{Mass of moisture per}\\ \text{unit quantity of fuel}\end{array}\right\} \times \left\{\begin{array}{c}\text{Specific enthalpy}\\ \text{of evaporation}\end{array}\right\}$$

For general calculations the moisture formed is taken from the hydrogen content of the fuel and free moisture of the fuel, neglecting the vapour from supply air. If H is the hydrogen fraction of the fuel, water formed from this hydrogen is 9H kg/kg fuel. The specific enthalpy of evaporation (h_{fg}) should be taken at the partial pressure of the water vapour in the products of combustion. Since the pressure is not precisely known, the value of h_{fg} may be taken from the steam table at room temperature.

For ash-fired fuel there will be some moisture present. Let M = Mass fraction of fuel moisture, then,

$$LCV = HCV - (9H + M) \times h_{fg} \text{ at room temperature.}$$

For dry fuel,

$$LCV = HCV - (9H) \times h_{fg} \text{ at room temperature}$$

The determination of calorific value of fuels is carried out in specially designed calorimeters. In the case of solid and liquid fuels, the calorific value is usually determined in a bomb calorimeter whereas that of gaseous fuels and some liquid fuels it is determined in a gas calorimeter.

All fuels for determining calorific value should be dry so that the HCV can be stated as 'on dry basis'. This is necessary because moisture content of a fuel varies. In addition, it is also stated as 'on ash-free basis' since ash content of a fuel widely varies. Let a fuel have A and M as ash and moisture fractions (kg/kg fuel) respectively and HCV be available for dry and ash-free sample.

Then HCV for ash received sample = HCV for dry and ash-free sample × (1 − M − A)

Most tables list higher calorific values for coal because lower calorific value for each value of moisture content will be different. LCV can be obtained by calculation taking into account the moisture and hydrogen content of the fuel.

If an experiment value is not available, it can be estimated for better grades of coal by **Dulong's** formula viz.

$$HCV = 34000\,C + 144000\left(H - \frac{O}{8}\right) + 9400\,S \text{ kJ/kg}$$

where C, H, O and S are mass fractions of carbon, hydrogen, oxygen and sulphur respectively in fuel. The mass fractions may be for actual sample or for dry ash-free sample and the value of HCV obtained is for corresponding sample.

The Dulong's formula is not very accurate as it assumes that all the combustible elements are in their free state. Considerable energy is required to break up the chemical structure of the elements and hence the actual calorific value realised is less than that calculated by Dulong's formula.

6.3 Types of Fuels

Fuels can be grouped under three categories viz. solid, liquid and gaseous. Examples of solid fuels are wood, charcoal, etc. whereas liquid fuels are derived from crude petroleum. Natural gas and other by-product gases come under gaseous category. Except wood all of these fuels are called fossil fuels since they are the result of fossilization (decomposition) of vegetable and organic matter. The fossil fuels are composed of hydrocarbon compounds along with sulphur, and metallic compounds. The hydrocarbon compounds and sulphur are combustibles in fuel and produce heat. The metallic compounds are non-combustibles and produce ash.

6.4 Solid Fuels

Wood:

This fuel played an important role prior to the commercial use of petroleum. Today, its use is limited to space heating in developed countries and to cooking in developing countries. Its supply is limited unless forestation is undertaken on large scale. Wood is also used in furniture and as a building material.

The fire wood contains cellulose, lignin, sulphur, tar, moisture and non-combustibles. Green wood contains 50% moisture which can be reduced to 20% on drying. Chemically, wood contains carbohydrates represented by the formula $C_x(H_2O)_y$. On an average wood has 50% carbon, 6% hydrogen and the rest is made up of oxygen, nitrogen and other components. The calorific value of dry wood is around 18000 kJ/kg.

Although wood is not an industrial fuel, it is the mother of coal in that huge forests buried under the earth transformed the carbohydrates of wood into hydrocarbons (C_xH_y) due to pressure and heat. Charcoal is also produced from wood by its incomplete combustion.

Coal:

This is the most abundant fossil fuel, obtained from fossilization (meaning stone like) of vegetation. It is estimated that at least 20 m of compacted vegetation was necessary to produce 1m thick steam of coal. This compacted vegetation, in the absence of air and under the influence of pressure and temperature is converted into coal. The various stages of conversion are as follows:

Wood → Peat → Brown coal → Lignite → Sub-bituminous coal → Bituminous coal → Anthracite.

This conversion takes 10 million to 300 million years; the peat being the youngest product and anthracite the oldest one. As the ageing process progresses, coal becomes harder, the hydrogen and oxygen content decrease, while the moisture content usually decreases and the carbon content increases.

6.4.1 Coal Analysis

The two basic coal analyses are the proximate analysis and the ultimate analysis. Both of these analyses give mass or gravimetric fractions of the components in the coal. The proximate analysis can be done in ordinary laboratories with simple apparatus and gives a general guideline for selection of fuel. It gives the mass fractions of fixed (or free) carbon (FC), volatile matter (VM), moisture (M) and ash (A) in coal.

The following is the procedure for proximate analysis of coal.

6.4.2 Proximate Analysis

Proximate analysis is helpful to find fixed carbon percentage in the coal sample.

1. A powdered coal sample (m gm) is weighed and then heated at 110°C for 20 minutes. The sample is again weighed (m_1 gm). The difference of mass ($m - m_1$) is the moisture evaporated. Hence,

$$\% \text{ moisture in coal sample } (\% M) = \frac{m - m_1}{m} \times 100$$

2. The remaining sample (m_1 mg) is then heated in a closed container at 954°C for seven minutes. The sample is again weighed (m_2 gm). In this heating, volatile matter evolves (above 600°C) and leaves the sample. Hence,

% Volatile matter in the sample,

$$\% \text{ VM} = \frac{m_1 - m_2}{m} \times 100$$

3. The remaining sample (m_2 gm) is heated at 732°C in an open crucible until it is completely burned. The residue is the ash fraction which is weighed (m_3 gm).

Hence, % ash in the sample,

$$\% \text{ A} = \frac{m_3}{m} \times 100$$

The percentage of fixed carbon is obtained by subtracting the moisture, volatile matter and ash from 100.

∴ $\quad \% \text{ FC} = 100 - (M + VM + A)$

6.4.3 Ultimate Analysis

The ultimate analysis requires elaborate experimentation. It lists the mass fractions of carbon (C), hydrogen (H), oxygen (O), sulphur (S) and nitrogen (N) in the coal.

In any coal, there are two components that show significant variation from batch to batch. These components are ash and moisture. The reported analysis are ash and moisture free sample. Once the ash and moisture fractions have been determined the other mass fractions and calorific value can be obtained by multiplying by a fraction (1 − A − M), i.e.

Mass fraction for ash received coal

= Mass fraction for ash and moisture-free sample × (1 − A − M)

It may be noted that ultimate analysis can be estimated from the experimentally determined proximate analysis.

6.4.4 Types of Coal

The following are the main types of coal:

(a) Peat: Geologically and chemically, it is the youngest product of decomposition of accumulated plant residue. It is fibrous, brown in colour and highly moist. Its average composition is 55% carbon, 5.8% hydrogen, 34% oxygen and 0.2% nitrogen. It may contain upto 10% ash and 0.2 to 0.3% sulphur. Its calorific value is around 22000 kJ/kg. It is used as a fuel after drying. It disintegrates quickly and hence difficult to transport. It can be hydraulically pressed into briquettes and then transported. It can also be used in the manufacture of fertilizers and alcohol. There are no known reserves of peat in India.

(b) Lignite: Geologically, this type is older than the peat and dark brown in colour. Its average composition is 68.5% carbon, 5.5% hydrogen, 25% oxygen and 1% nitrogen. It contains volatile matter, about 50% and its average calorific value is 27000 kJ/kg. It may contain 10% ash and 1% to 3% sulphur. It is considered as a low grade fuel and used in power stations close to the mines. It is briquetted and then transported. Considerable deposits of lignite occur in Tamil Nadu and Rajasthan in India.

(c) Bituminous Coal: It is one of the most popular, all purpose fuels. It differs from earlier varieties in that it does not contain plant residue and it is black in colour, hard and strong. The word 'bituminous' is derived from bitumen which burns with a yellow flame. The average composition of this coal is 70-80% carbon, 5% hydrogen, 5-15% oxygen, 1.5% nitrogen and 1-2% sulphur.

The calorific value of bituminous coal may vary from 25000 kJ/kg to 39000 kJ/kg depending on the ash content, which may vary from 10-60%. Bituminous coal of the approximate quality is used to manufacture coke which is an essential raw material for metallurgical processes. Coke is produced by heating coal in absence of air so that thermal decomposition of coal takes place. The process is known as carbonisation. The moisture, carbon dioxide, carbon monoxide and volatile matter get released and coal turns into a fused cellular porous structure. The gas is collected from coke ovens and is called 'coke oven gas' which is used as fuel. The type of coal used to manufacture coke is called 'coking coal', which retains its shape and size, when heated. A good quality coal is called 'free burning coal' which tends to break apart as it burns, thereby exposing unburned coal for combustion. As against this a 'caking' coal produces a fused coal mass as it burns so that much of the fixed carbon is not burnt. To improve burning of this coal, the coal bed must be mechanically agitated to break up the fused coal masses.

(d) Anthracite: This is the oldest variety in the transformation of wood into coal, it contains more than 90% carbon, 2% hydrogen and about 5% ash. It is the best type of coal. However, due to low hydrogen content, its burning is poor and it is not a good fuel. Anthracite is mainly used for metallurgical processes. India has no anthracite reserves.

Coal reserves in India are 196 billion tonnes sufficient for the next 100 years.

Waste Solid Fuels:

Sawdust, refuse wood, bagasse (dried sugar cane fibres) and other agricultural waste products represent some of the waste fuels. Such products have high water content and low heating value (around 18000 kJ/kg). They are generally burnt locally. Solid city waste is burnt in incinerators either directly or after briquetting. Combustion of such materials may be improved by burning them in conjunction with coal or oil.

Advantages of Solid Fuels:
(i) These are abundantly available and their firing methods are well established due to their traditional use.
(ii) Low price.

There are many disadvantages of solid fuels:

(i) Difficulty in burning, resulting in carbon monoxide as a product of combustion.

(ii) High ash content.

(iii) Much more handling required.

(iv) Unclean operation as fine particles are quickly carried away.

6.4.5 Liquid Fuels

These are mainly derived from crude petroleum, which is believed to have formed from enormous quantities of marine life accumulated and buried under the earth. The debris is subjected to anaerobic bacterial action and gets decomposed and finally converted by heat and pressure under reducing conditions to a black viscous product known as crude oil. The approximate composition of crude petroleum is 82-85% carbon, 10-15% hydrogen, upto 1% nitrogen, upto 1.5% sulphur and 2% oxygen. The specific gravity of crude oil varies between 0.85 to 0.96.

The main elements of petroleum are carbon and hydrogen, forming a large number of hydrocarbon compounds. These compounds can be grouped in their basic families. Any given fuel consists of mixture of these compounds and it exhibits the characteristic of that type of hydrocarbon which forms a major portion of the fuel.

The following table shows the basic families:

	Family	Chemical formula	Molecular arrangement
1.	Paraffin	C_nH_{2n+2}	Straight or branched chain.
2.	Olefin	C_nH_{2n}	Unsaturated chain with one double bond.
3.	Diolefin	C_nH_{2n-2}	Unsaturated chain with two double bonds.
4.	Naphthene	C_nH_{2n}	Saturated ring.
5.	Aromatic	C_nH_{2n-6}	Unsaturated ring with alternate double bonds.

Compressed Natural Gas (CNG) presents an alternative to petrol and diesel fuels as it can be stored under pressure and carried in the vehicle.

1. **Liquefied Petroleum Gas (LPG):** This is also called refinery gas. It is primarily composed of propane and butane. LPG is heavier than air and has a higher calorific value 95340 kJ/m^3. It is stored in cylinders at a vapour pressure of 10-26 bar at 65°C. It is used for cooking. It can also be used in I.C. engines.

2. **High Octane Petrol:** This is also called white petrol and is used in high compression ratio piston engines. Its higher calorific value is 47600 kJ/kg.
3. **Ordinary Petrol:** Any petrol (gasoline) represents lighter fractions of crude oil. Ordinary petrol is distilled between temperature range 40°C to 215°C.
4. **Kerosene:** This is used as a domestic fuel for cooking and lighting. Its range is 150-300°C. It is inferior to petrol in combustion efficiency. Its supply is limited as its yield varies from 5% to 20% of crude processed. Its HCV is 45590 kJ/kg.
5. **Aviation Turbine Fuel (ATF):** This is a mixture of kerosene and naptha. It is used as a jet engine fuel for civil and military aircraft. It is also called jet fuel (JP). Its HCV is 46000 kJ/kg.
6. **Diesel Oil:** The High Speed Diesel (HSD) oil has HCV of 44750 kJ/kg and is used in high speed diesel engines. It has higher density and viscosity than petrol. The Light Diesel Oil (LDO) has still high density and viscosity and HCV 42300 kJ/kg. LDO is used in slow speed diesel engines and in package boilers.
7. **Furnace Oil:** This is the fuel for industrial boilers and furnaces. It is highly viscous and requires preheating for ease in firing. It contains particles of free carbon and ash. Its sulphur content varies between 3.5% to 4% and its gross calorific value is 43700 kJ/kg.

Liquid fuels which may be derived from stocks other than petroleum are the following:

1. **Benzol:** This is a byproduct of high temperature coal carbonization and mainly consists of benzene (C_6H_6) and toluene (C_7H_8). It has a high antiknock quality but a lower calorific value than petrol.
2. **Alcohol:** This is somewhat similar to the derivatives of petroleum but contains oxygen atoms in the molecule. Ethanol (C_2H_5OH), produced by the fermentation of grain, has long been proposed as a fuel for I.C. engines. The antiknock quality of low octane petrol can be improved by the addition of alcohol. Methanol (CH_3OH) can be also satisfactorily burnt in I.C. engines and gas turbines. Natural gas is a common source to produce methanol. Heavy residues from oil refineries, coal and biomass are other raw materials for methanol production. Because of a high octane number (106), methanol is an excellent fuel for high compression engines. However, production cost of both types is much higher than petrol at present. Although alcohols have lower energy (HCV for methanol 23800 kJ/kg and 30160 kJ/kg for ethanol), their air-fuel ratios are lower. This results in nearly the same energy in the charge inducted and consequently engine power is not reduced. Furthermore, when blended with petrol, alcohol tends to absorb water from the atmosphere, causing separation of petrol and alcohol into two layers.
3. **Ammonia:** The possibility of burning ammonia (NH_3) in I.C. engines and gas turbines has been studied. Although test results are satisfactory, ammonia does not appear to an appropriate engine fuel. There are certain operating problems with ammonia. The engine exhaust contains a large amount of water vapour and discharge of unburned ammonia in the engine exhaust cannot be tolerated. It has HCV of 22480 kJ/kg.

4. Waste Liquid Fuels: Spent liquors from wood pulping processes, distilleries etc. represent waste fuels. They are used in industry for firing in boilers. Disposal of these products by firing rather than discharging into rivers is an essential step in reducing pollution. The calorific value of such by-products is less but their use reduces demand of petroleum fuels and helps in energy conservation.

Advantages of Liquid Fuels:
(i) Calorific value is higher.
(ii) They are clean to use.
(iii) Storage space required is smaller.
(iv) Ease in controlling the rate of firing.
(v) Economy in handling the fuel.
(vi) Ease in lightening up and shutting off operations.

Disadvantages of Liquid Fuels:
(i) These fuels do need preparation prior to firing such as filtration, pumping and preheating.
(ii) The ash, solid content and soot produce finely dispersed particles which are difficult to remove from flue gas.
(iii) The additives of I.C. engine fuels produce harmful substances.

6.4.6 Gaseous Fuels

In comparison with solid and liquid fuels, availability of gaseous fuels is less. Storage of gaseous fuels in large quantities is ordinarily not feasible either physically or economically. Other limitations in handling gaseous fuels are economical limits on transportation and energy value per unit volume. This restricts their use in vehicles and are largely used in stationary power plants located near abundant supply. Natural gas is the principal gaseous fuel and has been discussed. In addition to fuel it is also used in the manufacture of fertilizers and petrochemicals. Natural gas burns readily with a blue flame. It is an ideal fuel for power stations, industrial and residential heating as well as for I.C. engines.

Other gaseous fuels are of the following:

1. Blast Furnace Gas:

This is a by-product from blast furnace which is used to convert iron ore into pig iron. The gas results from burning of coal with insufficient air. A typical volumetric analysis of this gas may be: Carbon monoxide 26.5%, Nitrogen 57%, Carbon dioxide 12.7%, Methane 0.2%, Hydrogen 3.6% and has HCV of 300-3600 kJ/m^3. This is a low quality fuel gas and it is used in boilers and gas engines where considerable variation is observed in the composition of blast furnace gas.

2. Coke Oven Gas:

It is derived from the distillation of bituminous coal in the manufacture of coke. Mainly, it consists of volatile matter from coal. A representative sample may consist of Methane 34%, Ethane 3%, Carbon monoxide 7%, Hydrogen 47%, Carbon dioxide 2% and the rest is nitrogen and small amount of oxygen by volume. Its higher calorific value is around 11500 kJ/m^3.

3. Biogas:

Municipal waste generally contains 50 to 60% combustible material. The organic waste can be converted to gaseous fuel by hydrogenation, pyrolysis or by bioconversion. Hydrogenation is a chemical reduction process whereas pyrolysis is a destructive distillation process. The bio-conversion is a bacterial method of anaerobic digestion; the product of this process is called biogas. It is obtained by a process of fermentation in a digestor in the absence of oxygen. The biogas may be obtained from municipal sewage, cattle waste, farm waste etc. A typical composition of sewage gas is: Methane 62%, Carbon dioxide 35% and Nitrogen 3% and its calorific value is about 12000 kJ/m^3.

4. Producer Gas:

Producer gas is formed by burning low grade coal seams in the ground with insufficient air. Only enough air is added to maintain the bed at a high enough temperature to drive off some of the hydrogen and to oxidize some of the carbon to carbon monoxide. The method permits utilisation of low grade coals which cannot be economically mined. This gas is manufactured for on-site industrial use. The general composition of producer gas is: Methane 4%, Hydrogen 11%, Carbon monoxide 24%, Carbon dioxide 5% and the rest is nitrogen. Its HCV is 5000 to 5500 kJ/m^3.

5. Hydrogen:

Hydrogen is an all purpose fuel and is presently receiving serious attention. Steam reforming with hydrocarbons obtained from fossil fuels is presently the most economical method for commercial production of hydrogen. Water may be converted to hydrogen and oxygen by electrolysis, thermal dissociation at high temperatures or thermochemical splitting.

Hydrogen is a clean burning fuel and has highest heating value of all other fuels (HCV = 1,42,000 kJ/kg and 11,900 kJ/m^3). When hydrogen is burned the products of combustion consist of water, oxygen and nitrogen. In comparison with burning of petrol, the emission of nitrogen oxides is far less for engine fuelled with hydrogen. Thus, near absence of pollutants is the main advantage of using hydrogen as a fuel.

Advantages of Gaseous Fuels:

(i) Combustion of gaseous fuels permits exact control of combustion parameters such as quantity of fuel, length of flame, nature of flame (oxidizing/reducing) and fuel-gas temperature.

(ii) Ease in distribution and handling.

(iii) Absence of smoke and ash.

(iv) Cleanliness.

(v) Suitable for furnaces where product should not be contaminated or where furnace atmosphere is closely regulated.
(vi) Gaseous fuels do not require fuel preparation.

Disadvantages of gaseous fuels are difficulty in storing them in large quantities and fire hazard.

The following tables list some of the properties of fuels.

Table 6.1: Calorific Value of Fuels

Fuel	Higher Calorific Value	
	kJ/m^3	kJ/kg
Hydrogen (H_2)	11908	142097
Carbon (C) (burning to CO_2)	–	32778
Carbon (C) (burning to CO)	–	10110
Sulphur (S)	–	9257
Hydrogen sulphide (H_2S)	23720	16506
Carbon monoxide (CO)	11802	10110
Methane (CH_4)	37204	55529
Methyl alcohol (CH_3OH)	31827	23858
Ethane (C_2H_6)	65782	51920
Ethylene (C_2H_4)	58877	50322
Ethyl alcohol (C_2H_5OH)	58714	30610
Propane (C_3H_8)	95103	50399
n-butane (C_4H_{10})	123725	49589
Isobutane (C_4H_{10})	123435	49472
Benzene (C_6H_6)	137410	42293
Toluene (C_7H_8)	165021	43030
Xylene (C_8H_{10})	191769	43377
Ammonia	16166	22484
Gaseous Fuels:		
Natural gas	36000 to 42780	
Producer gas	5000 to 5525	
Blast furnace gas	3000 to 3600	
Coke oven gas	2000 to 21590	
Refinery gas	53900	
Liquid Fuels:		
Petrol (Gasoline)		47100
Kerosene		45560
Diesel oil		45330
Furnace oil		43700
Coal:		
Lignite		17000

Fuel	Higher Calorific Value	
	kJ/m³	kJ/kg
Sub-bituminous		20000 to 25000
Bituminous		26000 to 33000
Anthracite		30450

Table 6.2: Composition of Solid Fuels (% by mass)

Fuel	C	H	O	N + S	ash
Wood	42.5	6.8	49.9	0.8	–
Peat	54.7	5.8	34	1.5	4.0
Lignite	60.5	5.7	25	1.6	7.2
Bituminous coals	85-81	5-6	6-21	2	Variable
Anthracite	90.3	3.0	2.3	1.4	3.0

Table 6.3: Specific Gravity and Composition of Liquid Fuels (% by mass)

Fuel	Specific Gravity	C	H	S	O + N + Ash
Petrol	0.72-0.76	85-88.5	11.5-15.0	0.1	–
Diesel oil	0.83-0.84	86.5	13.2	0.3	–
Kerosene	0.78	85.8	14.1	0.1	–
Crude oil	0.93-0.95	85.6	11.6	2.5	0.3
Furnace oil	0.95-0.96	85.4	11.4	2.8	0.4

Table 6.4: Specific Gravity and Composition of Fuel Gases (% by volume) on an average

Fuel Gas	Specific Gravity (w.r.t. air)	CO_2	CO	H_2	N_2	CH_4	C_2H_6	C_3H_8	C_4H_{10}	Other C_xH_y
Natural Gas	0.6-0.8	–	–	–	2-14	82-95	3-7	0.5-2	0.2	–
Commercial propane	1.523	–	–	–	–	–	1.5	91	2.5	5.0
Commercial butane	1.941	–	–	–	–	0.1	0.5	7.2	88.0	4.2
Blast furnace gas	1.04	17.5	24.0	2.5	56.0	–	–	–	–	–
Producer gas	0.89	5.0	29.0	11.0	54.5	0.5	–	–	–	–
Coal gas	0.48	4.0	18.0	49.4	6.6	20	–	–	–	2

6.5 Mass and Mol Fraction

In combustion calculations, use of mass, mol and their fractions is always made. A brief review of their definitions is given below:

(a) Mass fraction: It is defined as the ratio of the mass of a constituent (m_i) of a mixture to the total mass of the mixture (m). The value of the mass fraction of a constituent (m_i/m) is less than unity and sum of mass fractions of constituents of a mixture equals unity. Mass fractions may be converted to percent values by multiplying them by 100. Hence the sum of percent values of constituents of a mixture equals one hundred.

A fuel is a mixture of carbon and hydrogen atoms chemically bonded. One can determine mass fractions of constituents of a fuel from its chemical formula. Let the fuel be benzene (C_6H_6). Chemically, it is a combination of six carbon atoms and six hydrogen atoms. By using atomic masses, we have

Mass of carbon atoms in the fuel = $6 \times 12 = 72$

and Mass of hydrogen atoms = $6 \times 1 = 6$

The total mass of the fuel molecule = $72 + 6 = 78$

Hence, mass fraction of carbon in the fuel = $\dfrac{72}{78} = 0.923$

and mass fraction of hydrogen in the fuel = $\dfrac{6}{78} = 0.077$

The sum of mass fractions equals = $0.923 + 0.077 = 1.000$

% wise, % carbon in the fuel = $0.923 \times 100 = 92.3$

and % hydrogen in the fuel = $0.077 \times 100 = 7.7$

The sum of percent masses equals = $92.3 + 7.7 = 100.00$

(b) Mol and Mol-Fraction

One mol of a substance equals the number of its molecular mass. The unit of mol depends on the system of units used. If gramme is the unit of mass, the unit of mol is gram-mol and if the unit of mass is kilogram (MKS and SI), the mol unit is kg-mol or simply k-mol. While dealing only in a single system of units, the repetitive use of k or gram may be dropped and only "mol" may be written instead of k-mol. Thus 1 k-mol of oxygen equals 32 kg, 1 k-mol of carbon equals 12 kg, 1 k-mol of benzene equals 78 kg and 1 mol of air equals 28.97 kg.

The number of mols of a substance can be obtained by dividing the given mass by its molecular mass. Thus 6 kg of carbon equals $n = \frac{6}{12} = 0.5$ mols of carbon and 6 kg of hydrogen equals $n = 6/2 = 3.0$ mols of hydrogen.

In a mixture there are number of mols of different constituents. Mol fraction is defined as *the ratio of number of mols of a constituent (n_i) to the total number of mols of the mixture ($n = \Sigma n_i$)*. As for mass fractions, sum of the mol fractions of the constituents of a mixture equals unity.

i.e. $\quad\quad\quad \Sigma m_i = 1 = \Sigma n_i$

Let a gas mixture have a pressure p, volume v and temperature T. Each constituent of the mixture occupies the entire volume independently and has the same volume as that of the mixture. All constituents of the mixture have the same volume and temperature and only their partial pressures are different. Let a constituent (i) have its partial pressure p_i. Applying the molar equation for the molar constituent and for the mixture, we have,

$$p_i \cdot v = n_i \bar{R} T \text{ (for the constituent)}$$

$$p \cdot v = n \bar{R} T \text{ (for the mixture)}$$

and

$$p \cdot v_i = n_i \bar{R} T \text{ (for the constituent)}$$

where $\quad\quad G$ = Universal gas constant

Taking the ratio of these equations, we get,

$$\frac{p_i}{p} = \frac{n_i}{n} \text{ and } \frac{v_i}{v} = \frac{n_i}{n}$$

Thus the mol fraction of a constituent equals the ratio of its partial pressure to the pressure of the mixture and volume fraction equals mol fraction.

Summarising these derivations, we have,

$$\frac{n_i}{n} = \frac{p_i}{p} = \frac{v_i}{v}$$

Thus in a mixture of ideal gases, the mol fraction, the partial pressure ratio and the volume fraction are all equal.

According to Avogadro's hypothesis, *'equal volumes of all gases at the same temperature and pressure contain the same number of molecules'*. Accordingly, the molecular volume of all gases at the same temperature and pressure is the same. Also equal volumes of gases at the same temperature and pressure will have masses proportional to their molecular masses.

Let a gas have molecular mass M. Applying the characteristic gas equation to this mass, we have,

$$pv = mRT \text{ and } p\bar{v} = MRT$$

Let the product $MR = \bar{R}$, where $\bar{R}$ is called as universal gas constant and is the same for all gases. Hence,

$$p\bar{v} = \bar{R}T \text{ for unit mol, also } p\bar{v} = \bar{R}T$$

and
$$p\bar{v} = n\bar{R}T \text{ for n moles of gas, where } v = n\bar{v}$$

At NTP conditions, $T = 273.15$ K and $p = 101.325$ kPa

($\bar{R} = 8.314$ kJ/kgmol·K),

$$\therefore \quad \text{Molar volume } \bar{v} = \frac{8.314 \times 273.15}{101.325} = 22.41 \text{ m}^3/\text{mol}$$

Thus mol may be considered as a unit of volume, and may be defined as a volume of 22.41 m³ at NTP. Obviously if a gas at NTP occupies a volume of 2.241 m³, it has number of moles n = 2.241/22.41 = 0.1.

This can be verified by using the mol equation,

$$n = \frac{p\bar{v}}{\bar{R}T} = \frac{101.325 \times 2.241}{8.314 \times 273.15} = 0.10$$

This proves that *'mols and volumes are proportional.'* Extrapolating this for a mixture of perfect gases, *'mol fractions of constituents equal volume fractions'*.

$$\therefore \quad \frac{n_i}{n} = \frac{v_i}{v}$$

This is the same result as proved earlier.

Average molecular mass of a gas mixture:

Let a gas mixture contain a number of components. For i^{th} component,

$$n_i = \frac{m_i}{M_i}$$

i.e. $m_i = n_i \times M_i$

∴ Mass of the gas mixture $= \Sigma \, n_i M_i$

and Number of mols of the gas mixture $n = \Sigma \, n_i$

∴ Average molecular mass of the gas mixture,

$$M_{av} = \frac{\text{Mass of the mixture}}{\text{Number of moles of the mixture}}$$

$$= \frac{\Sigma \, n_i M_i}{\Sigma \, n_i}$$

$$= \frac{n_1 M_1 + n_2 M_2 + n_3 M_3 + \ldots}{n_1 + n_2 + n_3 + \ldots}$$

Also characteristic gas constant for the mixture

$$R_{av} = \frac{\bar{R}}{M_{av}} \left[\frac{(kJ/kmol \cdot K)}{(kg/kmol)} = \frac{kJ}{kg \cdot K} \right]$$

If $\bar{c}_p$ and $\bar{c}_v$ are the specific heats at constant pressure and constant volume in kJ/kmol-K basis (molar specific heats).

$$\bar{c}_p - \bar{c}_v = \bar{R}$$

∴ $$\frac{\bar{c}_p}{M} - \frac{\bar{c}_v}{M} = \frac{\bar{R}}{M}$$

$$c_p - c_v = R$$

Also $\dfrac{\bar{c}_p}{\bar{c}_v} = \dfrac{c_p}{c_v} = k$, the adiabatic index.

For a gas mixture, the average values of molar specific heat can be obtained by,

$$\bar{c}_{pav} = \frac{\Sigma \, n_i \bar{c}_{pi}}{\Sigma \, n_i}$$

$$= \frac{n_1 \bar{c}_{p1} + n_2 \bar{c}_{p2} + n_3 \bar{c}_{p3}}{n_1 + n_2 + n_3 + \ldots}$$

and

$$\bar{c}_{v\,av} = \frac{\Sigma \, n_i \bar{c}_{vi}}{\Sigma \, n_i}$$

$$= \frac{n_1 \bar{c}_{v1} + n_2 \bar{c}_{v2} + n_3 \bar{c}_{v3} + \ldots}{n_1 + n_2 + n_3 + \ldots}$$

6.6 Stoichiometric Combustion Equation

In a combustion process, combustion is said to be complete when the fuel is completely oxidized, the elements of the fuel are completely converted to their oxides. e.g. carbon in fuel is burned to carbon dioxide, hydrogen to water vapour and sulphur to sulphur dioxide, alongwith production of heat. If the combustion process is incomplete, hydrogen and sulphur usually burn completely while a part of carbon burns to carbon monoxide and the rest to carbon dioxide. With incomplete combustion, heat evolved during the process is less and hence attempt is always made to effect complete combustion of fuel. The purpose of combustion chemistry is to determine the air required for combustion and finding out the products of combustion quantitatively.

The combustion reaction is written in the form of a chemical equation expressing the conservation of mass in terms of conservation of atoms.

For complete combustion of carbon in fuel, the equation is

$$C + O_2 \rightarrow CO_2 + \text{Heat energy}$$

Above equation means that one molecule of carbon reacts with one molecule of oxygen to produce one molecule of carbon dioxide along with heat. The quantity of heat may not be written every time. **The amount of oxygen given by the above equation is just enough for complete combustion of carbon. Such a balanced equation with the minimum oxygen requirements is called *stoichiometric equation*.** Since the oxygen for combustion is invariably supplied from air the stoichiometric equation is useful to determine the theoretical or minimum air required for combustion. It may be noted that the number of carbon and oxygen atoms are the same before and after the reaction.

The minimum quantity of air needed for complete combustion of fuel is known as stoichiometric air.

The above equation can be interpreted in different ways as follows:

(a) On molar basis:

1 mol of carbon + 1 mol of oxygen → 1 mol of carbon dioxide.

Note that mols before and after the reaction are different i.e. mols are not conserved during combustion reaction.

(b) On volume basis:

1 volume of carbon + 1 volume of oxygen → 1 volume of carbon dioxide.

The volume of carbon (a solid) is too small in comparison with the volume of oxygen (a gas) and hence one volume of oxygen with negligible volume of carbon produces one volume of carbon dioxide. Again note that volumes are not conserved during combustion.

(c) On mass basis:

The chemical equation on mol or volume basis can be converted to mass basis by multiplying the number of mols (or volumes) by the respective atomic mass. Hence oxidation of carbon can be written as

1×12 kg of carbon + 1×32 kg of oxygen → 1×44 kg of carbon dioxide.

Thus the total mass of reactants (12 + 32 = 44 kg) equals the mass of the products (conservation of mass theorem).

Since air is supplied for combustion, nitrogen is simultaneously supplied to the process. Although nitrogen does not contribute to the oxidation reaction, it affects the composition of products of combustion and leaves the reaction at a much higher temperature, taking away sensible heat from the reaction.

Air contains 21% of oxygen and 79% of nitrogen by volume (or mol). Hence each mol of oxygen is accompanied by 79/21 = 3.76 mols of nitrogen and 100/21 = 4.76 mols of air.

i.e. 1 mol of O_2 + 3.76 mols of N_2 → 4.76 mols of air.

Thus stoichiometric equation for complete oxidation of carbon can be written on mol basis as:

1 mol of C + 1 mol of O_2 + 3.76 mols of N_2 → 1 mol of CO_2 + 3.76 mols of N_2

On mass (or gravimetric) basis, composition of air is oxygen 23.2% and nitrogen 76.8%. Hence each kg of oxygen is accompanied by 76.8/23.2 = 3.31 kg of nitrogen and 100/23.2 = 4.31 kg of air.

i.e. 1 kg of O_2 + 3.31 kg of N_2 → 4.31 kg of air.

Hence stoichiometric equation for complete oxidation of carbon can be written on mass basis as:

12 kg of C + 32 kg of O_2 + (3.31 × 28) kg of N_2 → 44 kg of CO_2 + (3.31 × 28) kg of N_2

Usually composition of air may be taken on mass basis as O_2 = 23% and N_2 = 77%.

The mass of N_2 associated with unit mass of O_2 is therefore

$$\frac{77}{23} = 3.35 \text{ kg } N_2/\text{kg } O_2$$

and Mass of air $= \dfrac{100}{23} = 4.35 \dfrac{\text{kg}}{\text{kg } O_2}$

Note: Amount of nitrogen may not be always written in the equation.

6.7 Minimum Air Requirement on Mass Basis

Any fuel contains carbon, hydrogen, sulphur and oxygen along with nitrogen and non-combustibles called as ash. Combustion equations are written for complete oxidation of combustible elements and net oxygen requirements are determined. From this minimum air required for combustion is calculated. The minimum air is also called as theoretical or stoichiometric air.

For carbon, we have,
$$C + O_2 \rightarrow CO_2$$
$$12 \text{ kg C} + 32 \text{ kg } O_2 \rightarrow 44 \text{ kg } CO_2$$

Dividing both sides of the equation by 12, we get,
$$1 \text{ kg of C} + \frac{32}{12} \text{ kg of } O_2 \rightarrow \frac{44}{12} \text{ kg of } CO_2$$
i.e. $1 \text{ kg of C} + 2.67 \text{ kg of } O_2 \rightarrow 3.67 \text{ kg of } CO_2$ ... (6.1)

Thus the mass of oxygen required for complete combustion of carbon is 2.67 times that of carbon producing 3.67 times its mass, the mass of carbon dioxide. For oxidation of hydrogen,
$$2H_2 + O_2 \rightarrow 2H_2O$$
i.e. $2 \times 2 \text{ kg of } H_2 + 32 \text{ kg of } O_2 \rightarrow 2 \times 18 \text{ kg of water vapour.}$

Dividing both sides by 4, we get,
$$1 \text{ kg of } H_2 + 8 \text{ kg of } O_2 \rightarrow 9 \text{ kg of } H_2O$$ ... (6.2)

Hence the mass of oxygen required for complete combustion of hydrogen is 8 times that of hydrogen, producing 9 times its mass, the final product of water vapour.

For combustion of sulphur, the following equation can be written,
$$S + O_2 \rightarrow SO_2$$
$$32 \text{ kg of S} + 32 \text{ kg of } O_2 \rightarrow 64 \text{ kg of } SO_2$$

Dividing both sides by 32, we get,
$$1 \text{ kg of S} + 1 \text{ kg of } O_2 \rightarrow 2 \text{ kg of } SO_2$$ ... (6.3)

It means that the mass of oxygen required for complete combustion of sulphur equals the mass of sulphur and produces sulphur dioxide of twice its mass.

Let a fuel contain C mass fraction of carbon, H mass fraction of hydrogen, S mass fraction of sulphur and O, the mass fraction of oxygen. From equations (6.1), (6.2) and (6.3), we can write the minimum oxygen required for complete combustion = 2.67 C + 8 H + S for combustible elements. Since the fuel already contains 'O' kg mass per kg fuel, actual oxygen to be supplied externally,

i.e. Minimum O_2 = 2.67 C + 8 H + S – O kg/kg fuel

Minimum air necessary for complete combustion would be in the proportion $100/23.2 = 4.31$ per kg oxygen

$\therefore$ Minimum air $= 4.31 (2.67 C + 8 H + S - O)$ kg/kg fuel ... (6.4)

A fuel may contain some non-combustibles for which no oxygen is required and hence their account should not be taken for calculation of minimum air.

Important Note:
1. **The formula for minimum air is useful when ultimate analysis of fuel is given.** When fuel is given by a chemical formula, stoichiometric equation should be written each time for calculating minimum air.

Suppose the fuel is methane (CH_4) for which minimum air is to be calculated. Stoichiometric equation for methane is

$$\text{Fuel + Oxygen} \rightarrow \text{Products of combustion}$$
$$CH_4 + 2O_2 \rightarrow CO_2 + 2H_2O$$

i.e. $(12 + 4)$ kg of methane + (2×32) kg of oxygen
$$\rightarrow 44 \text{ kg of } CO_2 + (2 \times 18) \text{ kg of } H_2O$$

Dividing both sides by 16, we have

1 kg of CH_4 + 4 kg of oxygen $\rightarrow$ 2.75 kg of CO_2 + 2.25 kg of H_2O

$\therefore$ Minimum air required per kg methane

$= 4.31 \times$ Minimum oxygen required/kg methane

$= 4.31 \times 4$

$= 17.24$ kg

The complete oxidation reaction discussed above takes place under ideal conditions. If a fuel particle finds insufficient air, it will partly burn to carbon monoxide which may or may not oxidize to carbon dioxide depending on the availability of oxygen in the latter part of combustion process. In case of premixed combustible mixture, hydroxyls get converted to aldehydes first which then completely oxidize. If for some reason, oxygen is not available for their burning, aldehydes become a part of combustion products. Also at temperatures above 1200°C, some of the molecules dissociate. Some such reactions are the following:

$O_2 \rightarrow 2O$, $N_2 \rightarrow 2N$ and $2CO_2 \rightarrow 2CO + O_2$

The dissociated elements are very active and they may again associate at low temperatures. But if the conditions do not permit they may form other products such as nitrogen oxides.

The non-ideal conditions described for the combustion process lead to reduced heat of combustion as well as emission of products of incomplete combustion to the atmosphere. These products are harmful to the environment and are called as atmospheric pollutants.

6.8 Actual Air

Combustion of fuel seldom completes with stoichiometric air since all the conditions mentioned are not available for each particle of fuel. Air may not be evenly distributed with respect to fuel for which reason actual air supplied for combustion should exceed the minimum air. The difference in the actual air supplied and the minimum air calculated is called as 'excess air'. All the values of air quantity are generally taken in kg air/kg fuel. The ratio of excess air to the minimum air when stated on percent basis is called as percent excess air. The ratio of actual air to the minimum air is called as excess air coefficient (α) or dilution coefficient. The above mentioned definitions may be summarised as follows:

$$\text{Excess air, } A_{excess} = (\text{Actual air supplied} - \text{Minimum air required})$$

$$= (A_{act} - A_{min}) \frac{kg}{kg \text{ fuel}}$$

$$\% \text{ Excess air} = \frac{\text{Excess air}}{\text{Minimum air}} \times 100$$

$$= \left(\frac{\text{Actual air} - \text{Minimum air}}{\text{Minimum air}}\right) \times 100$$

$$= \left(\frac{A_{act}}{A_{min}} - 1\right) \times 100$$

$$= (\alpha - 1) \times 100$$

where Excess air coefficient (α) = $\dfrac{\text{Actual air (kg/kg fuel)}}{\text{Minimum air (kg/kg fuel)}}$

If say, 20% excess air is supplied, actual air is 120% of minimum air or 1.2 times the minimum air and α = 1.2. The mass of excess air on unit basis is

$k = 1.2 - 1 = 0.2$ ($\alpha - 1$) × Minimum air = $(k) \times$ Min air.

6.9 Air : Fuel Ratio

This is a parameter which gives the relative proportion of air and fuel on mass basis. It is defined as the ratio of mass of air to the mass of fuel for combustion i.e.

$$\text{Air to fuel ratio (A : F)} = \frac{\text{Mass of air (kg)}}{\text{Mass of fuel (kg)}} = \frac{m_a}{m_f} = \frac{A}{m_f}$$

The ratio may be taken either for minimum air (i.e. on stoichiometric basis) or for actual air and accordingly, we may write,

$$\text{Minimum air to fuel ratio, (A : F)}_{min} = \frac{\text{Mass of minimum air (kg)}}{\text{Mass of fuel (kg)}} = \frac{A_{min}}{m_f}$$

$$\text{Actual air to fuel ratio, (A : F)}_{act} = \frac{\text{Mass of actual air (kg)}}{\text{Mass of fuel (kg)}} = \frac{m_f}{A}$$

The reciprocal of air to fuel ratio is called fuel to air ratio (F: A) i.e.,

$$\text{(F : A) ratio} = \frac{1}{(A:F)} = \frac{\text{Mass of fuel (kg)}}{\text{Mass of air (kg)}} = \frac{m_f}{m_a} = \frac{m_f}{A}$$

6.10 Products of Combustion

6.10.1 Products of Combustion with Stoichiometric Air

When stoichiometric air is supplied to burn a fuel with ideal conditions in the combustion chamber, the products of combustion consist of CO_2, H_2O, SO_2 and N_2. The products consisting of water vapour are called wet products (WP) while the products without water vapour are called dry products (DP). Sulphur dioxide and water vapour generally combine to form sulphurous and sulphuric acid and settle out of the gas. Hence it is reasonable to delete SO_2 and H_2O in dry product analysis.

From the stoichiometric equations, one can find out mols (i.e. volumes) or mass of a constituent. By calculating the total number of mols of the products and dividing mols of the constituent by mols of the products, the molar (or volumetric) analysis of dry or wet products can be obtained. Likewise calculating the mass of each constituent of the gas and of the products, mass analysis of dry or wet products can be obtained.

Let a fuel have C, H and S as the mass fractions of carbon, hydrogen and sulphur. By supplying stoichiometric air (A_{min}) for complete combustion, there are $0.23 \times (A_{min})$ kg of oxygen and $0.77 (A_{min})$ kg of nitrogen entering the process of combustion. This nitrogen appears as a product of combustion while oxygen combines with combustible elements. Thus the products of combustion consist of CO_2, H_2O, SO_2 and N_2.

Calculation of minimum air and analysis of products on mass basis can be conveniently done in a tabular form as shown below:

Combustion with stoichiometric air on kg/kg fuel basis:

Constituent (a)	Mass fraction (b)	Min. O_2 (c)	Products (d)	Mass of product (e)	% Product (P) by mass $= \dfrac{e}{\Sigma e} \times 100$
Carbon	C	2.67C =	CO_2	3.67C = ...	......
Hydrogen	H	8H =	H_2O	9H = ...	......
Sulphur	S	1 × S =	SO_2	2S = ...	......
Min. air (A_{min})	$N_2 = 0.77 \times A_{min}$	= ...	$N_2 = 0.77 \times A_{min}$	$0.77 \times A_{min}$	......
Total		Σ Min. O_2 = ...		Σe =	ΣP = 100

Note: Here Σ p is actually Σ wp as it contains water vapour.

For getting the gravimetric analysis of dry products (DP) of combustion, only CO_2 and N_2 will be the constituents. Thus the following table can be prepared:

Constituent (a)	Mass fraction (b)	Min. O_2 (c)	Dry products (d)	Mass of dry products (e)	% DP by mass $= \dfrac{e}{\Sigma e} \times 100$
Carbon	C	2.67C = ...	CO_2	3.67C = ...	......
Hydrogen	H	8H =	–	–	
Sulphur	S	S = ...	–	–	
Min. air (A_{min}) = 4.35 × Min. O_2	$N_2 = 0.77 \times A_{min}$		N_2	$0.77 \times (A_{min})$	......
Total				$\Sigma e =$	% Σ DP = 100

6.10.2 Products of Combustion with Excess Air

Amount of oxygen supplied for combustion is totally utilized for oxidation with stoichiometric air. And hence no oxygen appears in the products. When excess air is supplied, oxygen from excess air is not completely utilized for combustion and appears in the products along with nitrogen from excess air. The following table gives the analysis in this case.

Combustion with excess air for wet products (kg/kg fuel):

Constituent (a)	Mass fraction (b)	Min. O_2 (c)	Dry products (d)	Mass of dry products (e)	% WP by mass $= \dfrac{e}{\Sigma e} \times 100$
Carbon	C	2.67 C = ...	CO_2	3.67C = ...	......
Hydrogen	H	8H = ...	H_2O	9H = ...	......
Sulphur	S	S = ...	SO_2	2S = ...	......
		Σ Min. O_2 =		$\Sigma e =$	
			N_2	0.77 (A_{min} + A_{excess}) = ...	......
			O_2	$0.23 \times A_{excess}$	......
			Total	Σ WP	% Σ WP = 100

In the same way, analysis of dry products consisting of CO_2, N_2 and O_2 can be tabulated.

6.10.3 Volumetric Analysis of Products

Since the products of combustion are a mixture of gases, it is appropriate to state composition of products by volume. The combustion equation when written on mol basis, the products are available on volume base as well. Let a hydrocarbon fuel be C_xH_y which is burnt with excess air ($k \times A_{min}$). The following combustion equation can be written for one mol of fuel.

$$\underset{\text{Fuel}}{C_xH_y} + \underset{\text{Min. air}}{(zO_2 + 3.76zN_2)} + \underset{\text{Excess air}}{(kzO_2 + 3.76\,kzN_2)}$$
$$\underset{\text{products}}{}$$

$$\rightarrow xCO_2 + \frac{y}{2} H_2O + kzO_2 + 3.76\,(z + kz)\,N_2$$

Since volumes are proportional to mols, the analysis of products by volume can be done by using the mols of products.

Total number of mols (or volume) of wet products

$$\Sigma\,WP = x + \frac{y}{2} + kz + 3.76\,(z + kz)$$

∴ % of a constituent by volume = $\dfrac{\text{Mols of constituent in products}}{\Sigma\,WP} \times 100$

i.e. % CO_2 by volume in the wet products = $\dfrac{x}{\Sigma\,WP} \times 100$

% H_2O by volume in the wet products = $\dfrac{(y/2)}{\Sigma\,WP} \times 100$

% O_2 by volume in the wet products = $\dfrac{kz}{\Sigma\,WP} \times 100$

and % N_2 by volume in the wet products = $\dfrac{3.76\,(z + kz)}{\Sigma\,WP} \times 100$

For analysis of dry products,

Number of mols (or volume) of dry products

$$= \text{Mols of } CO_2 + \text{Mols of } O_2 + \text{Mols of } N_2$$

i.e. $\Sigma\,DP = x + kz + 3.76\,(z + kz)$

∴ % CO_2 by volume in the dry products = $\dfrac{x}{\Sigma\,DP} \times 100$

% O_2 by volume in the dry products = $\dfrac{kz}{\Sigma\,DP} \times 100$

% N_2 by volume in the dry products = $\dfrac{3.76\,(z + kz)}{\Sigma\,DP} \times 100$

Conversion from Mass to Volume:

When product analysis is made on mass basis, we have to convert the mass fractions of products into proportional volumes. This can be done by dividing the mass of product by their molecular mass to obtain proportional or relative mol figures.

The following table can be prepared for this conversion.

Conversion table from mass to volume

Product constituent (a)	% by mass (b)	Molecular mass (c)	Proportional volume (PV) (d) = b/c	% by volume (e) = $\dfrac{d}{\Sigma d}$
(1) CO_2	p	44	p_1 = p/44	......
(2) O_2	q	32	q_1 = q/44	......
(3) N_2	r	28	r_1 = r/28	......
Total			Σd =	100.00

In place of proportional volume, one may use the term Relative Volume (RV), as the molecular masses are relative to one another.

Conversion from Volume to Mass Basis:

When gaseous fuels are burnt, relative volumes of products are directly obtained from mol fractions of constituents. Also flue gas analysis is made on volumetric basis. To convert volumes to masses, we multiply the volumes by molecular masses to obtain relative masses (RM). The ratio of relative mass of the constituent to the total mass of the mixture gives the volume fraction of the constituent. The following table is useful to obtain this conversion.

Conversion table from volume to mass

Constituent (a)	Volume of the constituent (b)	Molecular mass (c)	Relative mass (RM) d = b × c	% by volume $e = \dfrac{d}{\Sigma d}$
(1) CO_2	p_1	44	p = $p_1 \times 44$	......
(2) O_2	q_1	32	q = $q_1 \times 44$	......
(3) N_2	r_1	28	r = $r_1 \times 28$	......
Total			$\Sigma RM = \Sigma d$	100.00

Alternatively, in a mixture of gases, the mass fraction of a constituent (i) can be obtained from the equation,

$$\text{Mass fraction of } i^{th} \text{ component} = \frac{M_i \times V_i}{\Sigma M_i \cdot V_i}$$

$$= \frac{M_i V_i}{M_1 V_1 + M_2 V_2 + M_3 V_3 + \ldots}$$

where M_i and V_i are molecular mass and volume of ith component of the mixture.

6.11 Incomplete Combustion

Although incomplete combustion of fuel is undesirable and uneconomical for a power plant, it also leads to pollution. When carbon oxidizes to carbon dioxide, it releases 33900 kJ of heat per kg while carbon burning to carbon monoxide heat released is only 10000 kJ/kg. Thus nearly 70% heat is wasted due to incomplete combustion and also carbon monoxide produced is irritant and poisonous. Incompleteness of combustion is due to non-uniform relative distribution of fuel and air and non-ideal conditions in the combustion chamber. Even with sufficient excess air, combustion may not be complete due to these reasons and high amount of excess air does not solve the problem. Air less than the stoichiometric quantity definitely results in incomplete combustion.

The composition of the products of combustion due to incompleteness of combustion depends on the proportion of air. If deficient air is supplied to a hydrocarbon fuel, the products would consist of CO_2, CO, H_2O and N_2. In case of excess air and incomplete combustion, the products would consist of CO_2, CO, H_2O, O_2 and N_2. As stated earlier, hydrogen and sulphur having high reactivity with oxygen would always oxidise completely and carbon would partly burn to CO and partly to CO_2. Thus a balance of oxygen supplied and oxygen utilized as well as that of carbon is necessary to solve the problem of incomplete combustion.

6.12 Effect of Air : Fuel Ratio on Products of Combustion

With stoichiometric air: fuel ratio, all the carbon burns to carbon dioxide and it results in the maximum percentage of CO_2 in flue gases under ideal conditions. Neither CO nor O_2 are then be present in the flue gas. If excess air is supplied, excess oxygen appears as a product of flue gases; higher the amount of excess air, higher is the O_2 content of flue gas. This results in lowering the content of CO_2. Thus with A : F ratios greater than stoichiometric, there is an increase in O_2 content and a reduction of CO_2 content of flue gas.

On the contrary when air supplied is less than the stoichiometric proportion, incomplete combustion of part of carbon produces carbon monoxide. There is no oxygen in flue gases then. As proportion of air decreases, CO part of flue gases increases, due to which, CO_2 decreases.

The effect of A : F ratio variation on the content of flue gases is shown by the graph of Fig. 6.1.

The use of this graph can be made to estimate how best are the conditions in the combustion chamber. For a given fuel, the maximum CO_2 content of flue gas under ideal conditions of working is known. If CO_2 content of flue gases falls, it can be inferred that conditions have departed from ideal. Depending on whether O_2 or CO percent has increased in flue gas, one can predict the actual A : F ratio used for combustion.

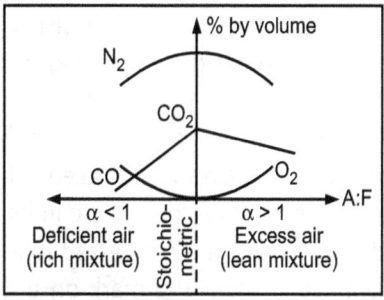

Fig. 6.1: Deficient air and excess air

6.13 Orsat Apparatus

Analysis of flue gases is required to assess how best the combustion of fuel is achieved. Orsat apparatus is a simple and handy apparatus to determine CO_2, O_2, CO and N_2 in flue gas by volume. Since the flue gas sample is collected over water i.e. at low temperature, the constituents of only dry flue gas are obtained; water vapour and SO_2 are absorbed in water.

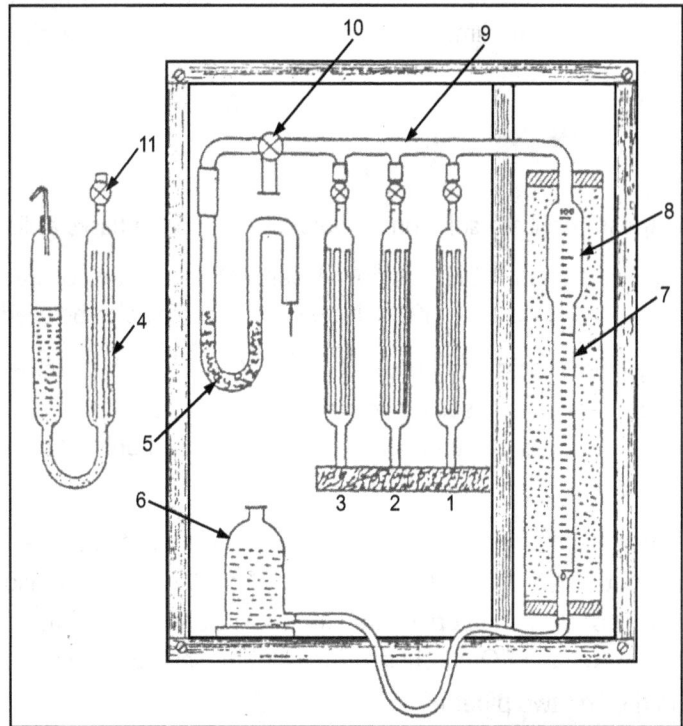

1.	Pipette 1 – Caustic potash solution.	7.	Water jacket
2.	Pipette 2 – Alkaline pyrogallic solution.	8.	Eudiometer (Burette)
3.	Pipette 3 – Cuprous chloride solution.	9.	Glass header cock
4.	Pipettes (side view)	10.	Three way cock
5.	Filter cum drier	11.	Stop cock
6.	Aspirator bottle		

Fig. 6.2: Orsat apparatus

Essentially the apparatus consists of three pipettes or flasks containing chemical solutions to absorb different gases (See Fig. 6.2). The pipettes are made of two flasks joined together at the bottom by a short U-tube as shown in the end view. The front pipette contains small diameter glass tubes to increase the area of absorbing solution while the back side pipette serves to contain the displaced solution when gas is admitted in the front pipette. The back pipette has a bent glass tube in its stopper for maintaining atmospheric pressure in it. All of the front flasks are connected to a common header by means of a stop cock on the neck of connecting tube. The mark on the necks serves to maintain a constant level of solution in the pipette. The header is connected on one side to inlet connection for flue gas sample via a three way cock while to an eudiometer on the other side. The eudiometer tube is a burette, calibrated 0-100 cc, and connected at the bottom to an aspirator bottle by means of a rubber tube. The aspirator bottle is open to atmosphere and contains water with methyl red. Taking the aspirator bottle up, increases the level of water in the eudiometer and pushes the gas out of it while lowering the aspirator, decreases the level of water in the eudiometer and helps to induct gas sample in it. A water jacket around the eudiometer helps to maintain a constant temperature of gas sample. The whole apparatus is enclosed within a wooden frame with removable doors on either side. The size of the case is approximately 22.5 cm × 60 cm.

Procedure:

Before using the apparatus, fresh solutions should be filled in the flasks as listed below.

Pipette No. 1: Caustic potash (KOH) solution; 1 part KOH to 2 parts of water by mass. This solution absorbs only CO_2. In place of KOM, NaOH solution may also be used.

Pipette No. 2: Pyrogallic acid solution; one part of pyrogallol to three parts of water together with 24 parts of caustic soda or caustic potash in 16 parts of water by mass. This solution absorbs O_2 as well as CO_2 and hence it should be used only after absorption of CO_2 in pipette No. 1.

Pipette No. 3: Cuprous chloride solution in hydrochloric acid. It is prepared by dissolving copper oxide in about 20 times its mass of strong hydrochloric acid and allowing it to stand in a corked vessel containing copper-wire, until the solution becomes colourless. This solution absorbs CO_2, O_2 and CO and hence the solution should be used only after passing the gas sample in the first two pipettes.

The level of solutions should be brought to a mark on the neck of the pipettes just below the one way tap (by lowering the aspirator bottle). The three way cock allows the glass header to be connected either to gas sample or to atmosphere or to closed position. The aspirator bottle is now raised to bring water in the burette to 100 cc mark. The three way cock is now connected to gas sample and aspirator bottle slowly lowered to induct flue gas.

The gas is drawn through the filter in U-tube which prevents soot, ash and carbon particles to enter the glass header. The U-tube may also contain a water absorbing agent like silica jel so that only dry flue gas sample of about 100 cc of gas is initially drawn and expelled to atmosphere by turning the three way cock to atmospheric side.

This is done two to three times so that no residual air remains in the glass header.

Now the apparatus is ready for testing a fresh gas sample. The aspirator is brought closer to eudiometer and water level in both brought to 100 cc mark. This ensures that pressure of gas in the burette is atmospheric. A fresh gas sample is now drawn in the burette by slowly lowering the aspirator bottle until water level falls to '0' cc mark. The level of water in the aspirator and that in the burette is made equal to ensure constancy of pressure in the burette each time volume is measured. The three way cock is now closed and stop cock on first pipette opened. The aspirator is slowly raised to push the gas sample into the pipette. As the gas comes in the front side pipette, the absorbing solution gets displaced in the back side pipette. The glass tubes retain some solution which reacts with the gas sample to absorb CO_2 from the gas. The aspirator is now slowly lowered to bring the gas back to the burette. This action of raising and lowering the aspirator is repeated at least five times to ensure that all CO_2 content of the gas is absorbed by the solution. The aspirator is finally brought down so that the solution in the first pipette rises to the mark on the neck. The stop cock is immediately closed as otherwise the solution may jump in the glass header. The volume of gas sample is now measured by bringing the level of water in the burette and the aspirator equal. The volume of gas is read on the scale of the burette. Let this reading be 10 cc. It means that 10 cc of gas has been absorbed by the solution in pipette No. 1 or 10 cc of CO_2 was originally contained in the gas sample of 100 cc. Thus the original dry gas sample contained 10% of CO_2 by volume.

To ensure complete absorption of CO_2, the procedure is again repeated in the first pipette by passing the gas sample two to three times in the same solution. The volume of the remaining gas is again measured. If this reading is the same as the last reading, all of the CO_2 in the sample has been absorbed. If the new reading is say 11 cc, the procedure should be repeated again until a constancy of the reading is obtained. When the third trial again gives 11 cc reading, the % volume of CO_2 is 11% and not 10%.

For finding out oxygen content of the gas sample, stop cock on the second pipette is opened and procedure repeated until a repeatable constant reading of gas sample is observed. Let the second reading be 14 cc, which means 14 – 10 = 4 cc of O_2 was contained in the original sample of 100 cc. Thus the flue gas sample contained 4% of O_2 by volume on dry basis.

Finally the gas is passed through the third pipette to determine the volume of CO in the flue gas. Let the third reading be 18 cc which means that the gas sample of 100 cc contained

18 – 14 = 4 cc of CO. In other words, the original gas sample contained 4% of CO by volume on dry basis.

Since any SO_2 will react with water, the gas sample left is only N_2. Hence, the percentage of N_2 in the sample is 100 – 18 = 82 by volume on dry basis. The trace gases, if any, cannot be determined by this apparatus.

In some units, a fourth pipette may be available to determine unsaturated hydrocarbons in the flue gas. A suitable reagent such as bromine water can be used for this determination.

Although Orsat apparatus is handy, easy to use and portable, it is not very accurate. Also trace gases in flue gas cannot be determined.

Gas chromatography is used for very accurate determination of flue gas constituents. But it is a sophisticated and costly equipment.

Now-a-days flue gas analysis is done with the help of a solid state gas analyser. It consists of a probe which is inserted to draw flue gas sample. It shows the O_2 and CO_2 content of the gas directly on liquid crystal display. By taking additional readings of temperature of air supplied and flue gas temperature, combustion efficiency and percent excess air supplied are also determined by the analyser.

Using flue gas analysis, air-fuel ratio actually used for combustion can be determined.

Determination of actual air to fuel ratio:

Let the percent volumetric figures of dry products as determined by Orsat apparatus be CO_2, CO and N_2 respectively for carbon dioxide, carbon monoxide and nitrogen. Let C be percent carbon by mass in the fuel. It is assumed that all carbon in flue gas is derived only from fuel and all nitrogen in flue gas comes only from air supplied. Hence ratio of nitrogen to carbon in flue gas equals the ratio of nitrogen in air supplied to carbon in the fuel burnt.

Mass of nitrogen in flue gas = Volume of N_2 in flue gas × Molecular mass of N_2

$$= N_2 \times 28$$

Similarly,

Mass of carbon monoxide in flue gas = $CO \times 28$, and

Mass of carbon dioxide in flue gas = $CO_2 \times 44$

The proportion of carbon in CO = $\dfrac{12}{28}$ by mass and

proportion of carbon in CO_2 = $\dfrac{12}{44}$ by mass.

$\therefore$ Mass of carbon in flue gas = $\dfrac{12}{28} \times (CO \times 28) + \dfrac{12}{44} \times (CO_2 \times 44)$

$$= 12 \, (CO + CO_2)$$

Hence,

$$\frac{\text{Mass of nitrogen in flue gas}}{\text{Mass of carbon in flue gas}} = \frac{N_2 \times 28}{12(CO + CO_2)} \text{ (from above)}$$

This ratio equals the ratio $\dfrac{\text{Mass of nitrogen from air}}{\text{Mass of carbon in the fuel}}$ both being taken per kg fuel.

$$\therefore \quad \frac{N_2 \times 28}{12(CO + CO_2)} = \frac{\text{Nitrogen supplied per kg fuel}}{C/100}$$

$$\therefore \text{ Nitrogen supplied per kg fuel} = \frac{N_2 \times 28}{12(CO + CO_2)} \times \frac{C}{100}$$

$$\therefore \text{ Actual air supplied per kg fuel} = \left(\begin{array}{c}\text{Nitrogen supplied}\\ \text{per kg fuel}\end{array}\right) \times \frac{100}{77}$$

$$= \left[\frac{N_2 \times 28}{12(CO + CO_2)} \times \frac{C}{100}\right] \times \frac{100}{77}$$

$$= \frac{N_2 \times C}{\frac{12 \times 77}{28}(CO + CO_2)}$$

$$\therefore \quad (A:F)_{actual} = \frac{N_2 \times C}{33(CO + CO_2)} \text{ kg/kg fuel}$$

This formula is very useful to determine actual air: fuel ratio from flue gas analysis.

If fuel contains any nitrogen (N_f kg/kg fuel), then corresponding air mass $\left(= \dfrac{N_f}{0.77}\right)$ should be subtracted from this quantity.

i.e.

$$A:F_{actual} = \frac{N_2 \times C}{33(CO + CO_2)} - \frac{N_f}{0.77} \text{ kg/kg fuel}$$

6.14 Determination of Carbon from Fuel Burning to CO or CO_2 from Orsat Analysis

Let CO and CO_2 be volumes of carbon monoxide and carbon dioxide in dry flue gas.

$$\text{Mass of carbon in CO} = \frac{12}{28} \times \text{Mass of CO} = \frac{12}{28} \times (28 \times CO) = 12(CO)$$

$$\text{Similarly, mass of carbon in } CO_2 = \frac{12}{44} \times \text{Mass of } CO_2$$

$$= \frac{12}{44} \times (44 \times CO_2) = 12(CO_2)$$

∴ Total mass of carbon in flue gas = 12 (CO + CO_2)

∴ Fraction of carbon from fuel burning to CO

$$= \frac{12 \,(CO)}{12\,(CO + CO_2)} = \frac{CO}{CO + CO_2}$$

and fraction of carbon from fuel burning to CO_2

$$= \frac{12\, CO_2}{12\,(CO + CO_2)} = \frac{CO_2}{CO + CO_2}$$

If C part of carbon from fuel actually burns, then part of carbon burning to CO is given by,

$$C_1 = \frac{CO}{CO + CO_2} \times C \text{ kg/kg fuel, and}$$

Part of carbon burning to CO_2 is given by,

$$C_2 = \frac{CO_2}{CO + CO_2} \times C \text{ kg/kg fuel}$$

Dry flue gas formed per kg fuel:

Mass of dry flue gas formed can be calculated by the ratio,

$$\frac{\text{kg dry flue gas formed}}{\text{Mass of carbon/kg fuel}} = \frac{\text{Mass of carbon/kg fuel}}{\text{Mass of carbon/kg dry flue gas}}$$

Let CO, CO_2, O_2 and N_2 be volumetric compositions of dry flue gas.

∴ Mass of dry flue gas = (28 CO + 44 CO_2 + 32 O_2 + 28 N_2) kg

Carbon in dry flue gas = 12 (CO + CO_2) kg

$$\text{Mass of carbon/kg dry flue gas} = \frac{12\,(CO + CO_2)}{(28\, CO + 44\, CO_2 + 32\, O_2 + 28\, N_2)}$$

If C is mass of carbon per kg fuel, then, mass of dry flue gas formed per kg fuel

$$= \frac{C}{\frac{12\,(CO + CO_2)}{[28\, CO + 44\, CO_2 + 32\, O_2 + 28\, N_2]}}$$

$$= \frac{C\,[28\, CO + 44\, CO_2 + 32\, O_2 + 28\, N_2]}{12\,(CO + CO_2)}$$

6.15 Determination of Calorific Value of Fuels

6.15.1 Bomb Calorimeter

Introduction:
This is one of the best methods for determining calorific value of solid and liquid fuels. The method has been recommended in many standards. The fuel is burnt in a strong steel chamber, known as the bomb which is immersed in a known mass of water. The fuel is placed in a crucible inside the bomb which is filled with oxygen under a pressure of 25-30 atmospheres. It is then electrically ignited by a platinum or magnesium wire. The heat liberated is measured by the rise in temperature of water surrounding the bomb from which calorific value is obtained. The following advantages are claimed for the procedure:

(1) Due to high oxygen content, combustion is complete.
(2) As the burning takes place in a sealed chamber, the products of combustion cannot fail to give up all their heat.
(3) The added substances in the bomb do not have any action on the constituents of the fuel and
(4) The general arrangement employed favours the accurate computation of the temperature loss correction.

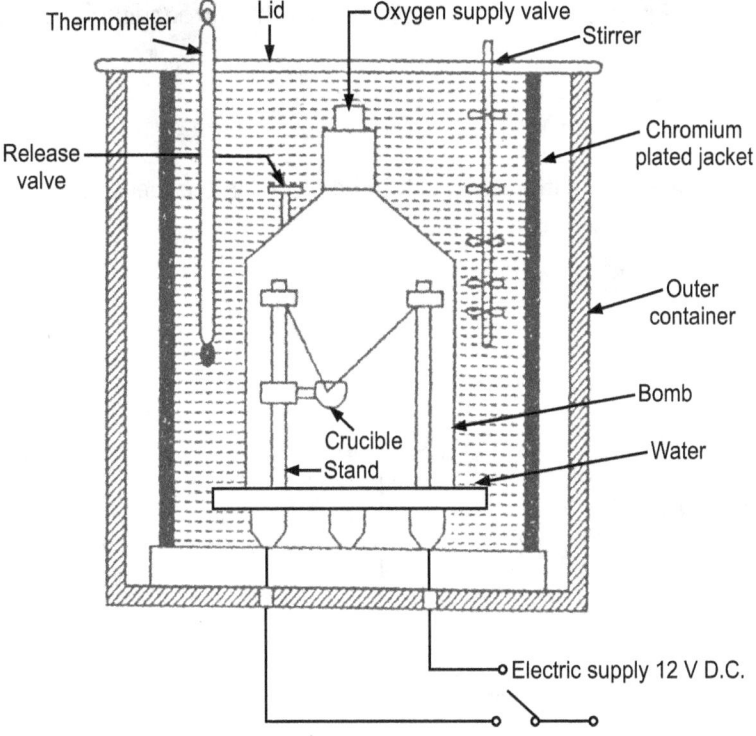

Fig. 6.3: Bomb calorimeter

Apparatus:

It consists of a strong stainless steel vessel, called the bomb, placed in a calorimeter vessel (chromium plated jacket) which contains water. A stirrer is provided to agitate water in the calorimeter to maintain uniform temperature of water. A thermometer having accuracy not less than 0.01°C is inserted into the water around the bomb. A crucible supported on the stand is kept inside the bomb. Electrical lead wires from the supply are also brought to the crucible so as to ignite the fuel sample placed in the crucible. For filling the bomb with pure oxygen, a stand for bomb, copper tubing, a pressure gauge on the line and control valve on the oxygen cylinder are necessary.

Experimental Procedure:

(1) A sample of the fuel (usually 1 gm) is placed in the crucible.
(2) Oxygen gas is admitted through the oxygen supply valve till the pressure inside the bomb raises 25 to 30 bar.
(3) The bomb is then completely submerged in the water of chromium plated jacket space.
(4) This vessel is placed inside the insulated outside container.
(5) The fuel is ignited to burn completely, at the same time stirring of water is carried out continuously till it reaches the uniform steady temperature.
(6) Heat released during combustion is absorbed by the surrounding water and apparatus itself.
(7) The rise of temperature of water is noted.

To ignite the fuel a very minute fuse wire is to be placed in the fuel to which electric supply is given.

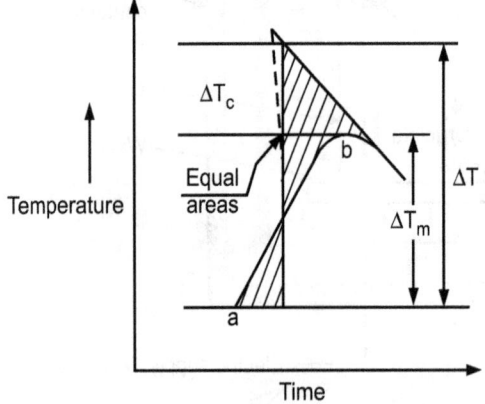

a - Firing
b - Maximum temperature
ΔT_c - Cooling correction
ΔT_m - Measured temperature rise

Fig. 6.4: Graph for cooling correction

With the help of thermometer, temperatures are noted at regular intervals for 10 minutes till the maximum temperature is reached. After this, the temperature starts falling slowly. When the temperature fall shows a steady rate, the temperature readings are taken at regular intervals for an additional five minutes. The cooling correction can be found by plotting time versus temperature graph as shown in Fig. 6.4.

Further, the detailed procedure to find cooling correction is not explained here.

The cooling correction should be added to the measured temperature rise. Also following observations are noted.

(1) m_f = Mass of fuel burnt in kg.

(2) m_w = Mass of water in calorimeter, kg.

(3) m_c = Water equivalent of calorimeter, kg.

(4) T_1 = Initial temperature of water and apparatus in °C.

(5) T_2 = Final temperature of water and apparatus in °C.

Apply heat balance equation.

Neglecting the mass of fuse wire,

Heat liberated by fuel due to its combustion

$$= \text{Heat absorbed by water and apparatus}$$

$$\therefore \quad m_f \times HCV = (m_w + m_c) \cdot (T_2 - T_1) \cdot C_p$$

$$= (m_w + m_c) \times \theta \times C_p$$

where θ = Corrected temperature rise

C_p = specific heat, kJ/kg·K

$$\therefore \quad HCV = \frac{(m_w + m_c) \cdot \theta}{m_f} \quad \ldots (6.5)$$

This equation gives HCV of the fuel because steam, if any formed, is condensed and therefore, heat is recovered from it.

Note: Heat is released by the fuel due to its combustion. This heat is absorbed by the water, at the same time water is loosing heat to the surroundings.

Thus, the actual temperature rise 'ΔT' is less than the theoretical value. Therefore, actual temperature is to be corrected by a factor, known as cooling correction.

∴ Theoretical or corrected temperature rise (θ) is

$$\theta = \Delta T_m + \text{Cooling correction } \Delta T_c$$

SOLVED PROBLEMS

Problem 6.1: A bomb calorimeter was used to determine the calorific value of a coal sample and the following readings were recorded.

Mass of coal sample	= 1.01 gm
Mass of water	= 2.5 kg
Water equivalent of apparatus	= 744 gm
Temperature rise of water	= 2.59°C
Temperature correction for cooling	= + 0.016°C

Determine the calorific value of sample in kJ/kg. Take c_p for water = 4.186 kJ/kg·K.

Solution:

Given: $m_f = 1.01 \times 10^{-3}$ kg, $m_w = 2.5$ kg, $m_c = 0.744$ kg, $\Delta T = 2.59°C$

Cooling correction = + 0.016°C

$\therefore \quad \begin{bmatrix} \text{Heat released due to} \\ \text{combustion of fuel} \end{bmatrix} = \begin{bmatrix} \text{Heat absorbed by} \\ \text{water and apparatus} \end{bmatrix}$

$\therefore \quad m_f \times HCV = (m_w + m_c) \times c_p \times \theta$

$\therefore \quad 1.01 \times 10^{-3} \times HCV = (2.5 + 0.744) \times 4.186 \times (2.59 + 0.016)$

$\therefore \quad HCV = \mathbf{35{,}044 \text{ kJ/kg}}$

Problem 6.2 (Considering mass of fuse wire): The following observations were made during the test for finding the HCV and LCV of a solid fuel on a bomb calorimeter:

Mass of fuel in crucible	= 0.78 gm
Mass of fuse wire	= 0.02 gm
C. V. of fuse wire	= 6688 kJ/kg
Mass of water in calorimeter	= 1.88 kg
Water equivalent of calorimeter	= 0.37 kg
Observed temperature rise	= 2.98°C
Cooling correction	= 0.02°C

Assume the fuel contains 90% carbon and 4% hydrogen, the rest being ash.

Solution:

Given: $m_f = 0.78$ gm, m_{fw} = Mass of fuse wire = 0.02 gm,

$m_w = 1.88$ kg, $\quad m_c = 0.37$ kg

$\Delta T = 2.98°C \quad \theta = 2.98 + 0.02 = 3°C$

Energy equation is

$\begin{bmatrix} \text{Heat developed} \\ \text{by the combustion} \\ \text{of fuel} \end{bmatrix} + \begin{bmatrix} \text{Heat released} \\ \text{by the combustion} \\ \text{of fuse wire} \end{bmatrix} = \begin{bmatrix} \text{Heat carried by} \\ \text{the water} \\ \text{and apparatus} \end{bmatrix}$

$$\therefore\ m_f \times HCV + m_{fw} \times CV = (m_w + m_c) \cdot \theta \times c_p$$

$0.78 \times 10^{-3} \times HCV + 0.02 \times 10^{-3} \times 6688$

$\qquad = (1.88 + 0.37) \times 3 \times 4.186$

$\therefore \quad HCV = \mathbf{36{,}000\ kJ/kg}$

$$LCV = HCV - \frac{9 \times H}{100} \times \text{Latent heat of steam}$$

$$= 36000 - 9 \times \frac{4}{100} \times 2640$$

$$= \mathbf{35{,}114\ kJ/kg}$$

Problem 6.3: The following data refers to an experimental determination of C.V. of a sample of coal:

(i) Mass of coal sample = 0.8 gm
(ii) Mass of fuse wire = 0.02 gm
(iii) Calorific value of fuse wire = 7000 kJ/kg
(iv) Mass of water in calorimeter = 2000 gm
(v) Water equivalent of calorimeter = 350 gm
(vi) Observed temperature rise = 2.9°C
(vii) Cooling correction = 0.07°C

Calculate higher calorific value of coal sample. Take c_p for water = 4.18 kJ/kg·K.

Solution:

Given:

$m_f = 0.8 \times 10^{-3}$ kg

Mass of fuse wire = $m_{fw} = 0.02 \times 10^{-3}$ kg

C.V. of fuse wire = 7000 kJ/kg

$m_w = 2.0$ kg, $m_c = 0.35$ kg, $\Delta T = 2.9°C$

$\theta = (2.9 + 0.07) = \mathbf{2.97°C}$

Heat balance is

$m_f \times HCV + m_{fw} \times CV = (m_w + m_c) \times \theta \times c_p$

$\therefore\ 0.8 \times 10^{-3} \times HCV + 0.02 \times 10^{-3} \times 7000 = (2 + 0.35)(2.97)(4.18)$

$\therefore \quad HCV = \mathbf{36292.8\ kJ/kg}$

6.15.2 Boy's Gas Calorimeter

This is suitable for determining the calorific value of gaseous fuel.

It consists of a suitable gas burner B; a gas supply pipe; a flow-meter to measure the flow rate of gas; a thermometer to measure the supply gas temperature and a manometer to measure its pressure (h_w). This burner is kept inside a cylindrical container which is surrounded by a cooling coil. Cooling water is supplied to the cooling coil from a constant head tank. Its flow rate is also measured.

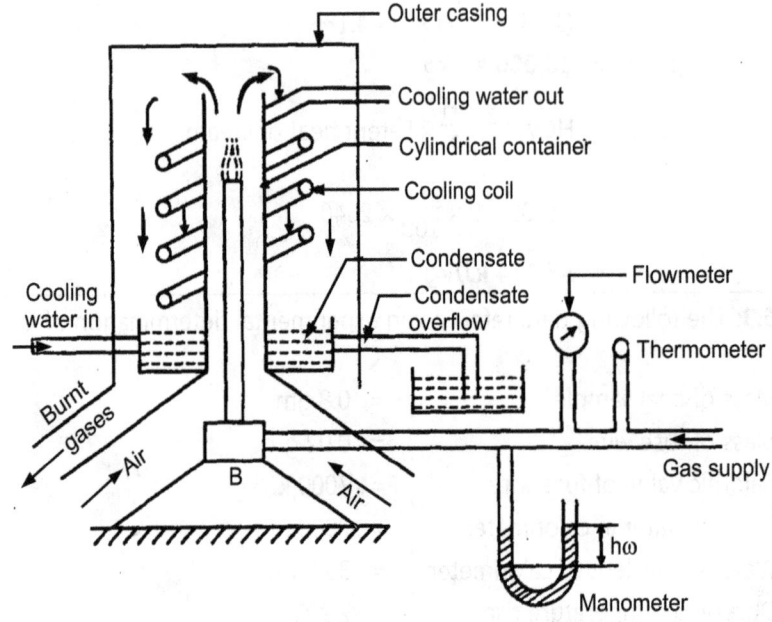

Fig. 6.5: Boy's gas calorimeter

The burnt flue gas moves up in the cylindrical container and then it flows down from the top of the container as shown in Fig. 6.5. The steam formed due to the combustion of hydrogen in the fuel and carried with the gases condenses around the cooling coil and drips down into the trap. The overflow of the condensate is taken out in a glass beaker. Before starting the test, water must be poured through the holes provided into the trap until it begins to overflow the condensation spout.

The outer casing of the calorimeter is provided with heavy insulation to prevent any heat loss to the surrounding.

During the experimentation, following observations are noted:
(1) Time of run
(2) Pressure of gas supplied = h_w c_m of water above atmosphere
(3) Volume of gas burnt during the test (v_g) in m³.
(4) Mass of water circulated (m_w); kg
(5) Inlet water temperature (T_{w_1}) °C
(6) Outlet water temperature (T_{w_2}) °C

(7) Mass of condensate collected (m_c)

(8) Barometer reading (h_b) cm of Hg

(9) Temperature of gas supplied (T_g) °C

If the volume of gas supplied is to be converted to NTP conditions, then the volume of gas at NTP conditions is given by

$$V_g = V_g' \times \frac{273}{T_g} \times \frac{\left(h_b + \frac{h_w}{13.6}\right)}{76}$$

The heat balance equation for the apparatus is,

Heat given out by flue gas = Heat taken by circulating water

$$V_g \cdot HCV = m_w \cdot c_{pw} \cdot (T_{w_2} - T_{w_1})$$

∴
$$HCV = \frac{m_w \cdot c_{pw}(T_{w_2} - T_{w_1})}{V_g} \text{ kJ/m}^3 \text{ at NTP}$$

In calculating this calorific value, it is assumed that the flue gas temperature at the calorimeter exit is equal to the air temperature entering into the calorimeter.

h_{fg} = Specific enthalpy of evaporation of water at its partial pressure = 2442 kJ/kg

∴
$$LCV = HCV - \left(\frac{m_c}{V_g}\right) \times 2442 \text{ kJ/m}^3 \text{ at NTP}$$

The values obtained above are generally accurate for engineering purposes.

SOLVED PROBLEMS

Problem 6.4: The following observations were made during the test for finding the C.V. of the gaseous fuel with the help of Boy's gas calorimeter.

(i) Gas consumed = 60 litres

(ii) Gas pressure = 4 cm of water above atmospheric pressure

(iii) Barometer reading = 750 mm of Hg

(iv) Temperature of gas = 30°C

(v) Water circulated in the calorimeter = 20 kg

(vi) Rise in temperature of water = 10°C

Condensate collected during the test = 60 gm

Find the HCV and LCV of the gas at 0°C and 760 mm of Hg pressure.

Solution:

Given: $v_g' = 60$ litres, $T_g = (30 + 273) = 303°C$

$h_b = 75$ cm of Hg, $h_w = 4$ cm of water

$m_w = 20$ kg, $(T_{w_2} - T_{w_1}) = 10°C$

$$v_g = v_g' \times \frac{273}{T_g} \times \frac{1}{76}\left(h_b + \frac{h_w}{13.6}\right)$$

$$= 60 \times \frac{273}{303} \times \frac{1}{76}\left(75 + \frac{4}{13.6}\right)$$

$$= 53.5 \text{ litres}$$

$$= 0.0535 \text{ m}^3$$

$$\therefore \quad HCV = \frac{m_w \cdot c_{pw} (T_{w_2} - T_{w_1})}{v_g}$$

$$= \frac{20 \times 4.186 \times 10}{0.0535}$$

$$= 15{,}626 \text{ kJ/m}^3 \text{ at } 0°C \text{ and } 760 \text{ mm Hg}$$

Condensate formed per m³ of gas

$$= \frac{60}{1000} \times \frac{1}{0.0535}$$

$$= 1.12 \text{ kg/m}^3$$

$$LCV = 15626 - 1.12 \times 2442$$

$$= 12890.9 \text{ kJ/m}^3$$

Problem 6.5: The following results were obtained from a gas calorimeter during a test to determine the calorific value of a gas.

Water collected = 4.7×10^{-3} m³

Inlet temperature of cooling water = 16°C

Outlet temperature of cooling water = 21°C

Gas temperature = 17°C

Gas consumed = 2.8 litres

Gas pressure = 786 mm of Hg

Determine the calorific value of the gas in MJ/standard m³ (measured at 15°C and 760 mm Hg)

Take specific heat capacity of water = 4.1868 kJ/kg·K

Solution:

Given: $m_w = 4.7$ kg, $T_{w_1} = 16°C$, $T_{w_2} = 21°C$, $T_g = 17°C$, $v'_g = 2.8$ litres,

Gas pressure = 786 mm Hg

$$v_g = v'_g \frac{(15 + 273)}{T_g} \times \frac{786}{760}$$

$$= 2.8 \times \frac{288}{290} \times \frac{786}{760}$$

$$= 2.87 \times 10^{-3} \text{ m}^3$$

Heat released by fuel = Heat carried by cooling water

$$v_g \cdot HCV = m_w \cdot c_{pw} (T_{w_2} - T_{w_1})$$

$$HCV = \frac{4.7 \times 4.1868 \times (21 - 16)}{2.87 \times 10^{-3}}$$

$$= 98389 \text{ kJ/m}^3$$

$$= \mathbf{98.389 \text{ MJ/m}^3}$$

Problem 6.6: The following readings were obtained during a test on bomb calorimeter.

Mass of fuel sample = 1.10 gm.

Water equivalent of calorimeter = 5.5 gm.

Water in calorimeter = 2441 gm.

Time (minute)	0	1	2	3	4	5 (fired)
Temperature	1.023	1.025	1.027	1.029	1.031	1.033
Time	6	7	8	9	10	
Temperature	2.75	3.45	3.56	3.58	3.583	
Time	11	12	13	14	15	16
Temperature	3.582	3.579	3.577	3.574	3.572	3.569

For Beckmann thermometer, 0°C = 7.8°C.

Calculate the calorific value of the fuel.

Solution: Observed temperature rise = 3.582 − 1.033 = 2.549°C.

Note that $T_o = 1.033$ and $T_n = 3.582$, after which the temperature drops uniformly.

To determine cooling correction:

Number of minutes elapsed between T_o and T_n are n = 6.

Mean temperature of initial period

$$= \frac{(1.023 + 1.025 + 1.027 + 1.029 + 1.031 + 1.033)}{6}$$

$$T' = 1.0275°C$$

∴ The product $n \cdot T' = 6 \times 1.0275 = 1.165$

Rate of fall of initial period $= (-)\dfrac{1.033 - 1.023}{5}$

$$v' = (-)\dfrac{0.010}{5} = (-) \, 0.002 \, °C/min$$

∴ $n \cdot v' = 6 \times [(-) \, 0.002] = (-) \, 0.012 \, °C$

Arithmetical sum of readings of main period

$$\sum_{1}^{n-1} (T) = 2.75 + 3.45 + 3.56 + 3.58 + 3.583$$

$$= 16.293°C$$

$$\dfrac{T_o + T_n}{2} = \dfrac{1.033 + 3.582}{2} = 2.3075°C$$

∴ $\left[\displaystyle\sum_{1}^{n-1}(T) + \dfrac{T_o + T_n}{2} - nT'\right] = 16.923 + 2.3075 - 6.165$

$$= 13.0655°C$$

v'' = Rate of fall of temperature in the final period (°C/min)

$$= \dfrac{3.582 - 3.569}{4}$$

$$= \dfrac{0.013}{5} = 0.0026$$

T'' = Mean temperature of the final period

$$= \dfrac{3.582 + 3.579 + 3.577 + 3.574 + 3.572 + 3.569}{6}$$

$$= \mathbf{3.575}$$

Cooling correction $= nv' + \dfrac{v'' - v'}{T'' - T'}\left[\displaystyle\sum_{1}^{n-1}(t)\dfrac{T_o + T_n}{2} - nT'\right]$

$$= -0.012 + \dfrac{0.0026 + 0.002}{3.575 - 1.0275}[13.0655]$$

$$= \mathbf{0.0116°C}$$

Corrected temperature rise = Observed temperature rise + Cooling correction

$$= 2.549 + 0.0116 = \mathbf{2.5606°C}$$

Writing for heat energy balance of the calorimeter, we have,

$$m_f \times HCV = (m_w + m_c) \, c_{pw} \, (\Delta T_c)$$

$$\therefore \quad HCV = \frac{(2441 + 559) \times 4.187 \times 2.5606}{1.1}$$

$$= \mathbf{29239.72 \ kJ/kg}$$

Alternatively the temperature correction can be calculated as follows:

From the observations the initial rate to fall of temperature is v' = (–) 0.0020 °C/min. Extrapolating this to a time of 1.5 minutes after firing, the temperature would have been 1.033 – [(–) 0.022 × 1.5] = 1.03°C.

The radiation correction after firing is v" = 0.0026°C/min. If all the energy released during firing had been instantaneously distributed, that temperature 1.5 minutes after would, therefore, have been

$$3.579 + (12 - 8.5) \times 0.0026 = 3.6011°C$$

Note that rate of fall of temperature is uniform after 12 minutes time.

Hence, the corrected temperature rise = 3.6011 – 1.03 = 2.5711

This rise is very close to that calculated by the more accurate formula of Regnault and Pfounder.

Another approach is to take one half the rate of cooling as the rate during latter half of main period of 6 minutes.

$$\text{i.e. temperature correction} = 6 \times \frac{1}{2} \times v''$$

$$= 6 \times \frac{1}{2} \times (0.0026)$$

$$= 0.0078°C$$

∴ Corrected temperature rise = 2.549 + 0.0078 = 2.5568°C.

This correction is less than that found above, but is on the safer side of the result.

Problem 6.7: The following readings were obtained from a gas calorimeter during a test.

Water collected	= 2.3 litres
Inlet temperature of cooling water	= 26°C
Outlet temperature of cooling water	= 31°C
Gas consumed	= 2.8 litres
Gas temperature	= 25°C
Gas pressure	= + 6 cm of water column
Barometer reading	= 716 mm Hg

Determine the calorific value of the gas at NTP.

Solution: Heat liberated by gas i.e.

$$= \text{Heat collected in water}$$
$$v_r \times HCV = m_w \times c_{pw} (T_{w2} - T_{w1})$$

where,
$$m_w = \rho_w \times \text{Volume of water}$$

The density ρ_w of water should be taken from tables at average temperature of $\dfrac{26+31}{2} = 28.5°C$. In the absence of this value, $\rho_w = 1$ kg/litre.

Also, $v = $ Volume of gas at NTP (760 mmHg and 0°C)

Under test condition,
$$v = 2.3 \times 10^{-3} \text{ m}^3$$
$$T = 273 + 25 = 298 \text{ K}$$

and
$$p = \frac{\left(716 + \dfrac{60}{13.6}\right)}{750} \times 100$$
$$= 96.05 \text{ kPa}$$

$\therefore \quad v_r = \dfrac{pv}{T} \times \dfrac{T_r}{p_r}$

$$= \frac{103.47 \times 2.8 \times 10^{-3}}{298} \times \frac{273}{101.325}$$

$$= 2.43 \times 10^{-3} \text{ m}^3$$

$\therefore \quad $ HCV (at NTP) $= \dfrac{2.3 \times 4.187 \times (31-26)}{2.43 \times 10^{-3}}$

$$= \mathbf{19815 \text{ kJ/m}^3}$$

Problem 6.8: The ultimate analysis of a dry and ash-free coal sample is: Carbon 79%, Hydrogen 8.5%, Oxygen 5%, Nitrogen 1.3% and Sulphur 6.2%. The higher calorific value is 33420 kJ/kg.

The coal as received contains 12% moisture and 15% ash. Calculate the ultimate analysis for this coal as fired.

Solution: For the received coal, moisture fraction $M = 0.12$ kg/kg coal

and Ash fraction $A = 0.15$ kg coal

The multiplier for conversion $= 1 - (M + A) = 1 - (0.12 + 0.15) = 0.77$

The ultimate analysis for received coal can be obtained by multiplying the values for dry and ash-free sample by 0.77. Hence the required coal analysis is:

Carbon	79 × 0.77	= 60.83%
Hydrogen	8.5 × 0.77	= 6.55%
Oxygen	5 × 0.77	= 3.85%
Nitrogen	1.3 × 0.77	= 1.00%
Sulphur	0.2 × 0.7	= 4.77%
		77.00
Moisture		12.00 % and
Ash		15.00%
	Total	100.00

The HCV for ash received coal = 33420 × 0.77 = **25733 kJ/kg**

Problem 6.9: Derive the partial pressure of water vapour in the combustion products having the following analysis by volume:

CO_2 = 12.4%, H_2O = 13.2%, N_2 = 74.4%

The products are at atmospheric pressure of 100 kN/m².

Solution:

V_i = Volume of water vapour in the mixture
  = 0.132 m³

V = Volume of mixture
  = 1.0 m³

Since $\dfrac{p_i}{p} = \dfrac{V_i}{V}$

we get, p_i = 100 × 0.132 = **13.2 kPa**

Problem 6.10: A sample of coal has the following composition by mass: Carbon 82%, Hydrogen 6%, Sulphur 1%, Oxygen 2% and the remainder is non-combustible. Calculate the minimum quantity of air required to burn 1 kg coal. If 20% excess air is used for combustion, calculate the actual air to fuel ratio.

Solution: The given mass fractions in the fuel are:

$$C = \frac{82}{100} = 0.82$$

$$H = \frac{6}{100} = 0.06$$

$$S = \frac{1}{100} = 0.01$$

and $$O = \frac{2}{100} = 0.02$$

The fractions are in kilograms per kilogram of fuel.

The mass of minimum or stoichiometric air per kg fuel can be calculated by the formula derived above, viz.,

$$\text{Minimum air, } A_{min} = 4.31 [2.67 C + 8H + S - O]$$
$$= 4.31 [2.67 \times 0.82 + 8 \times 0.06 + 0.01 - 0.02]$$
$$= \mathbf{11.462 \text{ kg/kg fuel}}$$

Now,
$$\text{\% Excess air} = \frac{\text{Excess air}}{\text{Minimum air}} \times 100$$

i.e.
$$\frac{20}{100} = \frac{\text{Excess air (kg/kg fuel)}}{11.462 \text{ (kg/kg fuel)}}$$

∴ Excess air per kg fuel,

$$A_{excess} = \frac{20 \times 11.462}{100} = 2.2924 \text{ kg/kg fuel}$$

Further actual air,
$$A_{act} = A_{min} + A_{excess}$$
$$= 11.462 + 2.2924$$
$$= \mathbf{13.7544 \text{ kg/kg fuel}}$$

Problem 6.11: Calculate the theoretical air to fuel ratios on mol and mass basis for the following fuels:

(a) Pure carbon (C), (b) Pure hydrogen (H_2), (c) Petrol ($C_{8.5} H_{18.4}$), (d) Heptane (C_7H_{16}), (e) Methanol (CH_3OH), and (f) Ethanol (C_2H_5OH).

Solution: For determining air : fuel ratio, we have to write the stoichiometric equation in each case.

(a) Combustion of pure carbon:

$$C + O_2 \rightarrow CO_2$$

One mol of carbon combines with one mol of oxygen to form one mol of carbon dioxide. Since each mol of oxygen is accompanied by 3.76 moles of nitrogen, molar air : fuel ratio for carbon = 1 + 3.76 = **4.76**.

Using molecular mass of fuel and air, we get,

Theoretical A : F ratio for carbon

$$= \frac{4.76 \times 28.97}{12} \frac{\text{(kg air)}}{\text{(kg fuel)}}$$
$$= \mathbf{11.49 \text{ kg/kg fuel}}$$

(b) Combustion of hydrogen:

$$2H_2 + O_2 \rightarrow 2H_2O$$

i.e. Two mols (or volumes) of hydrogen combine with one mol (or volume) of oxygen to produce two mols (or volumes) of water vapour. Since one mol of oxygen is supplied by 4.76 mols of air,

$$\text{Stoichiometric A : F molar or volume ratio} = \frac{4.76}{2} = \mathbf{2.38}$$

and stoichiometric A : F ratio by mass,

$$A_{min} = \frac{4.76 \times 28.97}{2 \times 2} \frac{\text{(kg air)}}{\text{(kg H}_2)} = \mathbf{34.47}$$

where 28.97 is the molecular mass of air – kg air/mol of air.

(c) For complete combustion of petrol, we have,

$$C_{8.5}H_{18.4} + 13.1\, O_2 \rightarrow 8.5\, CO_2 + 9.2\, H_2O$$

Thus one mol of this fuel requires 13.1 mols of oxygen.

$$\text{Hence, mols of air per mol of fuel} = \frac{13.1 \times 4.76}{1}$$

i.e. Molar A : F ratio for petrol = **62.356**

Further, one mol of $C_{8.5}H_{18.4}$ has mass of

$$8.5 \times 12 + 18.4 \times 1 = 120.4 \text{ kg}$$

$$\therefore \quad \text{Stoichiometric A : F ratio for petrol} = \frac{62.356 \times 28.97}{120.4} = \mathbf{15.00}$$

(d) Heptane fuel approximates the diesel fuel.

Now, $\quad C_7H_{16} + 11\, O_2 \rightarrow 7\, CO_2 + 8\, H_2O$

$\therefore$ Mols of air per mol of fuel = $11 \times 4.76 = 52.36$

and A : F ratio on molar basis = **52.36**

Each mol of heptane has $7 \times 12 + 16 \times 1 = 100$ kg mass

$$\therefore \quad \text{Minimum A : F ratio for heptane} = \frac{52.36 \times 28.97}{100} = \mathbf{15.17}$$

(e) Combustion of methanol:

$$CH_3OH + zO_2 = 1 \times CO_2 + 2H_2O$$

Balance of O_2 on both sides gives,

$$\frac{1}{2} + z = 1 + \frac{1}{2} \quad \therefore z = 1.5$$

Hence, 1 mol of CH_3OH combines with 1.5 mols of oxygen.

$$\therefore \quad \text{A : F ratio on mol basis} = \frac{4.76 \times \text{mols of oxygen}}{\text{mols of fuel}} = \frac{4.76 \times 1.5}{1}$$

$$= \mathbf{7.14}$$

One mol of CH_3OH has a mass of $(1 \times 12) + (1 \times 4) + (1 \times 16) = 32$ kg acid and out of the gas, hence it is reasonable to delete SO_2 and H_2O in dry air.

∴ A : F ratio for complete combustion of methanol

$$= \frac{7.14 \times 28.97}{32} \frac{\text{(kg air)}}{\text{(kg fuel)}} = \mathbf{6.46}$$

(f) Complete combustion of ethanol:

$$C_2H_5OH + zO_2 \rightarrow 2CO_2 + 3H_2O$$

Balancing O_2 molecules on both sides gives

$$\frac{1}{2} + z = 2 + \frac{3}{2}, \text{ i.e. } z = 3$$

Hence, 1 mol of C_2H_5OH combines with 3 molecules of O_2 for complete oxidation.

$$\therefore \quad \text{A : F ratio on mol basis} = \frac{3 \times 4.76}{1} \left(\frac{\text{mols of air}}{\text{mols of } C_2H_5OH}\right) = \mathbf{14.28}$$

One mol of C_2H_5OH has a mass of $2 \times 12 + 5 + 16 + 1 = 46$ kg

$$\therefore \quad \text{A : F ratio on mass basis} = \frac{14.28 \times 28.97}{46} = \mathbf{8.99}$$

Comment: Note that hydrogen has a very high value of A : F ratio. Most fuels have A : F ratio near about 15 while for alcohols it is much less.

By using the minimum values of A : F ratio by mass, one can determine A : F ratio for fuel when ultimate analysis of fuel is given.

Let a fuel have C = 0.86 and H = 0.14 kg/kg fuel.

Therefore for this fuel, $(A : F)_{min} = 0.86 \times 11.49 + 0.14 \times 34.47$

$$= \mathbf{14.7 \text{ kg air/kg fuel}}$$

Problem 6.12: During a boiler trial, a sample of coal gave the following analysis by mass: Carbon 89%, Hydrogen 4%, Oxygen 3%, Sulphur 1%, the remainder being incombustible. Determine the theoretical mass of air required/kg of coal for chemically correct combustion. If 60% excess air is supplied, estimate the percent analysis by mass of the dry flue gas.

Solution: Data: Mass fractions of fuel constituents:

C = 0.89, H = 0.04, O = 0.03, S = 0.01 kg/kg fuel. Here 60% excess air means k = 0.6.

The problem can be solved in the tabular form as shown below.

Combustion with excess air (kg/kg fuel)

Constituent (a)	Mass fraction (b)	Minimum O_2 (c)	Products (d)	Mass of products (e)
Carbon	C = 0.89	2.67 C = 2.67 × 0.89 = 2.3763	CO_2	3.67 C = 3.2663
Hydrogen	H = 0.04	8H = 8 × 0.04 = 0.32	H_2O	9H = 0.36
Oxygen*	O = 0.03	(−) 0.03	−	−
Sulphur	S = 0.01	1 × S = 0.01	SO_2	2S = 0.02
		Σ Min. O_2 = 2.7163	SO_2	2S = 0.02

$$\text{Minimum air } (A_{min}) = 4.35 \times \text{Min. } O_2$$
$$= 4.35 \times 2.7163 = 11.82 \text{ kg/kg fuel}$$
$$\text{Excess air } (A_{excess}) = 0.6 \times 11.82 = \mathbf{7.092 \text{ kg/kg fuel}}$$

% Analysis of the dry products with excess air by mass (kg/kg fuel)

Constituent of DP (f)	Mass of constituent of DP (g)	% DP by mass = $\frac{g}{\Sigma g} \times 100$
CO_2	3.2663	16.79
N_2	0.77 × (11.7 + 7.09) = 14.56	74.83
O_2	0.23 × (7.09) = 1.63	8.38
Total	Σ g = 19.4563	100.00

... **Ans.**

Problem 6.13: A fuel oil having a chemical formula $C_{12}H_{26}$ is burned with 50% excess air. Determine the stoichiometric air required and percent analysis of products of combustion including water vapour.

Solution: With stoichiometric air, the following equation can be written:

$C_{12}H_{26} + 18.5\ O_2 + (3.76 \times 18.5)\ N_2 \rightarrow 12\ CO_2 + 13\ H_2O + 3.76 \times 18.5\ N_2\ (= 69.56)$

Thus 18.5 moles of oxygen are required per mol of fuel.

∴ Minimum air required for complete combustion of 1 mol of $C_{12}H_{26}$

$$= 4.31 \times [\text{Min. } O_2 \text{(kg)}]$$
$$= 4.31 \times [18.5 \times 32] \text{ kg}$$

---

* Oxygen already present in the fuel reduces the quantity of oxygen to be supplied externally; hence a negative sign for O_2 in fuel.

One mol of $C_{12}H_{26}$ has a mass of $(12 \times 12) + 26 = 170$ kg

∴ Stoichiometric air : fuel ratio

$$(A:F)_{stoichio} = \frac{4.31 \times 18.5 \times 32}{170} = \textbf{15.00 kg/kg fuel}$$

Alternatively, $(A:F)_{stoichio} = \frac{18.5 \times 4.76 \times 28.97}{170} = 15.00$

Since 50% excess air is supplied, excess oxygen supplied = $0.5 \times 18.5 = 9.25$ mols per mol of fuel, along with $3.76 \times 9.25 = 34.78$ excess mols of N_2 per mol of fuel. Both of these constituents appear on product side. The following chemical equation can be written for combustion with excess air.

$C_{12}H_{26} + (18.5 + 9.25) O_2 + (69.56 + 34.78) N_2$

$\rightarrow 12 CO_2 + 13 H_2O + 9.25 O_2 + (69.56 + 34.78) N_2$

The following mass analysis of products can be done:

12 mols of CO_2 are produced per mol of $C_{12}H_{26}$.

∴ Mass of CO_2 produced per kg fuel $= \dfrac{12 \times (\text{Molecular mass of } CO_2)}{\text{Molecular mass of } C_{12}H_{26}}$

$= \dfrac{12 \times 44}{170} = \textbf{3.1 kg}$

13 mols of H_2O are produced per mol of $C_{12}H_{26}$.

∴ Mass of H_2O produced per kg fuel $= \dfrac{12 \times (\text{Molecular mass of } H_2O)}{\text{Molecular mass of } C_{12}H_{26}}$

$= \dfrac{12 \times 18}{170} = \textbf{1.376 kg}$

9.25 mols of O_2 are produced per mol of $C_{12}H_{26}$.

∴ Mass of O_2 produced per kg fuel $= \dfrac{9.25 \times (\text{Molecular mass of } O_2)}{\text{Molecular mass of } C_{12}H_{26}}$

$= \dfrac{9.25 \times 32}{170} = \textbf{1.741 kg}$

$69.56 + 34.78 = 104.34$ mols of N_2 are produced per mol of $C_{12}H_{26}$.

∴ Mass of N_2 produced per kg fuel $= \dfrac{104.34 \times (\text{Molecular mass of } N_2)}{\text{Molecular mass of } C_{12}H_{26}}$

$= \dfrac{104.34 \times 28}{170} = \textbf{17.18 kg}$

Using these masses of products, the percent analysis is as follows:

Product (a)	Mass of product, kg/kg fuel (b)	% WP by mass = $\frac{b}{\Sigma b} \times 100$
CO_2	3.1	13.25
H_2O	1.376	5.88
O_2	1.741	7.44
N_2	17.18	73.43
Total	$\Sigma b = 23.397$	100.00

Problem 6.14: Iso-octane (C_8H_{18}) is burned with 10% excess air. Calculate the volumetric composition of the products of combustion.

Solution: First stoichiometric combustion equation is written as:

$$C_8H_{18} + 12.5O_2 \rightarrow 8CO_2 + 9H_2O$$

Since 10% excess air is used, $k = 0.1$ and excess O_2 supplied is $0.1 \times 12.5 = 1.25$ mols accompanied by excess nitrogen. The following equation can be written for combustion of iso-octane with 10% excess air.

Fuel   Min air   Excess air

$C_8H_{18} + [12.5O_2 + (3.76 \times 12.5) N_2] + [1.25O_2 + (3.76 \times 1.25) N_2]$

Products

$\rightarrow 8CO_2 + 9H_2O + 1.25O_2 + 3.76 (12.5 + 1.25) N_2$

Mols or volume of products, $\Sigma WP = 8 + 9 + 1.25 + 3.76 (12.5 + 1.25)$

$= 69.95$

∴   % CO_2 in wet products by volume $= \dfrac{\text{Mols of } CO_2}{\text{Mols of WP}} \times 100 = \dfrac{8}{69.95} \times 100 =$ **11.44**

Similarly,

% H_2O in wet products by volume $= \dfrac{9}{69.95} \times 100 =$ **12.87**

% O_2 in wet products by volume $= \dfrac{1.25}{69.95} \times 100 =$ **1.99**

% N_2 in wet products by volume $= \dfrac{3.76 \times 13.75}{69.95} \times 100 =$ **73.90**

Note that while restricting the calculations to second decimal, inaccuracy of 0.01 is accepted. Hence, the total percent by volume may come either 100.01 or 99.99. In such cases, the second decimal of the percent figure for nitrogen should be adjusted to make the total 100.00, as it is the largest constituent.

Problem 6.15: A solid fuel suitable for boiler has following composition by mass:

C = 90%, H_2 = 3.5%, O_2 = 3%, N_2 = 1%, S = 1%.

The remainder is uncombustible. Determine the stoichiometric air quantity. Also determine mass analysis of the dry products of combustion.

If 40% excess air is actually supplied, determine volumetric analysis of products and the mass of the gases per kg fuel. Air contains 23% O_2 by mass.

Solution: (a) With stoichiometric air, the following table can be prepared for products of combustion (kg/kg fuel).

Fuel constituent	Mass fraction	Min. O_2	Product	Mass of product
Carbon	0.90	2.67 C = 2.403	CO_2	3.67 C = 3.303
Hydrogen	0.035	8H = 0.280	H_2O	9H = 0.315
Oxygen	(−) 0.03	(−) 0.03	–	
Nitrogen	0.01	–	N_2	N_2 = 0.010
Sulphur	0.01	S = 0.01	SO_2	2S = 0.02
		Σ Min. O_2 = 2.663		

$$\text{Stoichiometric air} = \frac{100}{23} \times \text{Min. } O_2 = \frac{100}{23} \times 2.663$$

$$= \mathbf{11.578 \text{ kg/kg fuel}}$$

Mass analysis of the dry products of combustion (kg/kg fuel):

Product	Mass of dry product	% by mass
CO_2	3.303	27.01
N_2	0.01 + 0.77 × 11.578 = 8.925	72.99
	Σ DP = 12.228	100.00

Note that nitrogen in the dry products appears from fuel and air supplied. Oxygen from fuel is consumed in combustion and does not appear as a product.

(b) With excess air, $\quad$ k = 0.4

∴ $\quad$ Excess air = k × Mass of minimum air

$\quad$ = 0.4 × 11.578 = 4.6312 kg/kg fuel

Total nitrogen from air = 0.77 (Minimum air + Excess air)

$\quad$ = 0.77 (11.578 + 4.6312) = 12.481 kg/kg fuel

Excess oxygen from excess air = 0.23 × Excess air = 0.23 × 4.6312

$\quad$ = **1.0652 kg/kg fuel**

The following table can be prepared for the products:

Constituent (a)	Mass of wet products (b)	Molecular mass (c)	Proportional volume d = b/c	% by volume (d/Σd) × 100
CO_2	3.303	44	0.0750682	13.04
H_2O	0.315	18	0.0175	3.04
SO_2	0.02	64	0.0003125	0.05
N_2	0.1 + 12.481 = 12.581	28	0.4493214	78.08
O_2	1.0652	32	0.033288	5.79
Total	Σ WP = 17.2842		Σ d = 0.5754896	100.00

Mass of flue gases per kg of fuel = Σ WP = **17.2842 kg/kg fuel**

Note: This value also equals mass of air supplied + Combustible part of fuel as the non-combustible is ash.

The figures of proportionate volume are always smaller and hence, for accuracy, 7 or 8 digit numbers are used. To avoid this difficulty, percent mass figures of products may be used instead of kg figures.

Problem 6.16: The results recorded during trial on gas calorimeter are as under.

Pressure of gas = 45 mm of water, Gas supplied = 0.10 m³ at 30°C, Water temperature at inlet and outlet = 28°C and 39°C respectively, Steam condensed = 0.07 kg, Mass of cooling water circulated = 22 kg.

Determine H.C.V. and L.C.V. of the fuel at 22°C. Take standard barometric pressure to be 760 mm of Hg.

Solution: Condition of gas supplied,

$$\text{Gas temperature, } T_g = 30°C = 30 + 273 = 303 \text{ K}$$
$$\text{Gas pressure, } p_g = 45 \text{ mm of water}$$
$$= 760 + \frac{45}{13.6} = 7633 \text{ mm of Hg}$$

Volume of gas, V_g = 0.10 m³

Let V be the volume of gas at S.T.P.

$$\frac{p_g \cdot V_g}{T_g} = \frac{pV}{T}$$

∴ $$\frac{763.3 \times 0.1}{303} = \frac{760 \times V}{(22 + 273)}$$

∴ V = 0.09778 m³ at 22°C

Rise in temperature of cooling water (ΔT) = 39 − 28 = 11°C.

For calorimeter,

Heat liberated by gas due to combustion = Heat utilized by cooling water

$\therefore \quad V \times (C.V.) = m_w\, c_{pw}\, \Delta T$

$\therefore \quad 0.09778 \times (C.V.) = 22 \times 4.18 \times 11$

$\therefore \quad C.V. = \mathbf{10345.26\ kJ/m^3}$

Higher calorific value = H.C.V. = 10345.26 kJ/m³

Amount of steam condensed is 0.07 kg for the fuel burnt 0.09778 m³

$\therefore$ Mass of steam formed/m³ of gas = $\dfrac{0.07}{0.09778}$ = **0.7159 kg**

Lower calorific value = L.C.V. = H.C.V. − Mass of steam × Latent heat

= 10345.26 − 0.7159 × 2449.48

= **8591.68 kJ/m³**

Problem 6.17: A sample of 1 kg of coal has the following composition: C = 0.78, H_2 = 0.05, O_2 = 0.08, S = 0.02, N_2 = 0.02, Ash = 0.05. It is burnt in a furnace with 50% excess air. The flue gases enter the chimney at 325°C and atmosphere is at 15°C. Calculate the quantity of heat carried away by the flue gases in kJ/kg of coal. Take c_p for O_2, N_2 and air as 1.008 kJ/kg·K and c_p for CO_2 and SO_2 as 1.05 kJ/kg·K.

Solution: Given:

1 kg of coal.

C = 0.78, H_2 = 0.05, O_2 = 0.08, S = 0.02, N_2 = 0.02 and Ash = 0.05.

50% excess air.

Flue gas temperature = 325°C.

Atmospheric temperature = 15°C.

$c_{p(O_2,\ N_2\ \text{and air})}$ = 1.008 kJ/kg·K, $c_{p(CO_2,\ SO_2)}$ = 1.05 kJ/kg·K

Constituent	Mass per kg of coal	Mass of O_2 required for complete combustion (kg)	Mass of products formed (kg)			
			N_2	CO_2	SO_2	H_2O
C	0.78	8/3 × 0.78 = 2.08	−	11/3 × 0.78 = 2.86	−	−
H_2	0.05	8 × 0.05 = 0.4	−	−	−	9 × 0.05 = 0.45
S	0.02	1 × 0.02 = 0.02	−	−	2 × 0.02 = 0.04	−
Total		ΣO_2 = 2.5	−	2.86	0.04	0.45
O_2	0.08	−0.08	−	−	−	−
N_2	0.02	−	0.02	−	−	−

Mass of air required for complete combustion (Theoretical)

$$= \frac{100}{23}(2.5 - 0.08) \text{ or } 4.35 \times (2.5 - 0.08)$$

$$= \textbf{10.522 kg/kg of coal}$$

Actual air supplied = Theoretical air + 50% of theoretical air
= 10.522 + 0.5 × 10.522 = 15.783 kg/kg of coal

Heat carried away by the flue gases leaving the boiler plant consists of:
(i) Heat with dry flue gases.
(ii) Heat with vapours formed due to moisture.

Heat carried by dry flue gases = $m_g \cdot c_{pg} (T_g - T_a)$

where, $c_{pg} m_g$ = (Mass of CO_2 and SO_2) × c_p + (Mass of O_2 and N_2) × c_p
= (2.86 + 0.04) × 1.05 + (1.21 + 12.153) × 1.008
= 2.9 × 1.05 + 13.363 × 1.008
= **16.515 kg/K**

Heat carried by dry flue gases = 16.515 × (325 − 15) = 5119.65 kJ per kg of coal

Now, heat carried by vapours = 9H × 3127.45
= 9 × 0.05 × 3127.45 = **1407.35 kJ/kg of coal**

∴ Total heat carried by exhaust or flue gases per kg of coal
= 5119.65 + 1407.35
= **6527 kJ/kg of coal**

Problem 6.18: The mass analysis of coal sample is as follows:

Carbon 80%, Hydrogen 6%, Oxygen 7% and remainder is incombustible matter. Orsat analysis of products of combustion gives the following results:

CO_2: 10%, CO : 1.5%, O_2 : 8% and remainder is N_2.

Find the mass of air supplied per kg of fuel burnt and the percentage of excess air supplied.

Solution:

The volumetric analysis of dry flue gases (DFG) can be converted into mass analysis as follows:

Constituent (a)	% by volume (b)	Molecular weight (c)	Proportionate mass (d) = (b) × (c)	% by mass (e) = Σ
CO_2	10	44	440.0	14.7059 = $\frac{440 \times 100}{2992}$
CO	1.5	28	42.0	1.4037 = $\frac{42 \times 100}{2992}$
O_2	8.0	32	256.0	8.5561 = $\frac{256 \times 100}{2992}$

Constituent (a)	% by volume (b)	Molecular weight (c)	Proportionate mass (d) = (b) × (c)	% by mass (e) = Σ
N_2	80.5	28	2254.0	75.3342 = $\dfrac{2250 \times 100}{2992}$
Total	100%		2992.0	100%

(i) Air supplied per kg of fuel:

Fuel contains 0.06 kg of H_2 per kg of which will produce steam.

$$m_s = [9 \times H] \text{ kg of water vapour}$$
$$= 9 \times 0.06 = \textbf{0.54 kg of water vapour}$$

From law of conservation of mass,

Mass of fuel + Mass of air supplied (m_a per kg of fuel) = Mass of DFG/kg of fuel + Mass of water

$$(0.8 + 0.06 + 0.07) + m_a = \frac{\text{Mass of carbon/kg of fuel}}{\text{Mass of carbon/kg of DFG}} + \text{Mass of water}$$

$$= \frac{0.8}{\dfrac{12}{44} \times 0.147059 + \dfrac{12}{28} \times 0.014037} + 0.54$$

∴ $$m_a = \frac{0.8}{0.040707 + 0.006016} = 0.54 - 0.93$$

$$= 17.88498 - 0.93$$

$$m_a = \textbf{16.95 kg/kg of fuel}$$

Stoichiometric air supplied per kg of fuel

$$= \frac{100}{23}\left[C \times \frac{32}{12} + H_2 \times \frac{32}{4}\right]$$

$$= \frac{100}{23}\left[0.8 \times \frac{32}{12} + 0.06 \times \frac{32}{4}\right]$$

$$= \textbf{11.36 kg/kg of fuel}$$

∴ Percentage of excess air supplied

$$= \frac{\text{Actual air} - \text{Stoichiometric air}}{\text{Stoichiometric air}} \times 100$$

$$= \frac{16.95 - 11.36}{11.36} \times 100$$

$$= \textbf{49.21%}$$

Problem 6.19: A bomb calorimeter was used to determine calorific value of coal sample having composition by mass as C = 85%, H_2 = 4.5%.

The following readings were recorded:
Mass of coal = 1.0 gm
Mass of water in calorimeter = 2.5 kg
Mass of fuse wire = 0.02 gm
Calorific value of fuse wire = 1800 kJ/kg
Water equivalent of calorimeter = 750 gm
Temperature rise = 2.61°C
Cooling correction = 0.019°C
Partial pressure of water vapour = 7 kPa.
Determine HCL and LCV of coal.

Solution:
Actual temperature rise of cooling water,
$$\Delta T = \text{Measured temperature rise} + \text{Cooling correction factor}$$
$$= 2.61 + 0.019 = \mathbf{2.629°C}$$

Let HCV be the higher calorific value of coal, then,
Heat given by (fuel + fuse wire) = Heat absorbed by (Calorimeter + Cooling water)

∴ Mass of coal × HCV + Mass of fuse wire × CV of wire

∴ $1 \times HCV + 0.02 \times 1800 \times 10^{-3} = c_{pw} \cdot \Delta T \left[m_w + \dfrac{m_c \, C_{pc}}{C_{pw}} \right]$

$= 4.18 \times 10^{-3} \times 2.629 \times [2.5 \times 10^3 + 750]$

∴ HCV = 35.7149 − 0.036
     = **35.68 kJ/gm**
   HCV = **35678.9 kJ/kg**

and   LCV = HCV − (Heat to moisture)

$= 35678.9 - \left(\dfrac{9 \times H}{0.895} \times 2400 \right) = \mathbf{3377.34 \ kJ/kg}$

Problem 6.20: The composition of a dry flue gas, as obtained by using Orsat apparatus was 10% CO_2, 1.8% CO, 7% O_2 and 81.2% N_2 by volume. What will be the percentage composition of the flue gas by weight?

Solution:
Mass of CO_2 = 0.1 × 44 = 4.4 kg
Mass of CO = 0.018 × 28 = 0.504 kg
Mass of O_2 = 0.07 × 32 = 2.24 kg
Mass of N_2 = 0.812 × 28 = 22.736 kg

∴ Total mass of the gas = 29.88 kg

∴ Percentage of CO_2 in gas = $\dfrac{4.4 \times 100}{29.88}$ = **14.77%**

∴ Percentage of CO in gas = $\dfrac{0.504 \times 100}{29.88}$ = **1.687**

$$\text{Percentage of } O_2 \text{ in gas} = \frac{2.24 \times 100}{29.88} = \mathbf{7.497}$$

$$\text{Percentage of } N_2 \text{ in gas} = \frac{22.736 \times 100}{29.88} = \mathbf{76.091}$$

Problem 6.21: During bomb calorimeter test on diesel oil according to BSS specifications, the following data were recorded:

Room temperature = 25°C.

Weight of crucible = 8.116 gm

Weight of crucible and oil = 8.702 gm

Weight of can = 1.051 kg

Weight of can and water = 3.492 kg

Water equivalent of can = 0.559 kg

Rise in temperature of can and water = 2.305°C

Find the higher calorific value of fuel.

Solution:

Weight of oil taken = 8.702 − 8.116 = 0.586 gm = 0.000586 kg

∴ Heat released by the combustion of oil

= HCV × 0.000586

Weight of water in the can = 3.492 − 1.051 = 2.441 kg

∴ Total equivalent of can and water

= 2.441 + 0.559 = 3.0 kg

∴ Heat received by can and water = $m_w \times c_{pw}$ × Rise in temperature

= 3 × 4.187 × 2.305 = **28.993 kJ**

∴ Equating heat evolved and received by water, we get

HCV × 0.000586 = 28.9531

∴ HCV = 28.9531/0.000586 = **49408 kJ/kg**

Problem 6.22: A S.I. engine uses octane (C_8H_{18}) as the fuel and the exhaust gas analysis gave the following composition:

CO_2 = 9.9%, CO = 7.2%, H_2 = 3.3%, CH_4 = 0.3%, N_2 = 79.3%.

Calculate air-fuel ratio.

Solution: We know that air contains oxygen 21% by volume.

Therefore, CO_2 in air can be written as,

$$N_2 \times \frac{21}{79} = \frac{N_2}{3.76}$$

The equation of the combustion,

$$zC_8H_{18} + \frac{79.3}{3.76} O_2 + 79.3 N_2 = 9.9 CO_2 + 7.2 CO + 3.3 H_2 + 0.3 CH_4 + 79.3 N_2$$

Making carbon balance, equating coefficients of carbon on both sides,

$$8z = 9.9 + 7.2 + 0.3 = 17.4$$

$$\therefore z = \mathbf{2.175}$$

Thus, the left hand side is,

$2.175\ C_8H_{18} + 21.09\ O_2 + 79.3\ N_2$

Molecular mass of air is '29' and molecular mass of fuel is,

$$12 \times 8 + 18 = 114$$

$$\therefore \text{Air : fuel ratio by mass} = \frac{\text{Mass of air}}{\text{Mass of fuel}}$$

$$= \frac{(21.09 + 79.3)\ 29}{2.175 \times 114}$$

$$= \mathbf{11.74}$$

Problem 6.23: In a bomb calorimeter test, the following observations were recorded:
(i) Weight of coal tested = 1.5 gm
(ii) Weight of water in calorimeter = 1.3 kg
(iii) Water equivalent of the calorimeter = 0.9 kg
(iv) Rise in temperature of jacket water = 8.925°C

If the coal contains 3% moisture by weight, the room temperature is 20°C and 1 kg of moisture at 0°C requires 2467 kJ of heat to evaporate to form dry and saturated steam, calculate LCV and HCV of the test fuel.

Solution: Given Data: Bomb calorimeter
Weight of coal = m_f = 1.5 gm
Weight of water in calorimeter = m_w = 1.3 kg
Water equivalent of the calorimeter = $(m_c c_{pc})$ = 0.9 kg
Rise in temperature of jacket water = ΔT = 8.925°C
Moisture in coal = m_m = 0.03 × 1.5 = 0.045 gm
Room temperature = T_a = 20°C
Enthalpy of vapour = h = 2467 kJ/kg.
Balancing the heat released by coal and heat gained by water,

Heat given by (coal) = Heat absorbed by (Calorimeter + Cooling water)

Mass of coal × HCV = $(m_c \cdot c_{pc} + m_w \cdot c_{pw})\ \Delta T$

$\therefore\quad 1.5 \times 10^{-3} \times$ HCV = (0.9 + 1.3) × 4.187 × 8.925

$\therefore\quad$ HCV = **54807 kJ/kg**

Lower calorific value (LCV) = HCV − $m_m \times h$

= $54807 - 0.045 \times 10^{-3} \times [2467 - 20 \times 4.187]$

LCV = **54307.723 kJ/kg**

Problem 6.24: Calculate the stoichiometric air : fuel ratio for the combustion of a sample of dry anthracite of the following composition by mass: Carbon = 88%, Hydrogen = 4%, Oxygen = 3.5%, Sulphur = 0.5% and Ash = 3%, Nitrogen = 1%. If 30% of excess air is supplied, determine:

(i) Air-fuel ratio
(ii) Dry analysis of products of combustion by volume.

Solution: Given data:

$$C = 88\% = 0.88$$
$$H = 4\% = 0.04$$
$$O_2 = 3.5\% = 0.035$$
$$S = 0.5\% = 0.05$$
$$Ash = 3\% = 0.03$$
$$N = 1\% = 0.01$$

Minimum amount of air required

$$= \frac{100}{23}\left[\frac{8}{3}C + 8H + S - O\right]$$

$$= \frac{100}{23}\left[\frac{8}{3}(0.88) + 8(0.04) + 0.005 - 0.035\right]$$

$$= \frac{100}{23} \times 2.636$$

= **11.46 kg of air/kg of fuel**

∴ Stoichiometric air-fuel ratio = 11.46 : 1.

Now, N_2 associated with this air = $0.77 \times 11.46 = 8.82$ kg.

With 30% excess air,

Actual A/F ratio = $11.46 \times 1.3 = 14.898 : 1 = 14.9 : 1$

∴ O_2 supplied = 14.90×0.23 = **3.427 kg**
and N_2 supplied = 14.90×0.77 = **11.473 kg**

∴ The products of combustion will have,

N_2 = 11.473 + 0.01 = 11.483 kg
and O_2 = 3.427 − 2.636 = 0.791 kg

Now, products of combustion per kg of anthracite fuel,

CO_2 = $0.88 \times \frac{44}{12}$ = **3.23 kg**

H_2O = 0.04×9 = **0.36 kg**

N_2 = 11.483 kg

$$SO_2 = 0.005 \times \frac{64}{32} = \mathbf{0.01 \text{ kg}}$$

$$O_2 = 0.791$$

Dry analysis of gases on volume basis:

Sr. No.	Products	Mass (kg) (a)	Molecular weight (b)	Relative volume (c) = (a)/(b)	% Compound by volume = $\frac{c}{\Sigma c}$
1.	CO_2	3.23	44	0.0734	14.43
2.	H_2O	0.36	–	–	–
3.	N_2	11.483	28	0.4101	80.67
4.	SO_2	0.01	64	1.566×10^{-4}	0.05
5.	O_2	0.791	32	0.0247	4.85
				$\Sigma c = 0.5083$	100%

Problem 6.25: In a bomb calorimeter, the following observations were recorded:

Weight of coal tested = 2.5 gm

Weight of water in the calorimeter = 1.3 kg

Water equivalent of calorimeter = 0.9 kg

Rise in temperature of jacket water = 7.515°C

The coal contains 3% moisture by weight and the room temperature is 25°C.

If 1 kg of moisture at 0°C requires 2470 kJ to evaporate to form dry and saturated steam, calculate the lower calorific value.

Solution:

Given Data:

m_f = 2.5 gm = 0.0025 kg

m_w = 1.3 kg

w_e = 0.9 kg

ΔT = 7.515°C

Moisture = 3% by weight

T_a = 25°C

By energy balance in bomb calorimeter,

Heat given by coal = Heat gained by water and calorimeter

$$HCV \times 0.0025 = (1.3 + 0.9) \times 4.187 \times 7.715$$

∴ HCV = **28426.38 kJ/kg**

Heat consumed to evaporate moisture = Mass of moisture × Latent heat

$$= 0.03 \times 2470$$

$$= 74.1 \text{ kJ/kg}$$

∴ Lower calorific value = LCV = HCV − 74.1

$$= 28426.38 - 74.1$$

$$= \mathbf{28352.28 \text{ kJ/kg}}$$

Problem 6.26: The ultimate analysis of a solid fuel is as follows:

C = 78%, O_2 = 3%, H_2 = 3%, S = 1%, Moisture = 5% and Ash content = 10%.

Calculate the mass of air supplied, also individual and total mass of products of combustion per kg of fuel if 30% of excess air is supplied for combustion.

Solution:

Data Given: C = 78%, O_2 = 3%, H_2 = 3%, S = 1%, Moisture = 5%, Ash = 10%.

Stoichiometric air required for complete combustion of 1 kg of solid fuel

$$= \frac{100}{23}\left[\frac{8}{3}C + 8H + S - O\right]$$

$$= \frac{100}{23}\left[\frac{8}{3} \times 0.78 + 8 \times 0.03 + 0.01 - 0.03\right]$$

= **10 kg/kg of fuel**

Actual air supplied = Stoichiometric air + Excess air

$$= 10 + 0.3 \times 10$$

= **13 kg/kg of fuel**

Now, we find amount of products of combustion namely CO_2, H_2O, N_2, O_2 and their % by mass.

(i) Amount of CO_2 formed = $\frac{H}{3} \times C = \frac{H}{3} \times 0.78$ = 2.86 kg/kg of fuel.

(ii) Amount of H_2O formed = 9H = 9 × 0.03 = **0.27**

The fuel contains 5% moisture.

∴ Total H₂O formed = 0.27 + 0.05 = 0.32 kg/kg of fuel

(iii) Amount of O_2 formed = 0.23 × 3 = 0.69 kg/kg of fuel

(iv) Amount of N_2 = 0.77 × Actual air

= 0.77 × 13

= **10.01 kg/kg of fuel**

Total mass of products of combustion

= 2.86 + 0.32 + 0.69 + 10.01

= **13.97 kg/kg of fuel**

Problem 6.27: The following results were obtained when sample of gas was tested in gas calorimeter. Gas burnt = 0.065 m³, Pressure of gas = 45 mm of water, Temperature of gas = 27°C, Water inlet temperature = 30°C, Water outlet temperature = 42°C, Mass of water passing through calorimeter = 17.5 kg, Barometric pressure = 750 mm of Hg, Steam condensed during test = 0.05 kg. Determine HCV and LCV of gas at 15°C and standard barometer of 76 cm of Hg.

Solution: The volume of the gas is measured at a temperature 27°C and pressure of 45 mm of water.

Let us reduce this volume to S.T.P. by using the general gas equation,

$$\frac{p_1 V_1}{T_1} = \frac{p_2 V_2}{T_2}$$

where, $p_1 = 75 + \left(\frac{4.5}{13.6}\right) = 75.331$ cm of Hg

T_1 = 273 + 27 = 300 K

V_1 = 0.065 m³

p_2 = 76 cm of Hg

V_2 = ?

T_2 = 273 + 15 = **288 K**

∴ $\frac{75.331 \times 0.065}{300} = \frac{76 \times V_2}{288}$

∴ V_2 = 0.06185 m³ = Volume of gas at S.T.P.

Heat received by water = 17.5 × 4.187 × (42 − 30)

= **879.27 kJ**

Higher calorific value (HCV) of fuel

$$= \frac{879.27}{0.06185}$$

$$= \mathbf{14216.17 \text{ kJ/m}^3}$$

The quantity of water vapour formed (i.e. steam condensed) per m³ of gas burnt

$$= \frac{0.5}{0.06185} = 0.808 \text{ kg.}$$

Lower calorific value (LCV) of fuel

$$= \text{H.C.V.} - 2465 \times 0.808$$

$$= 14216.17 - 2465 \times 0.808$$

$$= \mathbf{12224.45 \text{ kJ/m}^3}$$

Problem 6.28: C_7H_{16} is burnt with 10% excess air. Determine volumetric analysis of dry fuel and air-fuel ratio.

Solution: Mass of fuel C_7H_{16} = 84 + 16 = 100 kg.

∴ $\quad$ Mass of C $= \dfrac{84}{100} = 0.84$ kg for 1 kg fuel

$\quad$ Mass of H_2 $= \dfrac{16}{100} = 0.16$ kg for 1 kg fuel

∴ $\quad$ Minimum air required to burn 1 kg of fuel

$$= \frac{100}{23}\left[\frac{8}{3}C + 8H_2\right] = \frac{100}{23}\left[\frac{8}{3} \times 0.84 + 8 \times 0.16\right]$$

$$= 11 \text{ kg/kg of fuel}$$

Actual amount of air supplied = 1.1 × 11 = 12.1 kg

∴ $\quad$ Excess air supplied = 12.1 − 11 = 1.1 kg

Mass of CO_2 contained in 0.84 kg of carbon per kg of coal

$$= \frac{11}{3} \times 0.84 = \mathbf{3.08 \text{ kg}}$$

Mass of excess O_2 per kg of fuel $= \dfrac{23}{100} \times 1.1 = \mathbf{0.253 \text{ kg}}$

Mass of nitrogen per kg of fuel $= \dfrac{77}{100} \times$ Actual air supplied

$$= 0.77 \times 12.1 = \mathbf{9.317 \text{ kg}}$$

Total mass of dry fuel gases per kg of fuel

$$= 3.08 + 0.253 + 9.317 = \mathbf{12.65\ kg}$$

Percentage composition of dry fuel gases by volume:

Let us find out % composition of dry fuel gases by mass.

$$CO_2 = \frac{3.08}{12.65} = 24.35\%$$

$$\text{Excess } O_2 = \frac{0.253}{12.65} = 2\%$$

$$N_2 = \frac{9.317}{12.65} = 73.65\%$$

Now let us convert this analysis of dry fuel gases into volumetric analysis as below.

Constituent	% Mass analysis (a)	Molecular mass (b)	Proportional volume $c = \frac{a}{b}$	Volume in/m³ of fuel gas, $d = \frac{(c)}{\Sigma(c)}$	% Volumetric analysis
CO_2	24.35	44	0.5534	0.1705	17.05
Excess O_2	2.00	32	0.0625	0.01925	1.93
N_2	73.65	28	2.630	0.8102	81.02
Total	100.00		3.246		100.00

Hence, percentage of dry fuel gases is,

$$CO_2 = 17.05\%$$

$$\text{Excess } O_2 = 1.93\%$$

and

$$N_2 = 81.02\%$$

Now, Total air required = Minimum air + Excess air

$$= 11 + 1.1 = \mathbf{12.1\ kg/kg\ of\ fuel}$$

∴ A/F ratio = **12.1 : 1.**

Problem 6.29: A sample of coal has the following analysis by mass: Carbon = 34.4%, Hydrogen = 0.4%, Oxygen = 5.6% and remainder is ash. Determine higher and lower calorific value of fuel. One kg of carbon when burnt completely to CO_2 produces 35 MJ of heat. One kg of hydrogen when completely burnt to H_2O produces 143 MJ of heat. The enthalpy of condensation of water is 2.512 MJ/kg.

Solution: Air contains 23% O_2 by mass.

$$C + O_2 = CO_2$$
$$12 + 32 = 44$$
$$1 + 2\tfrac{2}{3} = 3\tfrac{2}{3}$$

∴ 1 kg of C requires $2\tfrac{2}{3}$ kg of O_2 to produce $3\tfrac{2}{3}$ kg of CO_2.

$$2H_2 + O_2 = 2H_2O$$
$$4 + 32 = 36$$
$$1 + 8 = 9$$

∴ 1 kg of H_2 requires 8 kg of O_2 to produce 9 kg of H_2O.

Constituents	Mass constituents kg/kg of fuel	O_2 required
C	0.844	$0.844 \times 2\tfrac{2}{3} = 2.251$
H_2	0.04	$0.04 \times 8 = 0.32$
O_2	0.056	$= -0.056$
Residual	0.06	–

∴ Total O_2 required = 2.571 − (0.056)

= 2.515 kg/kg of fuel

HCV = (0.844 × 35000) + (0.04 × 143000) kJ/kg

= 35260 kJ/kg

LCV = 35260 − (9 × 0.04 × 2512)

= **34,355 kJ/kg.**

EXERCISE

1. Explain various types of fuel giving their main properties and fields of use.
2. How calorific value of solid fuels is determined? Explain the apparatus and the procedure for the same.
3. What is HCV and LCV? Explain why LCV is preferred to HCV in most of the heating apparatus. Explain any gas calorimeter you have studied for measuring HCV and LCV.

4. Explain the combustion phenomenon of solid, liquid and gaseous fuels. Why solid fuels produce more soot and ash? What are the factors that contribute to atmospheric pollution?

5. How the flue gas is analysed? Explain the construction and working of Orsat apparatus. What precautions should be taken during experimentation?

6. Prepare a list of various hydrocarbon fuels obtained by cracking crude petroleum and show the products on a neatly drawn flow chart.

    The fuel used in an engine contains 85% carbon and 15% hydrogen. The air supplied for combustion is 80% of the theoretically required for complete combustion. Assuming all hydrogen is burnt and carbon is burnt partly to CO and CO_2 without any free carbon in the combustion products, find the volumetric analysis of dry products of combustion.

    (**Ans.** CO_2 = 6.95, CO = 10.89, N_2 = 82.15% by volume)

7. A bomb calorimeter is used to determine the calorific value of coal. The coal contains 6% hydrogen by mass. The following data is recorded during the test.

Mass of coal sample	=	1 gm
Mass of water in calorimeter	=	2500 gm
Water equivalent of calorimeter	=	744 gm
Initial temperature of water	=	17.5°C
Maximum temperature observed	=	20.15°C
Cooling correction	=	+0.015°C

    Determine higher and lower calorific value of coal. Assume enthalpy of vaporisation of water vapour in burnt gases as 2466.1 kJ/kg.

    (**Ans.** HCV = 36137 kJ/kg, LCV = 34806 kJ/kg)

8. The following measurements were taken on a gas calorimeter:

Volume of gas used	11 litres at 20°C
Gas manometer reading	10 cm W.L.
Mass of cooling water used during test	6.0 kg
Cooling water temperatures:	Inlet 19°C, Outlet 30°C

    Calculate the calorific value of fuel used.

    (**Ans.** HCV = 25122 kJ/m^3 under test conditions)

9. Determine chemically correct air: fuel ratio for the following fuels:
   (i) Hexane (C_6H_{14}), (ii) Ammonia (NH_3) and
   (iii) LPG (a mixture of 40% propane and 60% butane by volume)

   (**Ans.** (i) 14.78, (ii) 6.14, (iii) 15.81)

10. During a boiler trial, a sample of coal gave the following analysis by mass: Carbon 89%, Hydrogen 4%, Oxygen 3%, Sulphur 1%, the remainder being incombustible. Determine the theoretical mass of air required/kg of coal for chemically correct combustion. If 60% excess air is supplied, estimate the percentage analysis by mass of dry flue gas.

    (**Ans.** 11.64, CO_2 17%, O_2 8.4%, N_2 74.66%)

11. Following is the composition of a combustible gas by volume: CO 10%, H_2 15%, CO_2 2%, CH_4 26%, O_2 3% and N_2 44%. Determine minimum volume of air required for complete combustion of 1 m³ of this gas. If actual air supplied is 10% in excess, estimate volumetric composition of the dry products of combustion.

    (**Ans.** 2.928 m³/m³ gas, CO_2 11.1%, O_2 1.8%, N_2 87.1%)

12. The composition of a gaseous fuel is 60% methane, 30% ethane and 10% nitrogen by volume. Calculate the stoichiometric air : fuel ratio. If the fuel is burned with 8% excess air by volume, estimate the composition of the dry flue gas on % volume and % mass basis.

    (**Ans.** 16.69, CO_2 11.3, O_2 1.7, N_2 87.0% by volume;

    CO_2 16.64, O_2 1.82, N_2 81.54% by mass)

www.ingramcontent.com/pod-product-compliance
Lightning Source LLC
Chambersburg PA
CBHW080243170426
43192CB00014BA/2551